Investigating PSYCHOLOGY

Irene Taylor   Nicky Hayes

Longman

Acknowledgements

We are grateful to the following for permission to reproduce copyright material:
Edward Arnold Ltd, for extracts from *Psychology: The Science of Mind & Behaviour* by R D
Gross; Basil Blackwell Ltd for extracts from *Child Development: A First Course* by K Sylva
& I Lunt (1984); Brookes/Cole Publishing Company for extracts from *Social Psychology in
the 80s* (4th Edition) by K Deaux & L S Wrightsman (1984); Cambridge University Press
for extracts from *Simple Statistics* (2nd Edition) by F Clegg (1984); Harcourt Brace
Jovanovich, Inc for extracts from *Introduction to Psychology* (9th Edition) by Rita L
Atkinson, Richard C Atkinson, Edward E Smith & Ernest R Hilgard, copyright © 1987
by Harcourt Brace Jovanovich, Inc & extracts from *Psychology: An Introduction* by Jerome
Kagan, copyright © 1984 by Harcourt Brace Jovanovich, Inc; Harper & Row,
Publishers, Inc for extracts from *The Developing Child* (3rd Edition) by Helen Bee,
copyright © 1981 by Helen Bee & extracts from *Psychology: Being Human* by Zick Rubin,
copyright © 1985 by Zick Rubin; Holt, Rinehart & Winston, Inc, for extracts from
Psychology: Understanding Behaviour (2nd Edition) by Robert A Baron, Donn Byrne &
Barry H Kantowitz, copyright © 1980 by Holt, Rinehart & Winston, Inc, extracts from
A Survey of Social Psychology (3rd Edition) by Leonard Berkowitz, copyright © 1986 by
Holt, Rinehart & Winston, Inc & extracts from *Lifespan Human Development* (3rd Edition)
by David Brodzinsky, Anne V Gormly, Sueanne R Ambron, copyright © 1986 by Holt,
Rinehart & Winston, Inc; Longman Group UK Ltd for extracts from *Psychology: An
Introduction* by N Hayes & S Orrell (1987); MTP Press Ltd, Lancaster, England, for
extracts from *Introducing Psychology* by R B Burns & C B Dobson (1984); Midland
Examining Group for 'Source B' from the examination paper *GCSE Psychology (Mature)
Module 5* (1988); Thomas Nelson & Sons Ltd for an extract from *Animal Behaviour* by A P
Brookfield (1980), extracts from *A First Course in Psychology* by N Hayes (1984) & an
extract from *A First Course in Psychology* (2nd Edition) by N Hayes (1989); Northern
Examining Association for examination questions from *NEA Joint GCE/CSE Examination
Paper 1* (1987); Northcote House Publishers Ltd for extracts from *How To Pass
Examinations Without Anxiety* by David Acres (1987); the author's agents for extracts
from *How to Study Effectively* by C J Parsons (Arrow Books Ltd), copyright © 1976 C J
Parsons; Scott, Foresman & Co for extracts from *Psychology* by D Hothersall (1985) &
extracts & a table from *Psychology* by Henry L Roediger III, et al, copyright © 1984 by
Henry L Roediger III, J Philippe Rushton, Elizabeth D Capaldi, & Scott G Paris;
Tavistock Publications Ltd for an extract from *Understanding the Unemployed* by J Hayes
& P Nutman (1981); Wadsworth Publishing Company for an extract from *Sensation &
Perception* (2nd Edition) by E Bruce Goldstein © 1984 by Wadsworth, Inc; Worth
Publishers, Inc for extracts from *The Developing Person* by Kathleen Stassen Berger
(1980).

Plate 9 — Sanders, P. (1982), 'Your Guide to Methodology', in Brody, R, Hayes, N,
   Newton, J & Sanders, P, *Handbook for Psychology Students*, Leicester, Association for
   the Teaching of Psychology
Cartoon 4.2 — David Austin
Fig 2.1 — Kathy Sylva and Ingrid Lunt, *Child Development: A First Course*, Basil Blackwell
Cartoon 4.1 — First published in *The Psychologist*, bulletin of the British Psychological
   Society (1988) 1 (6)
Plate 2 — First published in *The Psychologist*, bulletin of the British Psychological
   Society (1988) 1 (9)
Reading 9.8 — F. Clegg, *Simple Statistics* (2nd Edition), Cambridge University Press
Cartoon 3.1 — *Daily Mail*
Plate 4, Fig 7.2 — Richard Gross; *Psychology, the Science of Mind and Behaviour*, Edward
   Arnold
Fig 6.1 — Adapted figure 'A Normal Distribution Curve', from *Introduction to Psychology*
   (8th Edition) by Rita L Atkinson, Richard C Atkinson, Ernest R Hilgard, copyright ©
   1983 by Harcourt Brace Jovanovich, Inc, reprinted by permission of the publisher
Cartoon 8.1 — Cartoon 'Remember When . . .', from *Introduction to Psychology* (8th
   Edition) by Rita L Atkinson, Richard C Atkinson, Ernest R Hilgard, copyright © 1983
   by Harcourt Brace Jovanovich, Inc, reprinted by permission of the publisher

Plate 3 — Figure 'The Human Brain', from *Introduction to Psychology* (8th Edition) by Rita L Atkinson, Richard C Atkinson, Ernest R Hilgard, copyright © 1983 by Harcourt Brace Jovanovich, Inc, reprinted by permission of the publisher

Fig 1.1 — Table 'Changing Definitions of Psychology', from *Introduction to Psychology*, (8th Edition) by Rita L Atkinson, Richard C Atkinson, Ernest R Hilgard, copyright © 1983 by Harcourt Brace Jovanovich, Inc, reprinted by permission of the publisher

Plate 1 — Figure 'Viewpoints in Psychology', from *Introduction to Psychology* (8th Edition) by Rita L Atkinson, Richard C Atkinson, Ernest R Hilgard, copyright © 1983 by Harcourt Brace Jovanovich, Inc, reprinted by permission of the publisher

Fig 3.4 — Figure 'Brain and Muscle Activity During Sleep', from *Psychology: An Introduction* (5th Edition) by Jerome Kagan, Julius Segal, copyright © 1988 by Harcourt Brace Jovanovich, Inc, reprinted by permission of the publisher

Reading 5a — Figure 'How Do You Perceive These Drawings?', from *Psychology: An Introduction* (5th Edition) by Jerome Kagan, Julius Segal, copyright © 1988 by Harcourt Brace Jovanovich, Inc, reprinted by permission of the publisher

Reading 5b — Figure 'Stroboscopic Motion', from *Psychology: An Introduction* (5th Edition) by Jerome Kagan, Julius Segal, copyright © 1988 by Harcourt Brace Jovanovich, Inc, reprinted by permission of the publisher

Reading 10 — From *Marriage and Family Development* by EM Duvall. Copyright © 1957, 1962, 1967, 1971, 1977 by Harper and Row

Reading 11 — From *The Psychology of Being Human* by Zick Rubin and Elton McNeil, copyright © 1977 by Marjorie McNeil and Zick Rubin

Act. 2.2 — From *The First Five Years* by Arnold Gesell, copyright © 1940 by Arnold Gesell, reprinted by permission of Harper & Row, Publishers, Inc

Cartoon 1.1 — Piet Hein, *More Grooks*, Hodder & Stoughton Ltd.

Cartoon 1.2 — Martin Honeysett

Figs 7.1 & 8.1 — A Birch & T Malim, *Developmental Psychology*, Intertext Ltd

Cartoons 2.1 & 10.1 — Knight Features

Cartoon 2.2 — *Manchester Evening News*

Cartoon 6.1 — Courtesy *Manchester Metro News*

Fig 6.2 — HJ Eysenck, *The Structure of Human Personality*, Methuen & Co Ltd

Fig 1 & R.8 — Midland Examining Group

Plate 6 — Reprinted with permission from *Psychology Today*, copyright © 1971 PT Partners.

Figs 10.2 & 10.3 — D Acres, *How to Pass Exams Without Anxiety*, Northcote Publishers Ltd

Fig 4.2 & Reading 6 — J Greene & C Hicks, *Basic Cognitive Processes*, 1984, Open University Press

Reading 2.10 — From *Sensation and Perception*, 2/E by E Bruce Goldstein, copyright © 1984 by Wadsworth, Inc. All rights reserved. Used by permission of the publisher

Fig 10.1 — Printed by permission of the publisher, *Visible Language*, from volume XV, number 1

Cartoon 5.1 — The Yaffa Newspaper Service Ltd

Plate 5 — J Allan Cash Ltd

Plate 7 — Sally & Richard Greenhill

Plate 10 — Sally & Richard Greenhill

No Trace Clause

We have been unable to trace the copyright holders in the following & would appreciate any information that would enable us to do so:

Psychology & You by J Berryman et al (Methuen & Co Ltd, 1987); *Developmental Psychology* by A Birch & T Malim (Intertext Ltd, 1988); *How to Study Effectively* by D Cocker (1987).

Cartoon 7.1 — Cartoon by Erika Stone/Peter Arnold, Inc.

Cartoon 3.2 — Cartoon on page   from *Today* newspaper, by Tom Johnston. We have made every endeavour to clear permission with the cartoonist, but have been unable to do so.

So many people have been involved in various ways that I am almost afraid to 'name' names because I may forget to mention someone!

My thanks go to Dr James Hartley for reading through the initial draft chapters and giving me the encouragement needed to continue! Also, to my many friends, family and colleagues who have read through the script and given me the benefit of their advice and comments. In particular I am grateful to Joy New and Denis Fishwick who have tested out the materials with students at Tameside College, and Kath Knowles who has done the same with students at Marple Evening Centre and Manchester Polytechnic.

A big 'thank you' must go to Nicky Hayes, who came in initially as an adviser and became my co-author. Not only has she contributed resource material but her expertise in examining has enabled me to standardise the questions. Also, her familiarity with publishing has allowed my introduction into this area to be less traumatic.

My family deserve commendations for letting both the book and myself take over the house and for giving me all-round support. My husband Frank has been involved in so many ways, including acting as a courier between Nicky and myself during a postal dispute. Thank you Veronica for typing back into the processor those chapters which I 'lost' when I accidently erased a disc instead of copying it! Adrian demonstrated great gender equality in ironing and taking over domestic chores when mother became 'author'.

Not least of all my thanks must go to my students who initially prodded me into starting the book and give me continued encouragement. They have helped me to identify areas of ambiguity and lack of clarity. Any such areas not identified are the responsibility of the author.

Irene Taylor

About this Book

'Can you recommend any resourcebooks we could use to practise/
develop/understand our psychology course?'

It was students asking questions like this that were to result in the
production of this book. The introduction of the new examination
structure for GCSE in the United Kingdom accelerated the process.

We decided to extend the original idea of resource material into a
format of topic-related chapters – the content of which would be
structured around introductory psychology courses and the syllabi of
the various examination boards for GCSE, A and A/S level Psychology.
Such a book could be used to complement introductory psychology texts
such as Hayes and Orrell (1987) *Psychology An Introduction* (Longman).
It is worth pointing out that this book, along with other textbooks in
psychology, is not like a novel. It is rare that anyone would recommend
that you sit and read the book from cover to cover at one sitting. Its use is
as a book for you to have on hand throughout your course, for reference
and revision. The earlier chapters give you 'back up' material on the
various topic areas, and the final chapter should prove more useful when
you are writing answers to questions and essays. Each chapter includes:

1 Readings
There are 10 source readings for each chapter with each reading followed
by structured questions. These questions include some which require you
to find information from the related reading and/or charts and graphs
(such as 7 and 8 in the example given below).

Other questions require psychological knowledge of the underlying
concepts and principles (such as required by question 9). You should be
able to find the information in your introductory psychology textbook(s)
and/or coursework notes. Remember to look carefully at the number of
marks given for each part of the question. Obviously the more marks
given, the more information required in the answer. Question 9 demands
twice as much effort (and time) as does question 8.

The position of these readings can be found at the beginning of each
chapter. Topic-related terms to define are also included to aid recall and
help in revision (see also Reading 10.1 Keywords and the Listing of Terms
to Define pages 10–12).

2 Suggestions for Further Reading
Main texts are identified at the end of each chapter along with other
suitable texts to extend your reading on the topics.

3 Activities
Three suggestions are made in each chapter of related activities which, in
many cases, could be developed into research or coursework reports. The
position of these activities can be found in the Listing of Activities page 12.

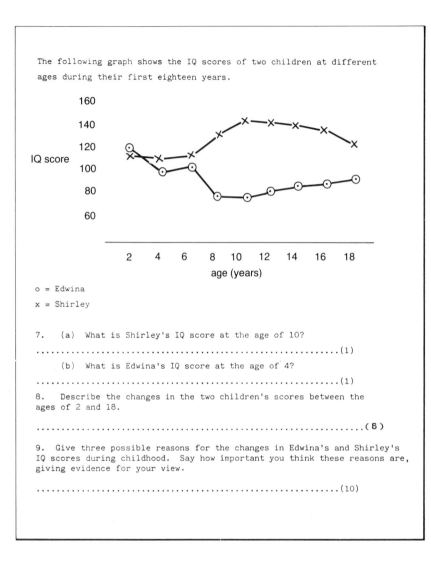

The following graph shows the IQ scores of two children at different ages during their first eighteen years.

o = Edwina

x = Shirley

7. (a) What is Shirley's IQ score at the age of 10?
....(1)

   (b) What is Edwina's IQ score at the age of 4?
....(1)

8. Describe the changes in the two children's scores between the ages of 2 and 18.

....(5)

9. Give three possible reasons for the changes in Edwina's and Shirley's IQ scores during childhood. Say how important you think these reasons are, giving evidence for your view.

....(10)

Figure 1 *A structured stimulus-response question*

4 Essays

There are three more advanced essays suggested for each chapter. These are intended to allow students intending to study psychology at A level and above the opportunity to think out possible essay plans on the topic areas. The position of these essays is indicated in the Listing of Essays on page 13.

For all chapters (except Chapter 10) there is also:

a) A **Methodology Question** which enables you to think through a possible research method related to a topic. This also allows some consideration of the possible advantages and disadvantages associated with the chosen method. The Listing of Methodology Questions can be found on page 14.

b) A **Stimulus Question** which describes a study and asks you to consider any methodological weaknesses and possible sources of bias. The Listing of Stimulus Questions can be found on page 13.

Both a) and b) should give you the necessary practice and confidence to pursue your own research in psychology, and are similar in form to questions that may be encountered in psychology exam papers.

In the last chapter, Chapter 10: Can Psychology Help You Study More Effectively? some **Objective Test Questions** are included to help you in revision. There are 10 questions for each of chapters 1−9 and another 10 general revision questions, making 100 questions in all.

   The stage is now set for you to become involved **actively** in learning about psychology. We hope you will find it an enjoyable experience.

Irene Taylor and Nicky Hayes

Contents

Listing of Chapters

Listing of Terms to Define

(the position of these words can be found by the reading source number in brackets)

A abnormal (6.9), accommodation (7.5), adaptation (7.5), addiction (3.9), adolescence (7.9), adoption (2.9), adrenalin/noradrenalin (3.8), age discrimination (8.6), aggression (2.8), alarm reaction (3.7), alpha/delta waves (3.4), analysis (10.4), anti-conformity (5.1), anxiety (10.9), assessment (6.1), aphasia (3.2), assimilation (7.5), attitude (5.8), attribution process (5.7), authoritarian personality (5.9), axons (3.6)

B behaviourism (1.3), bereavement (8.9), bi-polar constructs (6.7), body image (7.9), bonding (7.4), bottleneck theories (4.3), brainstorming (4.8), bystander apathy (5.3)

C case study (9.1), catharsis (2.8), centration (7.6), cerebral dominance (3.2), child-minder (8.4), classical and operant conditioning (1.3), coding (10.8), cognition (1.6), cognitive dissonance (5.8), cognitive maps (10.3), communication (2.3), comparative studies (3.5), compensatory education (6.3), compliance (5.2), compulsory retirement age (8.8), compulsory questions (10.10), computer simulation (4.7), concrete words (10.6), conditioning (6.5), confidant (8.3), conformity (5.1), confounding variables (9.6), conservation (7.6), control group (9.8), consciousness (3.4), coping strategies (10.9), correlation (2.9), cortex (3.1), creativity (4.8), critical/sensitive periods (2.1), cross-modal transfer (2.4)

D debriefing (9.10), demand characteristics (9.6), dependence (3.10), depersonalisation (5.4), deprivation (2.2), diffusion of responsibility (5.3), discrimination (2.6), disengagement (8.8), displaced vision studies (2.10), distribution of practice effect (10.7), double-bind (6.10), dual coding (10.6)

E EEG (3.3), egocentric (7.6), ego-defence mechanisms (1.5), empathy (6.8), environmental (8.5), episodic memory (4.5), essay plan (10.4), ethics (3.5), ethnocentrism (5.10), ethological (1.7), evolution (1.2), examination (10.10), excitatory and inhibitory synapses (3.1), existentialism (6.10), experiment (9.4), experimental and null hypothesis (9.4), experimenter expectancy effects (9.7), extraversion (6.4), extinction (2.6)

F family (8.1), family therapy (6.10), field experiment (9.9), figure/ground organisation (1.4), fixation (1.5), fluid/crystallised intelligence (6.2), forgetting curve (10.7), frustration-aggression hypothesis (2.7), functionalism (1.2), fundamental attribution error (5.7)

G gender (7.2), General Adaptation Syndrome (3.7), generalisation (9.1), generation gap (7.9), genetics (2.5), 'g factor' (6.2), grammar (2.3), group (5.10), group cohesiveness (5.10)

H halo effect (5.6), heuristics (4.7), hospice (8.10), humanistic (6.8)

I ideal self (6.8), identification (7.3), idiographic approach (9.1), imagery (10.6), imitation (7.1), implicit personality theory (5.6), imprinting (2.1), incubation (4.8), independent and dependent variables (9.4), information processing system (1.6), innate (2.4), insight learning (4.6), insight therapy (6.6), instinct (2.1), intelligence (6.1), interference theory (4.5), intergenerational (8.1), internalisation (5.1), intervention programme (6.3), introspection (1.1), introversion (6.4), irreversibility (7.6), IQ (6.2)

J job satisfaction (8.6)

K keyword (10.1), kinesics (5.5), kitten carousel (2.10)

L LAD (4.10), language (2.2), latent learning (4.6), learning set (4.6), leisure (8.8), levels of processing approach (10.8), life change units (8.2), lifestyle (8.1), linguistic relativity (4.9), linguistic universals (4.9), LTM (4.4)

M marriage (8.1), masking (4.3), mastery/symbolic/rule-bound play (7.7), maternal deprivation (7.4), maturation (2.5), means-ends analysis (4.7), micro-electrodes (3.3), mid-life crisis (8.6), MLU (2.3), mnemonics (10.6), modelling (7.1), morals (7.8), mortality (8.9), mourning (8.9), MZ and DZ twins (2.9)

N natural selection (1.2), nervous system (1.7), neurotic (6.4), neurotransmitter substances (3.6), non-conformity (5.1), non-verbal communication (5.5), norm (5.4), nursery (8.4)

O obedience (5.2), objective (1.1), occupation (8.5), Oedipal/Electra conflict (7.3)

P pacing/timing (10.10), palliation (3.9), paralanguage (5.5), patterned notes (10.2), perception (4.1), perceptual constancy (2.4), perceptual defence (4.2), perceptual set (4.2), performance (7.10), personal constructs (6.7), personality type (6.4), persuasion (5.2), PET (3.3), phenomenology (1.9), phenomenological (8.7), phi-phenomenon (1.4), phobia (6.5), play (7.7), playschool (8.4), population (9.5), positive/negative correlation (9.2), prejudice (5.9), preview (10.3), primacy/recency effects (5.6), privation (7.4), proxemics (5.5), psychoactive (3.10), psychoanalysis (6.6), psychobiological (1.7), psycholinguistics (4.9), psychometrics (9.3), psychotherapy (6.6), psychoses (6.9), pure/applied research (1.10)

R random and quota sample (9.5), reinforcement (2.6), relaxation techniques (10.9), relevant (10.4), reliability (9.3), REM sleep (3.4), Repertory Grid (6.7), replication (9.8), representative sample (9.5), retirement (8.8), retrieval (10.3), revision (10.5), role (8.2)

S scapegoat theory (5.9), scattergram (9.2), schedules of reinforcement (2.6), schema (7.5), schizophregenic (6.10), schizophrenia (6.9), scientific (1.1), selective attention (4.3), selective perception (5.9), self-actualisation (6.8), self-concept (8.7), self-esteem (7.9), self-fulfilling prophecy (9.7), self-monitoring (10.5), self-perception (5.2), semantic memory (4.5), semantics (2.2), sensation (4.1), sensory/motor/connector neurones (3.1), sensory-motor coordination (2.10), sex-role (7.2), sign learning (4.6), skill (7.10), social comparison (5.8), social facilitation (5.3), social influence (1.8), socialisation (2.7), social perception (1.8), Social Readjustment Rating Scale (8.2), social role (5.4), social support (8.3), socio-economic (8.5), S-O-R (1.6), species-specific (2.1), split-brain studies (3.2), S-R learning (1.3), standardisation (9.3), standardised instructions (9.6), statistics (9.8), stereotype (7.2), STM (4.4), stress (3.7), stroboscopic motion (1.4), sub-cortical areas (3.5), subjective (1.9), subliminal perception (4.2), superego (7.3), surface/deep structure (4.10), survey (2.7), symbol (2.3), sympathetic nervous system (3.8), synapses (3.6), synectics (4.8), systematic desensitisation (6.5)

T telegraphic speech (4.10), terminally ill (8.10), tests (6.1), timetable (10.5), tolerance (3.10), Type A behaviour (3.8)

U unconscious (1.5), unemployment (8.7)

V validity (9.3), variables (9.2), vicarious learning (7.1), visual discrimination (2.5), visual illusion (4.1)

W withdrawal (3.9), work (8.4), working memory (4.4)

Listing of Activities

Listing of Essays

Listing of Stimulus Questions

Listing of Methodology Questions

1

What is Psychology?

'. . . an ongoing process of trying to gain insights into the awe-inspiring complexity of human thought and action.'

J. Hassett (1984)

Plate 1

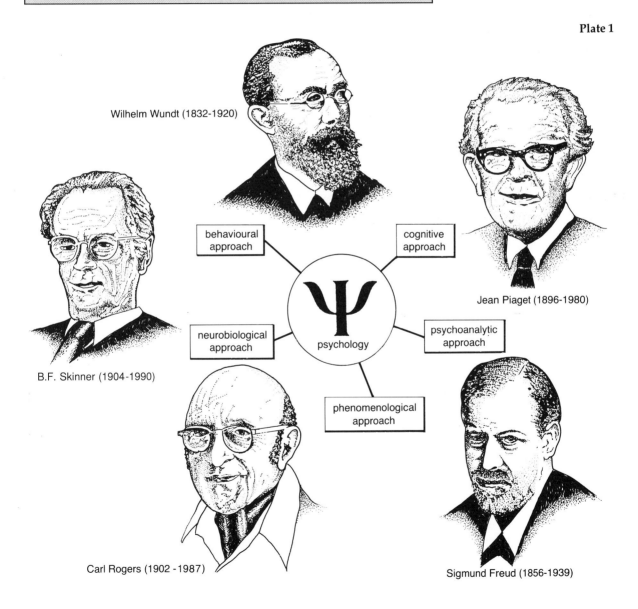

Wilhelm Wundt (1832-1920)

Jean Piaget (1896-1980)

behavioural approach

cognitive approach

Ψ

psychology

neurobiological approach

psychoanalytic approach

phenomenological approach

B.F. Skinner (1904-1990)

Carl Rogers (1902-1987)

Sigmund Freud (1856-1939)

Readings on 'What is Psychology?'

Psychology means different things to different people, as can be seen by the variety of definitions to be found in the literature. Figure 1.1 shows how these definitions have changed over the brief history of the science.

By looking into the historical development of psychology we can understand better the confusion which arises over its definition, and also see its specialisation into different branches of study. Prior to the late nineteenth century psychology was considered part of philosophy, and human behaviour was not usually seen as a suitable topic for systematic study. For partly religious and partly philosophical reasons, behaviour was often seen as a puzzle which we could never solve.

However, during the nineteenth century, many philosophers became convinced that all events (including human behaviour and mental processes) follow basic laws and could be studied by scientific means. Research in the fields of medicine and physiology using scientific methods promoted interest in whether they could also be used to advance the understanding of human behaviour. This might be a good point to explain what is meant by 'scientific methods'. These are usually seen as methods which use systematic observation and/or direct experimentation. If such requirements are fulfilled then the study can be seen to be **scientific.**

Although the early psychologists agreed that psychology should be scientific, they disagreed about what was to be the subject matter (*What shall we study?*) and the methods (*How shall we go about studying it?*). Because of this difference of opinion, psychology developed and separated into many schools of thought which differed in their choice of subject matter and methods of investigation. Each school has, however, handed down ideas and attitudes which are still of value to psychologists today.

Psychology is the Science of Mental Life, both of its phenomena and of their conditions . . . The phenomena are such things as we call feeling, desires, cognitions, reasonings, decisions, and the like.

William James, 1890

Psychology has to investigate that which we call internal experience – our own sensations and feelings, our thoughts and volition – in contradistinction to the objects of external experience, which form the subject matter of natural science.

Wilhelm Wundt, 1892

All consciousness everywhere, normal or abnormal, human or animal, is the subject matter which the psychologist attempts to describe or explain; and no definition of his science is wholly acceptable which designates more or less than just this.

James Angell, 1910

For the behaviourist, psychology is that division of natural science which takes human behaviour – the doings and sayings, both learned and unlearned – as its subject matter.

John B. Watson, 1919

As a provisional definition of psychology, we may say that its problem is the scientific study of the behaviour of living creatures in this contact with the outer world.

Kurt Koffka, 1925

Conceived broadly, psychology seeks to discover the general laws which explain the behaviour of living organisms. It attempts to identify, describe, and classify the several types of activity of which the animal, human or other, is capable.

Arthur Gates, 1931

Today, psychology is most commonly defined as 'the science of behaviour.' Interestingly enough, however, the meaning of 'behaviour' has itself expanded so that it now takes in a good bit of what was formerly dealt with as experience . . . such private (subjective) processes as thinking are now dealt with as 'internal behaviour'.

Norman Munn, 1951

Psychology is usually defined as the scientific study of behaviour. Its subject matter includes behavioural processes that are observable, such as gestures, speech, and physiological changes, and processes that can only be inferred as thoughts and dreams.

Kenneth Clark and George Miller, 1970

Psychology is the scientific analysis of human mental processes and memory structures in order to understand human behaviour.

Richard Mayer, 1981

Figure 1.1 *Definitions of psychology*

The founder of modern psychology is usually thought to be **William Wundt** (1832–1920) who is discussed in Reading 1.1.

Reading 1.1 William Wundt

Trained as a physiologist, Wundt wanted to study the human mind scientifically. In 1879 he established the world's first enduring psychological research laboratory at the University of Leipzig in Germany. At first, his laboratory was nothing more than a couple of rooms in the dining hall – modest beginnings backed, however, with Wundt's powerful vision. He saw psychology as an objective, experimental science, modelled on such established sciences as physiology, physics, and chemistry, but with the human mind as its own unique subject matter.

Even so, Wundt faced a problem that today's psychologists still confront. How was the mind to be observed? The solution Wundt offered was a method of self-observation called introspection. Under carefully controlled conditions, and after rigorous training, human observers reported the mental experiences they had under various circumstances. Wundt believed that the introspections of these highly trained observers would yield information about the contents of the mind that would be as valid as the information generated by the established sciences. Wundt aimed to use introspection to identify the basic elements of human consciousness just as Isaac Newton, in the seventeenth century, had used a prism to refract white light into its component colours – the colour spectrum.

As news of this undertaking spread, Wundt's laboratory began to attract students from all over the world. Although psychologists today do not accept introspection as an objective technique, Wundt's contemporaries saw it as an objective and scientific alternative to the purely subjective speculation of the philosophers – clearly an exciting development.

D. Hothersall (1985) *Psychology* Merrill

1 What is meant by 'scientific'? (2)

2 Name **two** sciences on which Wundt modelled the new science of psychology. (2)

3 a) What is introspection? (2)
   b) Describe **two** problems associated with the method of introspection. (6)

TERMS TO DEFINE

introspection   objective   scientific

In the early years psychologists such as Ebbinghaus (1850–1909), looking at memory, helped to demonstrate that psychological processes could be investigated objectively. This school of investigation into how conscious experiences were organised became known as **structuralism**. At Harvard, in America, William James (1842–1910) also tried to explain states of consciousness. This was the period of trying to find global or world-wide laws which would apply to experiences. The method of introspection was subject to a great deal of criticism. Other newly established laboratories came up with differing results and, because of the problems of checking subjective reports, there was no way of resolving the issue. The method was, therefore, criticised as unreliable.

Structuralism came under pressure from a new school who believed that the **function** of consciousness should be the subject investigated. Although consciousness was one of the topics studied, **functionalism** also looked at a variety of topics as can be seen in Reading 1.2.

THE ULTIMATE WISDOM

Philosophers must ultimately find their true perfection

in knowing all the follies of mankind – by introspection.

Reading 1.2   Functionalism

Just as the structuralists were concerned with the structure of mental life, the adherents of *functionalism* were concerned with the uses, or functions, of mental processes. During the late 1800s, Darwin's theory of evolution by natural selection swept intellectual circles in Europe and North America. It is not surprising that scientists began to ask about the adaptive significance of psychological processes, just as they did about biological processes. For example, they asked how these processes contributed to the individual's chance for survival. 'In examining mental processes, [functionalism] asked the questions of the practical man: "What are they for?" "What difference do they make?" "How do they work?"' (Heidbreder, 1933, p. 202).

John Dewey (1859–1952) was one of the founders of the functionalist school at the University of Chicago, and many others were attracted to these ideas. The functionalists never had a tight, tidy system like the structuralists, and they disagreed often. But they shared some basic beliefs: they thought that the functions of psychological processes were of primary interest and that behaviour should be studied as much as possible in a natural context. Functionalists also pointed out that psychological processes were continuous, ongoing events that could not usefully be stopped and dissected, as the structuralists proposed.

These ideas led to several healthy trends previously discouraged by structuralism. Functionalism broadened the subject matter of psychology to include a variety of types of people (children, the mentally ill) and species (chimpanzees, dogs) which could not be studied through analytic introspection. Another new trend was to apply research to practical problems.

H.L. Roediger et al (1984) *Psychology* Little, Brown and Co

1 What aspects of mental processes were investigated by the functionalists?   (2)

2 Describe **two** beliefs shared by all functionalists.   (4)

3 In what way did functionalism change the study of psychology?   (4)

TERMS TO DEFINE

evolution   functionalism   natural selection

William James also influenced this school. He was not committed to the philosophy of any one school. Instead he tried to understand the behaviour of human beings within a biological framework, and saw psychology as the study of the way in which people adapt to the environment. His theory of emotion still concerns psychologists today. His research was extensive and, although he used introspection, he also acknowledged the value of experimentation (even though he had little interest in using it himself).

Structuralists and functionalists played important roles in the early development of psychology because each viewpoint provided a systematic approach to the field. Both stressed the importance of the unconscious part of mental life and were concerned with discovering statements concerning similarities between people. They accepted the existence of **associations** in learning, aptly demonstrated earlier by the work of Ebbinghaus on memory learning. He had discovered that learning verbal material depends on repetition and understanding, and that we learn about this by adding on to our previous learning.

Topic-related Essays

1   Psychology is often defined as 'the scientific study of behaviour'. Critically discuss this statement.

2   'The Gestalt theory of perception has made no long-term contribution to research.' Discuss.

3   How far has the psychoanalytic approach helped us to understand behaviour?

Another early associationist was Ivan Pavlov (1849–1936), a Russian physiologist who discovered rules governing the association between external stimuli (such as sights and sounds) and internal physiological responses (such as autonomic responses like salivation). He became famous for his experiments with dogs, in which he taught them to salivate to the sound of a buzzer by creating an association between the buzzer and the presentation of food. This process is now known as **classical conditioning** (see Reading 6.6 Systematic Desensitisation, for a description of some of the practical applications of Pavlov's research in behaviour therapy).

Whereas Pavlov investigated the association of these **involuntary** responses, Thorndike (1874–1949) researched in America into the association of situations and **voluntary** responses. He created 'puzzle boxes' from which cats had to learn to escape. The hungry animals were motivated by the sight of food outside the box. Thorndike timed how long the animal took to escape and this time was seen as the measure of learning or remembering. This new school of psychology became known as **behaviourism** and is discussed briefly in Reading 1.3.

Watson saw the goal of psychology as describing, explaining, controlling and predicting behaviour. He intended to study learning in animals with a simple nervous system, whose environments could be

20

Reading 1.3   Behaviourism

The idea that behaviour could be learnt rather than being the result of some biological or neurological event, or a symptom of some psychodynamic force, was to revolutionise the study of psychology. The American psychologist, John Watson, took Pavlov's findings as the basis by which to understand all human activity and his article in 1913, 'Psychology as the behaviourist views it', laid the foundation for decades of further study. Simply, Watson argued that we are born with certain innate stimulus-response (S–R) reflexes. Through the process of classical conditioning more and more complex behaviours are learnt to produce our full behavioural repertoire. We know now that Watson's theories are too simplistic and an S–R model of human activity cannot provide all the answers. However, in deeming that behaviour (rather than introspection, for example) was the proper subject matter of psychology, Watson shaped the work of following generations of psychologists.

Whilst learning by association does not explain all learning, it does occur, as we all know. As a simple example: play a piece of music which you haven't listened to for a long time. Whilst it is playing see what memories you experience: people, places, emotions, conversations, images, may all trickle back to awareness. The music is linked with the events in memory and now becomes a stimulus to elicit the associated responses learnt in your past.

J. Berryman et al (1987) *Psychology and You* Methuen

1 What do behaviourists consider suitable subject matter?   (2)

2 Explain what is meant by S–R learning.   (3)

3 Briefly describe the procedure associated with:
   a) classical conditioning   (4)
   b) operant conditioning.   (4)

4 Describe **two** differences between classical and operant conditioning.   (6)

TERMS TO DEFINE

behaviourism   classical and operant conditioning   S–R learning

strongly controlled. For example, rats could be investigated in the laboratory maintaining the same light, temperature and background; when presented with a number of different stimuli their responses could be noted.

Skinner (1904–1990) followed Watson as leader of this school. He was also interested in the learning process and made an important contribution to our knowledge of how patterns of reward and punishment produce and modify connections between stimulus and response (S–R learning). He tried to find universal laws which would apply to all organisms (see Reading 2.6 Superstitious Behaviour, which demonstrates how such connections are learned).

By 1920 structuralism and functionalism were displaced by three new

schools, all very different in their approaches: **behaviourism**, **Gestalt psychology** and **psychoanalysis**. These were to dominate the field until World War II.

The behaviourists stated clear predictions which were testable by experimentation. This gave rise to the definition of behaviourism as 'the **scientific** study of human behaviour'. Behaviourism is still important in psychology today but many psychologists now refuse to reject mental and physiological explanations of behaviour. If the behaviourist approach appeals to you, perhaps you might like to try Activity 1.1.

Activity 1.1

You are a behavioural therapist who has been asked to help a child who is five years old to talk and communicate. All medical checks have found no physiological problem to exist and an early diagnosis of **autism** has been made. Such children often cut themselves off from the outside world and live in their own world.

Plan a suitable behaviour modification programme. What reinforcement will you use? What will be your first step? How will you build on this? Will you involve the parents? If so, when – at the beginning of the programme or later? Why?

Opposition to the behaviourist view came from the **Gestalt** school. This developed in Germany, initially as a reaction to the structuralist view of perception as the sum of many independent sensations. Gestalt psychologists argued that we perceive the world in unitary 'wholes' or 'gestalts' and believed that 'the whole is greater than the sum of the parts'. Learning and problem solving to the Gestalt school involves the reorganisation of what we see in the environment so that the mind can impose order on the information it receives. Some of these **Gestalt Laws** are discussed in Reading 1.4 (see also Chapter Four Figure 4.2).

This school of thought was often criticised because they described but did not explain. They were influential in areas such as perception, memory and thinking, and stimulated a great deal of research on the relative contribution of genetics and learning on perception.

Reading 1.4   Gestalt Laws

Apart from the figure/ground principle, the Gestalt psychologists identified some other ways in which we tend to organise our perception. Two of these were the principles of similarity and of proximity. By similarity they meant that, all other things being equal, we tend to group together things which look the same. So if we were looking at a line of figures, say, like this:

ooooooooxxxxxxxxxxoooooooooxxxxxxxxx

we would tend to group the similar ones together because they were like each other.

The principle of proximity is that we tend to group things together if they are near each other. So if, for instance, you saw a line of figures like this:

xxxxxxoo   oooxxxooo   oooxxxxxx

you would tend to see it as three groups of mixed 'o's and 'x's rather than seeing the similar ones grouped together. There are several other principles like this that the Gestalt psychologists identified, and they referred to them as the laws of Prägnanz (or meaning), because that was the way, they thought, that we give meaning to what we are able to see.

One of the most important of the Gestalt principles, and one which has much wider implications than just the way that we interpret drawings or visual stimuli, is known as the principle of closure. If you very briefly show someone an incomplete figure and then ask them to say or draw what they have seen, they will tend to draw the whole thing filling in the gaps. Often, in fact, they are not aware that there were actually any gaps at all. The principle of closure seems to be a very strong tendency in our perception.

The Gestalt psychologists identified another way that the principle of closure manifested itself, in an illusion known as the phi phenomenon. Briefly, this happens if, say, you flick two adjacent lights on and off in rapid succession. Instead of seeing the two lights, an observer will tend to see just one light moving backwards and forwards as we tend to join up the two distinct points. You have probably seen this happening often, in such things as advertisement lighting in streets, where illusions of movement are created by using the phi phenomenon.

Another example of the principle of closure is in the experience of stroboscopic motion. When we are shown series of pictures in rapid succession we tend to link them up and just see one picture moving. This is the basis of films and is one way that we can see the principle of closure in operation in our perception.

N. Hayes and S. Orrell (1987) *Psychology: An Introduction* Longman

1 Explain in your own words what the Gestalt psychologists mean by the principles of:
   a) similarity and proximity
   b) closure. (4)

2 Join together the following sentences:

The laws of Prägnanz refer to	when rapidly presented pictures become a moving picture
The phi-phenomenon is	the way we impose meaning on what we see
Stroboscopic motion is	when two flickering lights in close proximity appear to be one moving light

(3)

3 The Gestalt school believe . . . .   (3)

4 Critically, discuss **one** study which supports the Gestalt view of psychology.   (5)

TERMS TO DEFINE

figure/ground organisation   phi-phenomenon   stroboscopic motion

Another school of thought became known as the **psychoanalytic** school due to the methods used by its founder, **Sigmund Freud**, whose theory is discussed in Reading 1.5.

Reading 1.5   Sigmund Freud

Freud, often referred to as 'the father of psychoanalysis', was not a psychologist. Freud (1856–1939) was a Viennese physician who became interested in the role of unconscious mental processes in influencing people's behaviour and, in particular, their psychological problems. He was interested in exploring human behaviour, feelings and thoughts, but his ideas were based on his clinical work. He built up a view of what makes humans 'tick' from his deductions about the causes of the problems he saw in his patients. Thus his view of human nature was shaped by observing and trying to help those who had problems; he was not concerned with the 'normal' or average person but just a small number of rather unhappy people.

Essentially Freud believed that a large part of the mind was unconscious, and that our behaviour was 'driven' by instincts housed in this unconscious area of mind. The expression of these instincts was, he suggested, shaped by our early life experiences: thus, for example, a person who was deprived of adequate breast feeding, or mother love, might later show neurotic patterns of behaviour such as a craving for comfort, food or love.

In attempting to find the causes of psychological problems, Freud's approach, in psychoanalytic therapy, was to use a variety of techniques which were intended to give insights into a person's unconscious mental processes. Two of these techniques were free-association and dream analysis. In the former, a patient would lie on a couch and be asked to report freely whatever thoughts or feelings came to mind; in dream analysis the content of the patient's dreams were explored using free association with a dream event as the initial stimulus.

Freud believed that these techniques led him to the source of a patient's problems and, by bringing that source out into the open into conscious awareness, the emotional release (or catharsis) induced would assist in helping the patient towards a solution of the problem.

J. Berryman et al (1987) *Psychology and You* Methuen

1 Freud was a:
   a) chemist
   b) physician
   c) psychologist.   (1)

2 What did Freud believe motivates behaviour?   (2)

3 a) On what evidence did Freud base his theory?   (2)
   b) Which research method did Freud use?   (2)

4 In your own words describe **one** technique used by Freud to reach unconscious mental processes.   (3)

5 How might a psychoanalyst help someone with a sleeping problem? Describe **one** problem with this approach.   (6)

TERMS TO DEFINE

ego-defence mechanisms   fixation   unconscious

By the first decade of the twentieth century, Freud's theory and techniques for the treatment of mental disorders had emerged. Over the period since then it has been used by many of those treating the mentally ill. Personality is seen to progress through a number of **psychosexual** stages, so named because of the importance Freud placed on sexuality in development. There was, and still is, much opposition to Freud, especially due to his description of children having an early period of sexual interest at the age of four or five years (see Chapter Seven for a discussion of Freud's theory and also Reading 7.4 The Oedipal Conflict).

Psychoanalysis is a lengthy process. The analyst tries to help the patient, through **regression**, back to the psychosexual stage at which they have became **fixated** (unable to progress through). In this way the patient can come to terms with emotional anxiety and achieve emotional maturity. Freud reached his conclusions using a **case study** method, seeing his patients over a number of years, and also from self-analysis. Activity 1.2 also involves the use of the case study method.

Freud is often criticised in that his conclusions were biased by his own views and prejudices (see Reading 6.6 Does Psychotherapy Work? for further discussion on this topic).

Most **post-Freudians** do not go along with all of Freud's original theory. Some have modified his views to include the influence of society on personality, although many still find his techniques helpful in therapy. Often people outside psychology see the study of psychology in Freudian terms. Several years ago, on discovering that I was a psychology student, a

Activity 1.2

Perhaps you know a baby or a young child? If so, perhaps you could perform a case study on some aspect of their development, over a number of weeks or months? Check what you are planning to do with your tutor, and make sure you ask permission from the child's parents, assuring them that there will be nothing harmful or difficult in what you are going to do.

For example, suppose you decide to study social development. You could observe the child's reaction to people, especially noting different responses to familiar and unfamiliar people. Observe how this reaction changes with age. This is an interesting topic to study in a child of 5–6 months onwards. It might be interesting to study more than one infant so that individual differences can be noted, or perhaps you could compare notes with a friend doing a similar case study?

---

friend asked me to let him know when I graduated so that he could '*come and put my head on your couch and you can help me get to know myself better*'. This is how some view psychology – needless to say a view disputed by the behaviourists!

The goal of most psychologists is to **understand** and **predict** behaviour. To a lesser extent they can also **control** behaviour, as seen by the work of applied practitioners such as behaviour therapists. Most psychologists accept the complexity of the subject and the variety of routes which have resulted. The trend today is towards a **holistic** approach in trying to understand and solve human problems. It is often seen as a complex system of interacting parts. However, many still identify with various areas.

One area of growth in recent years is that of **cognitive psychology**, which is described in Reading 1.6. Here we see a swing back towards discussions of **internal** psychological processes in tasks such as reading. How do we learn about the environment? How do we store knowledge in our memory? How do we use it to act intelligently in new situations? These are the type of questions which cognitive psychologists try to answer.

Reading 1.6   Cognitive Psychology

Cognition refers to the mental processes of perception, memory, and information processing by which the individual acquires knowledge, solves problems, and plans for the future. Cognitive psychology is the scientific study of cognition. Its goal is to conduct experiments and develop theories that explain how mental processes are organised and function. But explanation requires that the theories make predictions about observable events, namely behaviour. As we shall see, one can theorise about cognitive processes and how they work without resorting to neurobiological explanations.

The cognitive approach to the study of psychology developed partly in reaction to the narrowness of the S–R view. To conceive of human actions solely in terms of stimulus input and response output may be adequate for the study of simple forms of behaviour, but this approach neglects too many interesting areas of human functioning. People can think, plan, make decisions on the basis of remembered information, and selectively choose among stimuli that require attention.

In its origin, behaviourism rejected the subjective study of 'mental life' in order to make psychology a science. It provided a valuable service by making psychologists aware of the need for objectivity and measurement. Cognitive psychology represents an attempt to investigate mental processes once again, but in an objective and scientific manner.

An analogy has been made between the S–R approach and an old-fashioned telephone switchboard: the stimulus goes in, and after a series of cross connections and circuits through the brain, the response comes out. The analogy for cognitive psychology is the modern high-speed computer – or what in its most general sense is called an information-processing system. Incoming information is processed in various ways: it is selected, compared and combined with other information already in memory, transformed, rearranged, and so on. The response output depends on these internal processes and their state at that moment.

Kenneth Craik, a British psychologist and one of the early advocates of cognitive psychology, proposed that the brain is like a computer capable of modelling or paralleling external events. He remarked.

> If the organism carries a 'small-scale model' of external reality and of its own possible actions within its head, it is able to try out various alternatives, conclude which is the best of them, react to future situations before they arise, utilise the knowledge of past events in dealing with the future, and in every way to react in a much fuller, safer and more competent manner to the emergencies which face it. (Craik, 1943)

The notion of a mental model of reality is central to a cognitive approach to psychology.

Cognitive psychology is not restricted to the study of thought and knowledge. Its early concerns with the representation of knowledge and human thought processes led to the label of cognitive psychology, but in recent years the approach has been applied to virtually all areas of psychology (Mandler, 1985).

R.L. Atkinson et al (1987) Introduction to Psychology
Harcourt Brace Jovanovich

1 What is cognition?   (2)

2 Name **one** cognitive psychologist.   (1)

3 Why did the cognitive psychologists disagree with the S–R view?   (4)

4 Describe **one** information processing system of cognition.   (6)

TERMS TO DEFINE

cognition   information processing system   S–R

After World War II more sophisticated instruments and equipment, including computers, became available for use in psychology. This encouraged the work of Simon and others in computer simulation of psychological processes. These are often referred to as **information processing systems.** The human organism is seen as an active seeker of knowledge and processor of information, from which is built a mental representation of the world. Cognitive psychologists reject S–R learning in favour of **organisation** by the human cognitive system. Today psychology is far more cognitive in nature; it could be seen as having come full circle.

Now we can see the use of more rigorous methods to gain objectivity and reproducibility. The definition of psychology can now be said to include this change in emphasis: '*the scientific study of behaviour and mental processes*'.

Today there has been increasing specialisation so that many psychologists identify with their area of research, although the schools of thought previously mentioned continue to exert their influence. Some of the main areas of research are identified in Reading 1.7 **Approaches in Psychology**.

The psychobiological/physiological approach just discussed demonstrated that mechanisms of the brain and nervous system are strongly involved in behaviour, and some researchers believe that all psychology will eventually be explained in terms of physiological events. This is known as a **reductionist** view. Other physiological psychologists stress the **interaction** of physiological and outside sources.

Social psychologists oppose the reductionist view, stressing that social factors and group processes affect behaviour. Social psychology is concerned with the structure and function of society and the individual's relationship with others. What are the social motivators? How do we measure attitudes and attitude change? What causes prejudice, aggression, conformity, obedience? These are a few of the many issues that researchers in this field have set about trying to resolve. Interpersonal attraction and non-verbal communication are also covered, as are many other wide-ranging topics, some of which are noted in Reading 1.8 **Social Psychology**.

Social psychologists tend to use cognitive and behavioural approaches although you will find a wide diversity of methods used both inside and outside the laboratory.

Humanistic psychology stresses the worth of the individual and the potential for personal growth and fulfilment. Humanistic psychologists oppose the reductionist view, and are similar to the Gestalt school in seeing human personality as a whole rather than trying to analyse it in small pieces. Such reductionism, in their view, dehumanises the individual. In many ways this approach can be seen as a revolt against the mechanistic scientific approach of modern psychology, which is seen as unsuitable for the study of human behaviour.

Rogers' self theory, the work of one such humanist, is discussed in Reading 6.8. Humanists believe that people will always grow and be motivated to reach their full potential if the environment allows them to do so. The involvement of subjective conscious experience gives the name **phenomenology** to this approach. Phenomenologists believe we are not affected by reality but rather by our perception/understanding of it. This approach is discussed in Reading 1.9.

Reading 1.7   Approaches in Psychology

Approach	Goal
Psychobiological	To discover and describe the structures and processes in the nervous system that underlie behaviour
Ethological	To study instinctive behaviour in its natural context, often by comparing behaviour of different species
Behavioural	To study behaviour, usually in controlled laboratory settings, and to examine how environmental conditions determine behaviour
Cognitive	To discover and study the mental processes that underlie knowledge and behaviour
Psychoanalytic	To determine the unconscious motivations of behaviour and to bring these motivations into conscious awareness
Humanistic	To examine the phenomena of experience and to help people maximise their potential for psychological growth

H.L. Roediger et al (1984) *Psychology*
Little Brown and Co

Complete the following summary table:

	Approach	Area of study	Name of ONE associated researcher	Description of research
1	Behavourist	Studies behaviour in controlled setting to identify determining variables	Skinner	operant conditioning – association of an action with its consequences
2		mental processes involved in knowledge and understanding		
3	Ethological			
4			Rogers	
5	Psychoanalytic			
6		structure and processes of nervous system involved in behaviour		
7				conformity studies – group effects on compliance

TERMS TO DEFINE

ethological   nervous system   psychobiological

Reading 1.8   Social Psychology

Gordon Allport (1968) suggested that 'social psychologists regard their discipline as an attempt to understand how the thought, feeling, and behaviour of individuals are influenced by the actual, imagined or implied presence of others'. In this useful definition, the term 'implied presence' refers to the fact that people often act with an awareness that they belong to particular cultural, occupational, or social groups. Furthermore, even when we are alone, our behaviour may be influenced by our awareness that we are performing a role in a complex social structure, thus reflecting the implied presence of others. If we fail at our job, if our physical appearance changes, or if we get arrested, our reactions are affected by awareness of others and our relationships to them.

The ramifications of Allport's definition are thought-provoking. Just how far does the concern of social psychology extend? Clearly within the domain of social psychology is the behaviour of a young man sitting on a crowded bus as a frail old woman stands wearily in the aisle beside him. Does he offer her his seat? Or does he pretend to be engrossed in a book or in the passing scenery? Does he feel any concern about what she thinks of him? About what others are thinking? When a young woman enters a doctor's office for an eye examination, her actions also may be affected by the presence of others. The ophthalmologist asks her to look at the eye chart, trying first one lens and then another. The young woman's task is a straightforward one of determining and reporting which lens gives a clearer image, but she may be thinking 'Am I giving the right answer? What if I really can't tell the difference? Does the doctor know if I'm making a mistake?' Such questions reflect her concern about the impression she is making; certainly they demonstrate that many responses in such a situation are social behaviour.

Not all activities carried out by humans are social behaviours. For example, if you pick an apricot off a tree, eat it, immediately get sick, and thereafter avoid eating apricots (at least those straight off the tree), your reactions occur whether other people are present or not and probably do not reflect an awareness of others. Reflex actions, such as removing your hand from a hot stove, are nonsocial; the immediate physical response is the same regardless of the presence or the awareness of others. However, your oral response to touching a hot stove may well be coloured by the presence of others. Certain internal responses – glandular, digestive, excretory – are generally considered to be beyond the realm of social psychology. However, nausea, constipation, or other physical responses may result from feelings associated with the actions or presence of other people. Even the time of dying may be a response to social considerations. David Phillips (1970, 1972) has suggested that Jews 'postpone' the date of dying until after significant events, such as Yom Kippur, the Day of Atonement. In Jewish populations in both New York City and Budapest, he found a 'death dip' – a significant decrease in death rates – during the months prior to Yom Kippur.

Thus, a great deal of any person's behaviour – perhaps more than you first realised – is social.

K. Deaux and L.S. Wrightsman (1984) *Social Psychology in the 80s* (4th edn)
Brooks/Cole

1 Describe **two** areas of research for social psychologists.   (2)

2 Give an example from the text of a behaviour which is **not** social.   (1)

3 What, according to Phillips (1970, 1972), is a 'death dip'?   (2)

4 a) Describe **one** social psychological experiment.   (4)
   b) Give **one** criticism of this experiment.   (4)

TERMS TO DEFINE

social influence   social perception

Reading 1.9 Phenomenology

The major implication is that each of us perceives the world in a unique way, although our perceptions might have points in common. And it is these perceptions, or the intentions to which they give rise, that determine how we react and what we are.

This can be expressed: $S \rightarrow O \rightarrow R$ rather than the behaviourist $S \rightarrow R$.

A stimulus impinges on the organism which perceives it, processes it, decides what to do about it and then attempts to carry out its intention. The O is an important intervening point between stimulus and response; it is where choices are made, on the basis of thinking, evaluating and expecting. Every subject in an experiment has his background of unique experiences which are causing him to view the situation in a unique way. His perceptions are determining his individual reactions. So psychologists should attempt to see the world through the other person's eyes.

The main themes of phenomenological psychology can be summarised as follows:

(1) Man is his consciousness. Consciousness is defined in this context as a feeling of being active, an awareness of one's identity and the understanding which this gives.

(2) Man lives in a subjective world of private experiences, emotions, feelings, and perceptions. So the proper study of psychologists is experience and perception. The important question, of course, is how is this achieved?

(3) Man is unpredictable. Man has choice, free will and makes active decisions. It should be remembered that this is just as much of an assumption as the alternative, that man is predictable.

(4) Man is irrational. He contradicts the laws of reason in what he does. He has faith, religions, beliefs, and makes value judgements, all of which are of importance to study.

(5) Man should be studied as a whole. If man is broken down into his parts and these parts are studied separately, something is lost from the true picture of man. The whole is greater than the sum of the parts.

(6) Man is unique, and should be studied as such.

Behaviourism and the phenomenological humanist approach represent two completely opposed viewpoints in psychology, or more properly, two

31

completely opposite models of man. One has led to the rules and methods of conventional science being applied to the study of man. The other has sprung up partly as a reaction to this, and seeks to put 'man' back into the picture and leave out the machine.

R.B. Burns and C.B. Dobson (1984) *Introducing Psychology* MTP Press

1 Give **two** characteristics of the phenomenological approach. (4)

2 Behaviourism and phenomenology are:
  a) directly opposed to one another
  b) in agreement with one another. (1)

3 Name **one** supporter of this approach. (2)

4 Can you find **one** criticism of the phenomenological approach? (4)

TERMS TO DEFINE

phenomenology   subjective

There are many areas in which psychologists work. The work they do includes both **pure** and **applied psychology** which is discussed in Reading 1.10.

The three main areas of applied psychology (**educational, industrial/occupational**, and **clinical**) all demand special training after the initial requirement of a degree in psychology. Educational psychologists are involved in planning educational programmes for children with special needs, such as mental and physical handicap. They administer psychological tests including tests of ability, such as intelligence tests, to help assess those with learning difficulties. They are often involved with research into teaching methods and educational programmes.

Industrial or occupational psychologists are often responsible for the selection and testing of people entering employment. They may find themselves designing training programmes, researching into the design of machinery, helping to develop communication networks or helping to sell products through advertising.

One of the largest groups of applied psychologists can be found working in clinical psychology. Clinical psychologists use psychological research to help people with behavioural problems. Most of their work is with the mentally ill in hospitals and also in the community. It might be helpful here to distinguish between **psychiatrists** and **psychologists**. Psychiatrists have undergone a degree course in medicine and then gone on to specialise in the treatment of mental disorders. Clinical psychologists have taken a degree course in psychology and then specialised in the study of abnormal behaviour. The two fields overlap and you will often find psychologists and psychiatrists working together on cases. However, due to the difference in their training, conflict between the two is sometimes inevitable. Psychiatrists with their medical background are involved in medical treatment, including drugs and sometimes surgical techniques; whereas psychologists are trained in other methods including cognitive

Reading 1.10 Pure and Applied Psychology

A distinction which may prove helpful is that between the academic and the applied branches of the subject. The academic psychologist carries out research (scientific investigation) in a particular area (e.g. perception) and is attached to a university, polytechnic or research establishment where they will also teach first degree students (undergraduates) and may supervise the research of postgraduates.

Research is of two major kinds: pure, i.e. done for its own sake and intended, primarily, to increase our knowledge and understanding; and applied, i.e. aimed at solving a particular problem, usually a social problem such as alcoholism or juvenile delinquency. Applied psychology is usually funded by a government institution, like the Home Office or the Department of Education and Science, or by some commerical or industrial institution.

The range of topics that may be investigated is as wide as psychology itself, but a way of classifying them has been suggested by Legge (1975), namely, those which focus on the processes or mechanisms underlying various aspects of behaviour, and those which focus more directly on the person.

The Process approach is much more confined to the laboratory, makes far greater use of animals as subjects, and makes the general and basic assumption that psychological processes (particularly learning) are essentially the same in all species; any differences that are found between members of different species are only quantitative (differences of degree). In contrast, the Person approach makes much greater use of field studies (e.g. observing subjects in their natural environments) and of non-experimental methods (e.g. correlational studies). In the main, human subjects are used and it is assumed that qualitative differences (differences in kind) exist between humans and other animals.

R.D. Gross (1987) *Psychology: The Science of Mind and Behaviour* Arnold

1 What is the difference between 'pure' and 'applied' research?   (4)

2 Describe **two** differences between the Process and Person approaches.   (4)

3 Discuss **one** example of research which has been 'applied' in psychology.   (4)

TERMS TO DEFINE

pure/applied research

and behavioural therapy. This can cause a difference of opinion such as on the relative value of intervention in the form of electro-convulsive therapy (ECT), where an electric current is passed through the brain simulating a severe epileptic fit. This treatment is sometimes used for severe depression. Many psychologists are concerned about the long-term effects on memory and concentration and would prefer the application of alternative behavioural treatments in most cases.

Psychology overlaps with many other disciplines. Much of the history of psychology can be seen as bringing philosophical problems into the area of scientific enquiry. At this point you might like to take a historical journey through psychology as suggested in Activity 1.3.

Activity 1.3

Draw up a chart noting the important dates in the history of modern psychology. Give the names of famous psychologists wherever possible and briefly note their findings.

When studying psychology we find topics separated into the various areas of research (e.g. cognitive, social, developmental etc.). However, it is worth bearing in mind that these areas all relate to human beings and do not exist in a vacuum; there is considerable interaction and overlap between them. As you progress through your studies of psychology some of these links should become apparent. It is only to help separate the important areas of research and make theories and topics more understandable that such divisions have been created. This book follows the usual segregated pattern, but occasional references will be made to links between the topic areas in the hope that you will become aware of interactions within and between areas.

One controversy which is central to the study of psychology, and found in all areas of research, is that of the influence of our genetic inheritance and/or the effects of learning on behaviour. Are we born with certain characteristics or are they shaped by our experiences? The resulting interaction of these processes, (known as the **nature and nurture** debate), will be discussed in Chapter Two.

SUGGESTIONS FOR FURTHER READING

R.L. Atkinson et al (1987) *Introduction to Psychology* (9th edn) Harcourt
    Brace Jovanovich
A. Gale (1985) *What is Psychology?* Edward Arnold
D. Hothersall (1985) *Psychology* Merrill
J. Radford and E. Govier (1982) *A Textbook of Psychology* Sheldon

Stimulus Questions

An organisational psychologist wanted to investigate the effect that working conditions have on how satisfied people are at work. She arranged for a number of employees at a bottle factory to fill in questionnaires about their working conditions. Among other topics, the subjects were asked to rate the canteen service, and the cleanliness of both the factory and the job that the person was doing.

The psychologist analysed the data by calculating the correlation between how satisfied people said they were with their job, and their responses to the other questions. The correlation coefficients obtained were as follows:

Cleanliness of working surroundings + ·73

Cleanliness of job itself + ·06

Efficiency of canteen service + ·53

Quality of canteen food + ·27

The employees were also asked to give their opinions about important factors in job satisfaction. In the final list, cleanliness of working surroundings was ranked tenth in order of importance, while the quality of canteen food was ranked fourth.

1.1 Which factor seemed to be most important to job satisfaction? (1)

1.2 Which factor seemed to be least important to job satisfaction? (1)

1.3 What is a correlation coefficient? (2)

1.4 All of the scores here are positive correlations. What is a positive correlation? (2)

1.5 What sort of diagram is normally used for showing correlations? (1)

1.6 Suggest a possible explanation for why the subjects' opinions and the psychologist's data appear to contradict each other. (4)

1.7 Outline **one** disadvantage of asking people directly what factors they think are most important at work. (3)

1.8 Suggest another way in which the psychologist could have found out what people think of their working conditions. (4)

1.9 What name is given to the problem of whether your research methods really measure what they are supposed to be measuring? (1)

1.10 If you were conducting a survey on job satisfaction, outline **two** controls or precautions that you would need to take, and explain why each one would be necessary. (6)

Methodology Questions

Freudian psychoanalysts believe that experiences in infancy and early childhood are the cause of adult personality characteristics. Imagine that you are about to conduct a retrospective study on this question, and that you have decided to focus particularly on the possible connection between very strict parental styles, and obsessive neatness and orderliness. You intend to ask 10 people about their early memories of their parents, and compare each of these with a friend's description of how tidy they are. In order to do this, you will ask them to use a rating scale ranging from 1 = extremely untidy to 10 = extremely neat. The ratings of how strict the parents were will be on a five-point scale which ranges from 1 = very easy-going to 5 = very strict indeed.

1.1 What is a retrospective study? (1)

1.2 Name **two** psychosexual stages described by Freud. (2)

1.3 What will your hypothesis be for this study? (3)

1.4 Give **one** disadvantage of having 10 subjects in the study. (2)

1.5 State **one** problem of using a 1–10 scale to rate neatness. (2)

1.6 Give **two** difficulties which can come from asking subjects to rate how strict their parents were. (4)

1.7 If you were drawing up a diagram to illustrate your findings from this study, what type of diagram would you choose? (2)

1.8 Part of Freud's evidence for his theory of the unconscious mind came from studies using **word-association tests**. What are these? (3)

1.9 Suggest an alternative method that you could use to obtain a reliable measure of neatness from your subjects. (2)

1.10 Give **two** criticisms which can be made of retrospective studies. (4)

2

Nature and Nurture

Plate 2

37

Readings on 'Nature and Nurture'

One controversy which has intrigued psychologists for many years is the relative contribution to behaviour of innate (**nature**) and learned (**nurture**) components. Natural forces have been appreciated throughout history. Many early developmental psychologists argued that biological maturation was the main principle of development. Conversely, the learning (empirical) school championed by John Watson early in the twentieth century opposed this view and further suggested that human development depended more importantly on environmental experiences. Today, most psychologists see development resulting from the **interaction** of both biological determinants and environmental experiences.

We shall examine evidence demonstrating the importance of innate and learned characteristics and also look at some of the examples demonstrating the interplay between the two.

Ethology is the study of behaviour in the natural environment. It is from this field of enquiry that behaviour patterns seen to be innately determined have been identified. Innate behaviour, specific to certain species where it appears in the same form for all members, is labelled as **instinctive**. One area where instinctive behaviour has been identified is that of **imprinting** (Lorenz, 1935). This refers to a type of early learning which forms the basis of a young animal's attachment to its parents. Lorenz saw imprinting occurring during a **critical period** early in the animal's life. Such **critical and sensitive periods** are discussed in Reading 2.1.

It has been suggested that many critical or sensitive periods occur in development. The psychoanalytic school of psychology headed by Sigmund Freud saw certain periods of early childhood as being critical for later development. More recently, this view was further investigated by

John Bowlby. A discussion of this can be found in Chapter Seven, especially Reading 7.5 Bonding.

Reading 2.1   Critical and Sensitive Periods

Lorenz borrowed the term 'critical period' from embryology, implying that there are periods in development during which the individual is especially impressionable or vulnerable, that is, when particular experiences exert a profound and lasting influence on later behaviour.

In relation to imprinting, 'critical' implies that unless learning occurs during a particular period after hatching, it will never occur; (it also conveys the second major characteristic of imprinting, namely, irreversibility). Imprintability, according to Lorenz, is genetically 'switched on' and then 'switched off' again at the end of the period; in the case of mallard ducklings the critical period lasts for the first few hours after hatching (Lorenz, 1935) and, more precisely, between 5 and 24 hours after hatching, with a peak between 13 to 16 hours (Ramsay and Hess, 1954). Hess (1958), studying chicks, ducklings and goslings, maintains that although imprinting could occur as early as one hour after hatching, the strongest responses occurred between 12 to 17 hours ('critical period peak'); after 32 hours, it was extremely unlikely to happen and it became increasingly difficult after 20 hours. Gottlieb (1961) reported a critical period of 8 to 27 hours (with no peak) for Peking ducklings.

Are these periods switched on and off in the way Lorenz believed?

Many researchers have shown that if a young bird is kept in isolation, it remains unimprinted (and still imprintable) beyond the end of the normal critical period (for instance, Sluckin, 1961 and Bateson, 1964, with ducklings). Also, if chicks are kept in an unstimulating environment (especially if it is visually unstimulating) they could imprint well after the critical period normally ends (Guiton, 1958); similar results were found by Moltz and Stettner (1961) who fitted translucent hoods to ducklings, thus preventing perception of patterned light.

In view of this evidence that the young bird's experience can extend the period of imprintability, Lorenz's original proposal that the termination (as well as the onset) of the critical period is under genetic control seemed untenable and this led Sluckin (1965) to coin the term sensitive period instead. A sensitive period is one during which learning is most likely to happen and will happen most easily but it is not as 'critical' or 'once-and-for-all' as the critical period concept suggests. It seems more useful to think in terms of the probability that imprinting will occur rather than 'whether-or-not' it will occur.

Hinde (1966) defines a sensitive period as, 'a time during an organism's development when a particular influence is most likely to have an effect', while according to Dworetzky (1981), 'there could be times in our life when we are genetically primed to respond to certain influences and other times when those influences would have little or no effect'.

R.D. Gross (1987) *Psychology: The Science of Mind and Behaviour* Arnold

1 a) What is meant by instinct?   (2)
   b) Name **two** patterns of maternal behaviour displayed by animals which demonstrate instinctive behaviour.   (2)

2 Imprinting refers to:
   a) a type of early learning related to attachment
   b) a maternal duty
   c) a particular environmental stimulus that sets off a species-specific behaviour. (2)

3 During which period of time is imprinting most likely to occur? (1)

4 a) With reference to **one** experimental study in animals, show what is meant by the term 'critical' period. (6)
   b) Why is the term 'sensitive' period now preferred by psychologists? (2)

TERMS TO DEFINE

critical/sensitive periods   imprinting   instinct   species-specific

Lenneberg (1970) believed that by puberty the child's brain had become specialised for language, and if a person had not developed language by this time then such acquisition would be difficult if not impossible. This early period of life was seen to be critical for language development in humans. He suggested that the brain is especially sensitive for the learning of language at this time. Research with isolated children, who have been deprived of human contact and human speech, has provided an insight into this topic. A report of children reared in partial isolation can be found in Reading 2.2 **Isolated Children**.

Reading 2.2   Isolated Children

'Isabelle' was hidden away, apparently from early infancy, and given only the minimal attention necessary to sustain her life. Apparently no one spoke to her (in fact, her mother was deaf and did not speak). Isabelle was six years old when discovered. Of course she had no language, and her cognitive development was below that of a normal two-year-old. But within a year, this girl learned to speak. Her tested intelligence was normal, and she took her place in an ordinary school (Davis, 1947; Brown, 1958). Thus Isabelle at seven years, with one year of language practice, spoke about as well as her peers in the second grade, all of whom had had seven years of practice.

Rehabilitation from isolation is not always so successful. A child, 'Genie,' discovered in California about twenty years ago, was fourteen years old when found. Since about twenty months, apparently, she had lived tied to a chair, was frequently beaten, and never spoken to – but sometimes barked at, for her father said she was no more than a dog. Afterwards, she was taught by psychologists and linguists (Fromkin et al., 1974). But Genie did not become a normal language user. She says many words, and puts them together into meaningful propositions as young children do, such as 'No more take wax' and 'Another house have dog.' Thus she has learned certain basics of language. Indeed, her semantic sophistication – what she means by what she says – is far beyond young children. Yet, even after many years of instruction, Genie did not learn the closed-class words, pronouns, auxiliary verbs, and so on, that appear in mature English sentences, nor did she combine propositions together in elaborate sentences (Curtiss, 1977).

Why did Genie not progress to full language learning while Isabelle did? The best guess is that the crucial factor is the age at which language learning began. Genie was discovered after she had reached puberty while Isabelle was only six. As we shall see later, there is some reason to believe there is a critical period for language learning. If the person has passed this period, language learning proceeds with greater difficulty.

H. Gleitman (1986) *Psychology* (2nd edn) W.W. Norton and Co

1 How old were Isabelle and Genie when they were discovered?   (2)

2 In your own words describe the language development of the two girls after discovery.   (4)

3 a) What method of investigation was used to determine the change in language behaviour of the children reported?   (1)
   b) Name **one** disadvantage of this approach.   (2)

4 Give **two** possible reasons for the different progress in language learning of Isabelle and Genie.   (4)

TERMS TO DEFINE

deprivation   language   semantics

Is language **species-specific**? Is human language unique and restricted to humans? Several researchers have suggested that there is a genetic component to language and language acquisition, thereby restricting its full use to humans. This view has been challenged by several psychologists who have endeavoured to teach language to non-humans, mainly apes. Some of this research is discussed in Reading 2.3 **Teaching Language to Apes**.

Reading 2.3   Teaching Language To Apes

David Premack (1971) taught the chimp Sarah to use plastic chips as symbols for words, and to communicate by rearranging chips into 'sentences'; Duane Rumbaugh (1977) taught a typewriter keyboard form of communication to a chimp named Lana. Among the most successful projects have been those based on American sign language, teaching the animals to sign manually the way deaf persons do. Two of the most famous of these animals are Washoe the chimpanzee, trained by Beatrice and Allen Gardner (e.g., 1969, 1975), and Herbert Terrace's (1979) 'Nim Chimpsky.' (There's an 'in joke' here – the noted linguist Chomsky's first name is Noam.)

A great deal of evidence about language acquisition has been accumulated in these projects. For obvious reasons, the most intriguing questions have been those comparing the chimps' language skills with those of normal human children. Until recently, these patterns were viewed as highly similar – suggesting that language is perhaps not as restricted to humans as has been believed for centuries. Washoe, for instance, seemed not only to master a large number of signs, but had some success in forming short 'grammatical' sentences with the signs. Francine Patterson's (1978) Koko, a gorilla, evidenced similar skills, and was observed to display other sorts of language-related behaviour like teasing, joking and even lying!

And yet as a recent critical review from the Rumbaugh team illustrates, the limitations of these projects are becoming apparent as initial enthusiasm has waned. It seems, for instance, that the chimps do not progress beyond a fairly elementary level in terms of the length of their sentences as measured by MLU, Mean Length of Utterance, a standard psycholinguistic measure of language complexity. While normal children show an ever-increasing pattern on MLU across age, the chimps seem to 'stall' at about a 3 to 4 word level. The chimps show no evidence of conversational 'turn taking,' while this is a fairly early development in human language (indeed, vocal turn taking among mothers and infants can be observed shortly after the infant begins to babble). And finally, the chimps tend merely to string symbols together, rather than achieve a more specific referent or idea for particular symbols. To quote the review by Savage-Rumbaugh, Rumbaugh & Boysen (1980): "chimpanzees have tended to form five- and six-word utterances such as 'you me sweet drink give me,' while children form six-word utterances such as 'Johnny's mother poured me some Kool-Aid'."

D. Hothersall (1985) *Psychology* Merrill

1 How were Sarah and Lana taught to communicate with humans?   (2)

2 a) What is the MLU?   (2)
   b) Describe **two** differences in language ability which distinguish human children from chimps.   (2)

3 Fill in the missing terms relating to Hockett's criteria of language:
   a) . . . . . refers to the ability to talk about people or objects not present.
   b) Traditional transmission is . . . . . .
   c) Telling lies or talking about impossibilities is known as . . . . . .   (3)

4 What criticisms have been made of studies which suggest that non-humans can acquire human language?   (6)

TERMS TO DEFINE

communication   grammar   MLU   symbol

You have probably noted the reliance on animal studies in many areas of psychology. The completion of Activity 2.1 could prove useful in evaluating their contribution.

Activity 2.1

Using this resourcebook, and any other psychological textbooks you have available, compile a list of animal studies. Include the following details:

1 Researcher's name and date
2 Purpose of the study
3 Results of the investigation.

Could human subjects have been used instead of animals?
Do you consider the research to be ethical?

Perhaps you could chart the information to make comparison of the reports easier. Did you notice any historical changes in the type of animal research performed (e.g. research performed recently compared with that of 20–30 years ago)? How can you explain this? If human subjects could have been used in some studies, why do you think that animals were used instead?

The role of nature and nurture in perception has been widely investigated to try and determine whether we have to learn to see, or whether we are born with perceptual abilities. Studies of young babies (**neonates**) have tried to distinguish processes which exist in the newborn before these are modified by learning experiences. Most of the evidence to date supports the view that many simple perceptual abilities are under genetic control, whereas more complex abilities are susceptible to environmental influences. This viewpoint gains supporting evidence from blind patients who have regained their sight, often due to the removal of cataracts (a film over the lens of the eye). The research of Von Senden (1932) has been often quoted and his work is discussed in Reading 2.4 **Perception: Innate or Learned?**

Reading 2.4   Perception: Innate or Learned?

Von Senden's original data was taken up again by Hebb in 1949, who analysed the findings in terms of: (i) *figural unity*, the ability to detect the presence of a figure or stimulus; and (ii) *figural identity*, being able to name or in some other way identify the object, to 'say' what it is. Hebb concluded that while (i) seems to be innate, (ii) seems to require learning.

Initially, cataract patients are typically bewildered by an array of visual stimuli (rather like the 'blooming, buzzing confusion' which William James believed was the perceptual experience of newborn babies). However, they can distinguish figures from ground (i.e. some object from its background), fixate objects, scan them and follow moving objects with their eyes. But they cannot identify by sight alone those objects which are already familiar through touch (and this includes faces), distinguish between various geometrical shapes without counting the corners or tracing the outline with their fingers, or say which of two sticks is longer without feeling them (although they can tell there is a difference).

They also fail to show perceptual constancy, that is, the recognition and perception of things as the same despite changes in their appearance (compare with Piaget's concept of conservation). For example, even after visual identification has occurred (i.e., things are recognised through sight alone) there may be little generalisation to situations other than that in which the object was originally recognised, e.g. a lump of sugar held in someone's hand may not be identified as such when suspended from a piece of string. Another example would be the failure to recognise a triangle as being the same geometrical shape when its white side is turned over to reveal a red side or when viewed under different lighting conditions. (Interestingly, Bower believes that size and shape constancy are probably innate; Hebb's findings suggest this is not so.)

So the more simple ability of figural unity seems to be available very soon after cataract removal and seems not to be dependent on prior visual experience, while the more complex figural identity seems to require a long period of training. Hebb believes that this is how these two aspects of perception normally develop.

Further evidence comes from a single case, that of a man named S.B., reported by Gregory and Wallace in 1963. S.B. was 52 when he received his sight after a corneal graft operation. His judgement of size and distance were good, provided that he was familiar with the objects in question. He could recognise objects visually if he was already familiar with them through touch while blind so, unlike most of the 65 cases analysed by Hebb, he displayed good cross-modal transfer, i.e., recognition through one sense modality (touch) being substituted by another (vision). However, he seemed to have great difficulty in identifying objects visually if he was not already familiar with them in this way: a year after his operation he still could not draw the front of a bus although the rest of the drawing was very well executed. S.B. was never able to use his new-found ability to see to its fullest extent; for instance, he did not bother to turn on the light at night but would sit in the dark all evening.

R.D. Gross (1987) *Psychology: the Science of Mind and Behaviour* Arnold

1 Explain what is meant by:
   a) figural unity
   b) figural identity.   (2)

2 Describe **two** perceptual abilities present when cataract patients regain their sight.   (4)

3 Discuss **two** perceptual problems which are encountered initially by most cataract patients on regaining their sight.   (4)

4 Describe **two** problems of interpreting evidence from studies of blind adults who have regained their sight.   (4)

5 Discuss, with evidence, the research on whether perception is innate or learned.   (10)

TERMS TO DEFINE

cross-modal transfer   innate   perceptual constancy

Determining whether abilities are innate or learned is far from easy, so many factors, or variables, have to be considered. Vurpillot (1976), investigating **maturation** of perceptual processes in children aged between 3½–7½ years, has shown how perceptual skills change with age. The children she studied were shown a standard drawing of a landscape including a house, shrub, pond and the sun in the sky. Similar drawings were then presented to the children who were asked to point out the differences between the two drawings. The standard drawing and four comparisons can be seen in Figure 2.1.

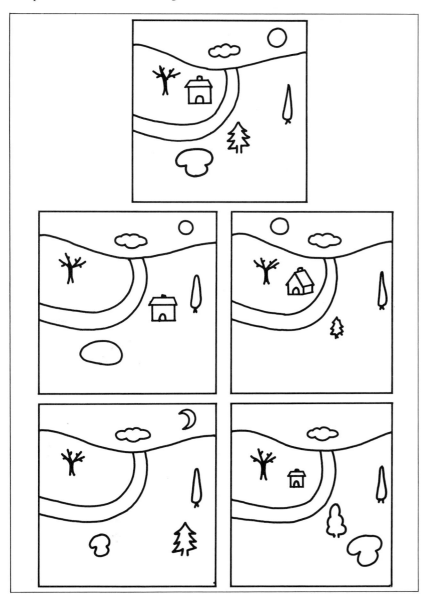

Figure 2.1 *The Vurpillot standard drawing (top) plus four comparisons*

Vurpillot found that perceptual discrimination may be present at birth but this may not be used correctly until **perceptual maturation** has taken place. This research is discussed in Reading 2.5.

Reading 2.5   Perceptual Maturation

Vurpillot found that children as young as three-and-a-half are quick to perceive differences in form (when a round sun is changed into a crescent one) and also when parts of the drawing are absent. By seven-and-a-half they are skilful at reporting changes in size, but still not proficient at detecting changes of location.

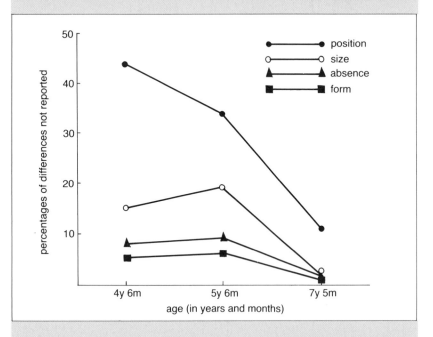

The above figure shows the proportion of children at each age who cannot yet detect these different kinds of disparity between the standard and the comparison.

Why did the younger children so blithely assume the drawing to be similar when an important element was moved to another location? Or reduced in size? Vurpillot argues that all children could discriminate these differences; their vision was certainly good enough. When discussing the greater skill of the older children she writes: 'as a general rule it seems that change in performance expresses . . . the adoption of a new decision criterion . . .'. In deciding whether or not the drawings were similar the younger children did not bother to compare size or location. For them, a yes/no decision hinged on form being the same in each drawing and also the sheer presence or absence of something. Vurpillot says that response to this task is determined by an understanding of what makes visual events similar. As long as the parts are present and in identical form, the young child is satisfied they are similar. The older child requires something more – that the components of the drawing be of the same size and in the same location. His understanding of perceptual similarity includes size and location as well as presence and form.

In sum, the younger child is not limited by lack of visual discrimination but by his capacity for gathering, recording and thinking about perceptual information. He relies on a few simple criteria for making perceptual judgements. What matures with age are decision rules for making visual comparison and strategies for selecting from a wealth of information. These are part of the mind's structure for deciding which visual information in the environment is necessary or important.

K. Sylva and I. Lunt (1982) *Child Development: A First Course* Basil Blackwell

1 Define maturation.   (2)

2 a) How many children aged 5½ years did not notice differences in the
        size of objects in the drawings?   (1)
    b) What difference in noting the changes of location occurred between
        the ages of 4½ and 7½ years?   (2)

3 How does Vurpillot explain the young child's lack of skill in detecting
   differences in the pictures?   (4)

4 Discuss, with the help of at least **two** studies, the role of maturation in
   development.   (8)

TERMS TO DEFINE

genetics   maturation   visual discrimination

Children mature in roughly the same sequence, with individual progress rates dependent on several factors including inherited potential and learning experiences. This can be seen in an observational study of young children, as suggested in Activity 2.2.

The role of learning in development has been investigated extensively by the behaviourist school of psychology (introduced in Chapter One). The early behaviourists investigated simple learning (or **conditioning**) of associations between a stimulus and a response. 'Operant' conditioning, so named by Skinner, is sometimes known as 'instrumental' conditioning because the animal's response becomes instrumental in acquiring reinforcement. The original experiments demanded the hungry animal either to press a lever (rats and other rodents), or peck a disc (pigeons and other birds/poultry) to gain a food reinforcer. This technique was extended to create entirely new or novel behaviour, often not associated with the normal behaviour of the animal. Such techniques have been used to train animals in 'circus tricks'. However, other stimuli which are present at the same time can become 'linked' and thus change the intended behaviour. This linking of stimuli present at the same time is known as **temporal contiguity** and is demonstrated in Reading 2.6 **Superstitious Behaviour.**

Activity 2.2

If time permits, and you have contact with someone with young children, a maturational study could prove interesting. Choose children aged between 15–36 months (if you know of two children of the same age a comparison could demonstrate individual differences). Study each child individually (with the parent present if possible), and note the occurrence of the motor abilities shown on the chart below. The average age (norm) for the occurrence of each activity is recorded on the chart as x. If the ability is not observed but is present according to the parent's report then record this as R.

	Months: 15	18	21	24	30	36
Motor development						
Walks						
– few steps, starts and stops without support	x					
– falls by collapse	x					
– seldom falls		x				
– fast, runs stiffly		x				
– squats in play			x			
– on tiptoe (D)					x	
Runs						
– without falling				x		
Jumps						
– with both feet					x	
– from bottom stair						x
Chair, small						
– seats self		x				
Chair, adult						
– climbs into		x				
– gets down, no help			x			
Stands on one foot						
– attempts					x	
– momentary balance						x
Book (children's picture)						
– helps turn pages	x					
– turn pages 2-3 at a time		x				
– turns page singly				x		

How does each child's developmental level compare with his/her chronological age? If two, or more, children of the same age were observed, what differences were found in their developmental level? Can you give a possible explanation for these differences?
On the basis of your observations, describe the general developmental sequence of locomotion.
This could be performed as a group exercise with results from several sources combined. Several other skills such as manual dexterity (e.g. in using building blocks), drawing, knowledge of digits, language, play etc. could also be observed.

Reading 2.6   Superstitious Behaviour

The association of the reinforcement with the behaviour immediately preceding it can have unexpected results. If an experimental animal is doing something else at the same time as it presses the lever in a Skinner box, then both the lever pressing and the something else will be reinforced. The animal learns the total pattern, one movement of which is useful, and the other movement which has no particular value. A monkey, for example, might well be scratching its head when it presses the lever, and it quickly learns to do this whenever it subsequently presses the lever. Skinner refers to the head scratching as 'superstitious' behaviour; it has nothing to do with the causal relationship of the lever and the food mechanism.

In one experiment a hungry pigeon was placed in a Skinner box in which it had learned to feed from a grain hopper. The food supply was then operated periodically, small quantities of grain appearing at 30 second intervals throughout several long experimental sessions. The appearance of the food was not now contingent on a particular behaviour pattern. However the pigeon was doing something at the time the food appeared, and this behaviour was reinforced. This gave a slightly increased chance that the pigeon would be doing the same thing when the next lot of grain appeared, and so the behaviour pattern became stronger. The pigeon gets trapped into a particular behaviour sequence which may appear to be completely bizarre. In some experiments Skinner found that the pigeons developed behaviour patterns which included turning sharply to one side, hopping from one foot to the other, bowing and finally lifting the head high.

Such a situation may seem amusing. With our greater wisdom we can laugh at the monkey 'knowing' that it must scratch its head in order to obtain food. We know there is no causal connection between these two actions. We must not be too condescending however; think of the frequency with which people behave in a similar way. A particular article of clothing worn during a day on which all goes well becomes lucky. Large numbers of people are convinced that their lives will run smoothly as long as they have their mascots with them. A widespread form of superstitious reinforcement occurs during illness. Many diseases run through a natural development, and a remedy given at the time when the patient is on the point of recovering naturally is reinforced by this recovery. So we have inherited some very strange folk remedies and beliefs, all of which have been 'proven' to work.

A.P. Brookfield (1980) *Animal Behaviour* Nelson

1 What do you understand by the following terms related to conditioning?
   a) reinforcer
   b) shaping
   c) generalisation
   d) positive and negative reinforcement.   (5)

2 How did Skinner explain superstitious behaviour?   (2)

3 Explain how an animal learns to discriminate between stimuli.   (4)

4 a) What are the main features of operant conditioning?   (6)
   b) Describe **two** possible applications of operant conditioning to human behaviour.   (8)

TERMS TO DEFINE

discrimination   extinction   reinforcement   schedules of reinforcement

The application of classical conditioning techniques in the treatment of phobias (abnormal fears) can be found in Chapter 6, Reading 6.6 Systematic Desensitisation, and the interested reader is referred to Suggestions For Further Reading at the end of the current chapter.

Many human characteristics are at the centre of the nature/nurture controversy. Aggression has been seen by many psychologists as inherited. Central to Freud's psychodynamic theory is belief in the existence of instinctual drives, including sex and life preserving instincts (the **libido**) and aggression (**thanatos** which represents the death instinct). He saw aggression as a strong motivating force which needs to be released or expressed in a manner acceptable to society.

Many researchers have questioned this view. Aggression can be seen to be dependent on environmental triggers. This is the basis of the **frustration-aggression hypothesis** which suggests that aggression is the result of frustrating circumstances rather than inherited disposition. The role of the environment and learning processes in the development of aggression during **socialisation** in childhood is discussed in Reading 2.7 **Socialisation and Aggression**.

Reading 2.7 Socialisation and Aggression

When playing in nursery school, children become very much more aggressive when they have only a small space to play in, and so are continually interfered with. Also, children behave more aggressively when they have just had a frustrating experience, for instance when they haven't been able to solve a puzzle. In adulthood, some people continue to react aggressively to frustrating events, while others don't. Why is this?

Newson and Newson, in a large study of child-rearing practices in Nottingham, in 1968, found that there were strong class differences in the amount of aggression which children showed. They found that middle-class parents tended to object to their children showing aggressive behaviour, while working-class parents tended to encourage their children to 'stand up for themselves', and to fight back if they were pushed around by other children. When they looked at mothers and infants, they found that, even in the first year of life, infants from working-class homes received more physical punishment than did middle-class infants, and showed more temper tantrums already.

Boys tend to show more aggressive behaviour than girls, and it is sometimes thought that this, too, is a result of parental treatment. A study by Rothbart and Maccoby, in 1966, used tape-recordings of family behaviour. When they analysed the tapes, they found that mothers were far more tolerant of aggressive acts committed by sons, than of aggressive acts committed by daughters. Young boys, it seems, are expected to be aggressive, whereas girls are not.

Another study, by Sears, Maccoby, and Levin, showed that, if children are punished by the parents for being aggressive – and particularly if it is physical punishment – aggressive acts can actually increase! It seems possible that this comes about as a result of 'modelling' – the parents, by their own behaviour, show the child that aggression can be used – because they, themselves, are using it when they punish the child. Since the children see punishment, and aggression, as being adult-type actions, the children increase their own aggressive behaviour.

N. Hayes (1984) *A First Course in Psychology* Nelson

1 Give **one** example from the text to illustrate how frustration in nursery school could make children more aggressive.   (1)

2 Complete the following sentences:
   a) . . . . class parents encourage their children to fight when other children behave aggressively towards them.
   b) . . . . class children receive less physical punishment from their parents.   (2)

3 a) How do psychologists explain the increase in aggression in children whose parents use physical punishment in child rearing?   (2)
   b) Describe **one** experiment which demonstrates how children may learn aggression through watching the actions of others.   (4)

4 Information on child-rearing may be gained from a survey. What are the problems associated with this method?   (8)

TERMS TO DEFINE

frustration-aggression hypothesis   socialisation   survey

The issue of whether aggression is innate or can be learned has become increasingly important with the growth of television and videos. Coverage of violence, both in documentaries and in films has been questioned. Most children today watch several hours of television daily and additionally may watch video films. Visits to the cinema are also likely. Many researchers have reported high levels of violence in such viewing, especially in children's cartoons (Gerbner et al, 1980). Perhaps you might like to investigate this yourself. If so, try Activity 2.3.

Activity 2.3

Are psychologists, and others, alarmist about the amount of violence on television? Select three or four early evening programmes (before 9 p.m.) which may be watched by children. Include one cartoon, and one 'educational' programme created for children (such as 'Sesame Street' or 'Blue Peter'). I suggest an observational period of 10 minutes for each programme.

1 For each programme, record the number of physical and verbal violent actions. (Make sure you define what you mean by 'violence' before you start!)
2 Were the violent actions performed by males or females?
3 What other behaviour may the children learn from each programme?

Make a note of any problems that you encountered in making these observations. How could you resolve these in future studies?

The supporters of the Freudian viewpoint did not believe that observation of violence would lead to aggression; indeed, many suggested that watching aggressive actions may allow the viewer to release pent-up aggressive urges, resulting in reduced aggression. This is known as the **cathartic effect**. However, recent evidence, such as that in Reading 2.8 **Violence and Television**, suggests that violence on the screen may encourage real-life aggression.

Reading 2.8 Violence and Television

There is now considerable evidence that violence on the screen often encourages real-life aggression.

Some of the effects represent a subtle change in attitude. One study found that people who watch a great deal of television tend to become distrustful of others and afraid of being victims of crime. They often try to protect themselves with extra locks on their doors, guard dogs, and guns (Gerbner and Gross, 1976). At the same time, they seem to become hardened to violence and less likely to be emotionally upset by real-life incidents of aggression (Thomas et al, 1977). It might be said that they begin to take violence for granted, as a standard part of human behaviour.

Other more direct effects have also been observed. One group of investigators found that preschool children who were heavy viewers of violent programmes became more aggressive during their play periods at day-care centres (Singer and Singer, 1980). Another study, of elementary school children in the United States, Finland, and Poland, found that in all three countries children who regularly watched programmes containing heavy doses of violence were rated by their peers as most aggressive. This was true of girls as well as boys (Eron and Huesmann, 1980). Still other studies revealed a significant increase in both verbal and physical aggression by children after television was introduced into their communities (Williams, 1978; Granzberg and Steinbring, 1980), though aggressive behaviour seems to decrease in children who watch television shows in which the characters solve their problems constructively, without resorting to violence (Leiffer, Gordon, and Graves, 1974).

It has been found that adults also tend to behave more aggressively after watching films that show aggressive acts (Hartmann, 1969). Moreover a number of violent crimes appear to be real-life imitations of television or movie stories (Mankiewicz and Swerdlow, 1977). Professional criminals sometimes learn new techniques from watching crimes on the screen (Hendrick, 1977).

J. Kagan et al (1984) *Psychology: An Introduction*
Harcourt Brace Jovanovich

1 Describe **one** change in attitude found in adults who watch a great deal of television. (1)

2 a) Watching high levels of TV violence has more effect on boys than girls.   TRUE/FALSE   (1)

   b) Children watching programmes where problems are solved without violence show less aggressive behaviour.   TRUE/FALSE   (1)

3 What psychological theory is being expressed in the research quoted in the text?   (2)

4 Describe **one** study carried out on the influence of television viewing on aggression in children.   (5)

5 Critically discuss **two** research examples demonstrating how psychologists measure changes in levels of aggression.   (8)

TERMS TO DEFINE

aggression   catharsis

A further discussion about the part played by imitation on development can be found in Chapter Seven, especially Reading 7.1 Observational Learning and Reading 7.2 Sex Roles.

Intelligence is another characteristic whose origin has been questioned. The measurement of intelligence known as the intelligence quotient (IQ) itself has been at the centre of much controversy, as can be seen in Chapter 6 Reading 6.1 Behavioural Assessment.

As we have seen, distinguishing between what is innate and what is learned has been shown to be difficult. One method which has been used in researching hereditary influences has involved studying identical (**monozygotic** or **MZ**) and fraternal (**dizygotic** or **DZ**) twins and adoption studies. Identical twins share their genetic potential whereas fraternal twins, who come from separate eggs, do not. Thus if identical twins appear more like one another than fraternal twins, this is surely evidence for the effects of heredity on IQ – or is it? It will become clear after Reading 2.9 **Adoption and Twin Studies** that this is not as straightforward as it appears.

Reading 2.9   Adoption and Twin Studies

Identical twins do have IQs that are more alike than fraternal twins (Loehlin and Nichols, 1976; Wilson, 1977, 1978, 1983). Robert Plomin (Plomin and DeFries, 1980), combining the results of all the studies of IQ in twins, estimates that the correlation between IQ scores of identical twins who have grown up together is .86 (a very high correlation), while the correlation between scores of same-sex fraternal twins reared together is about .60 – lower, but still fairly substantial. Score one point for heredity.

But wait a minute. Isn't it possible that identical twins are treated more alike than are fraternal twins, too? Maybe they are dressed alike, spend more time together, are disciplined alike, have more similar toys, and so on. In fact, this does seem to be true (Lytton, 1977), which means that at least some of the similarity between twins that has been ascribed to heredity may really be caused by the environment.

Studying a special subgroup of identical twins – those who have been reared apart from each other – can help us sort out these two influences. If such twins are still like each other in IQ, even though they have not been together, that would surely show a hereditary effect.

As you might imagine, there aren't many pairs of identical twins who have been reared in different families. But there are a few, and psychologists who have studied them (e.g. Shields, 1962) have generally found that the twins' IQ scores are still quite similar. Once again, though, the apparent support of a hereditary view that these data provide has been challenged by more recent analyses.

Leon Kamin (1974) went back and looked carefully at the cases involved in all studies of twins raised apart and found that, in the majority of instances, both twins were reared by relatives of the parents, such as two aunts or the grandmother and an aunt. In most cases, the children knew each other, went to the same schools, and knew they were twins. In those cases in which the twins were reared by unrelated families, ordinarily both children were placed in families of the same general social class. If we look at the correlation between the scores for identical twins raised in unrelated families only, we find that it is considerably lower (about .50 in the Shields study). Susan Farber (1981) has pursued this analysis still further and found that when the IQs of identical twins who were reared in the least-similar environments and for whom reliable and accurate data had been reported were compared, their IQs were the least similar as well. Thus, the twin data, which first appear to show an extremely strong hereditary influence on IQ, are not as clear-cut as they seem.
Results from adoption studies are equally two-sided. The most common finding is that adopted children's IQs can be predicted better from knowing the IQs or the level of education of their natural parents than from knowing the IQs or education of their adoptive parents (Horn, 1983; Scarr and Weinberg, 1983; Plomin and DeFries, 1983; Skodak and Skeels, 1945). Again, that sounds like a clear point for a genetic influence, but as usual, there are some confusions.

First of all, when two adopted children are raised in the same family, their IQs turn out to be more similar than you'd expect by chance, even though they have no shared inheritance at all (Scarr and Weinberg, 1977). The environment, in this case, seems to be moving both children in the same direction.

Second, adopted children, as a group, tend to have higher IQs than do their natural parents. The effect of most adoptive environments seems to be to raise the child's IQ 10 or 15 points over what it probably would have been if he had been raised by his natural mother (Scarr and Weinberg, 1977; Skodak and Skeels, 1945). So obviously, the adoptive environment has a major impact.

H. Bee (1985) *The Developing Child* Harper Row

1 What is meant by correlation? (2)

2 Chart the results of the Plomin and De Fries (1980) study on a bar graph, making sure that you label it clearly. (4)

3 Identify **one** problem found by Kamin (1974) which may bias the results of twin studies. (3)

4 Give **one** example of how the environment of the adopted child can affect IQ level. (3)

5 Discuss the advantages and disadvantages of using correlational techniques in research. (10)

TERMS TO DEFINE

adoption   correlation   MZ and DZ twins

The small portfolio of research into the origins of human characteristics demonstrates that in most cases features develop according to the **interaction** of heredity and learning experiences. Current research tries to determine the influence of each on the characteristic under investigation. Sometimes this relationship can be quite complex. Research into the area of **sensory-motor coordination** given in Reading 2.10 illustrates the importance of **active** interaction.

Reading 2.10   Sensory-Motor Coordination

Although you may often sit in one place to watch a film, a television programme, or even a lecture on perception, much of your visual experience occurs as you interact more actively with your environment. This active interaction with the environment – which ranges from simple actions, such as turning the pages in this book, to more complex actions, such as figure skating or gymnastics – involves sensory-motor coordination. Although many of your day-to-day tasks may seem easy to you now, you originally had to learn to coordinate your movements with your perceptions to do even the simplest things. How did you develop this ability?

Richard Held (1965) has suggested that a person must actively interact with the environment to develop sensory-motor coordination. To support this idea, Held did an experiment in which he disrupted sensory-motor coordination by having a person wear prism goggles that shift perception to the left or right. A person wearing the goggles often has trouble picking up things and often bumps into things, because they are not where they appear to be. Eventually, however, the person adapts to the displaced vision and can function while wearing the goggles.

That a person can adapt to displaced vision is nothing new – psychologists have been putting prism goggles on people (and on themselves) since before the turn of the century – but Held added something new. He had one person wear the goggles while walking along an outdoor path and another person wear them while being pushed in a wheelchair along the same path. Thus, both people were exposed to the same visual stimulation, but the walking person was active whereas the other was passive. After this trip along the path, Held tested the extent of adaptation to the goggles and found that the active person adapted to the goggles but the passive person did not. This result supports the idea that active or self-produced movement is necessary to adapt to the displaced vision caused by prism goggles.

To show that self-produced movement is important not only for the sensory-motor coordination involved in an adult's adaptation to prism goggles but also for a newborn's development of sensory-motor coordination, Held and Alan Hein (1963) did an experiment in which two dark-reared kittens were given their first visual experience in the 'kitten carousel' shown in the figure. As the active kitten walked, it transported the passive kitten riding in the gondola. Just as in the goggles experiment described above, both kittens received the same visual stimulation, but this stimulation was caused by self-produced movement only for the active kitten. As predicted, the active kitten developed good sensory-motor coordination, as indicated by its ability to blink at an approaching object, to put out its paws to ward off collision when carried downward toward a surface, and to avoid the deep side of a visual cliff; the passive kitten, however, had poor sensory-motor coordination, as indicated by its inability to do any of these things.

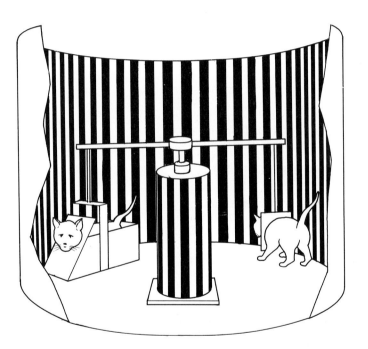

Thus, to develop sensory-motor coordination, it is necessary not only to be exposed to changing visual stimulation but also to cause the scene to change by means of self-produced movement. It is this interaction between changes in visual stimulation and the movement which produces these changes that helps you to coordinate what you do with what you see.

E.B. Goldstein (1984) *Sensation and Perception* Wadsworth

1 a) In your own words describe Held's (1965) research involving
      displaced vision. (3)
   b) State the hypothesis. (2)

2 What psychological explanation can be given for the finding that the inactive kitten had poor sensory-motor coordination?   (2)

3 Describe **one** research example which demonstrates the role of learning in perception.   (5)

4 Animals are often used in deprivation studies such as described above. Critically discuss the use of animals in psychological research.   (10)

TERMS TO DEFINE

displaced vision studies   kitten carousel   sensory-motor coordination

Just as understanding the mechanics of a car may help the driver to use the car's potential, so does an understanding of human physiology help the student to recognise the possible constraints and potential of human behaviour. We shall turn to this area in Chapter Three: **Brain and Behaviour**.

Topic-related Essays

1   What evidence is there to support the existence of 'critical' or 'sensitive' periods in development?

2   Discuss, with evidence, the effectiveness of language learning in primates.

3   Critically discuss ways of investigating the influence of genetic and environmental factors on intelligence.

SUGGESTIONS FOR FURTHER READING

Main texts
R.L. Atkinson et al (1987) *Introduction to Psychology* (9th edn) Harcourt Brace Jovanovich
N. Hayes (1988) *A First Course in Psychology* (2nd edn) Nelson
N. Hayes and S. Orrell (1987) *Psychology: an Introduction* Longman

Other useful texts
H. Bee (1985) *The Developing Child* Harper Row (esp. social learning theory and aggression)
A.M. and A.D.B. Clarke (1976) *Early Experience: Myth and Evidence* Open Books (detailed accounts of isolation studies)
G. Davey (1981) *Applications of Conditioning Theory* Methuen (more advanced text showing how learning theory has been applied)
K. Sylva and I. Lunt (1984) *Child Development: A First Course* Basil Blackwell (esp. animal studies, imprinting and attachment, maturation)

Stimulus Questions

A psychiatrist decided to conduct a twin study to investigate the idea that the mental illness 'schizophrenia' is inherited. By looking through hospital records, he found 60 patients in mental hospitals who were twins. He arranged to interview these patients and their twin partners (who were not diagnosed as mentally ill). From these interviews, he assessed the pairs of twins as being either monozygotic (MZ) or dizygotic (DZ). Forty-five of the pairs were judged to be MZ twins.

At the beginning of the study, 50 per cent of the mentally-ill patients were diagnosed as schizophrenic. The psychiatrist found that several more patients in the study could be diagnosed as schizophrenic, and that many of their paired twins appeared to have 'suspected schizophrenia', or a schizoid personality. The psychiatrist said that this meant that they might develop schizophrenia in the future, even though they had not shown any symptoms or needed treatment up to that point. In order to make sure that his twin assessment did not affect his diagnosis, the psychiatrist made his diagnosis before he made a judgement about whether the twins were MZ or DZ. The judgement about what type of twins they were was on the basis of their physical appearance.

On the basis of his findings, the psychiatrist concluded that schizophrenia was an inherited mental disorder.

2.1 At the beginning of the study, how many patients were diagnosed as schizophrenic?   (1)

2.2 What is a monozygotic twin?   (1)

2.3 What is a dizygotic twin?   (1)

2.4 Give **one** criticism of the way that the MZ and DZ judgements were made.   (3)

2.5 Suggest **one** improvement that could have been made to the way that the MZ and DZ judgements were made.   (3)

2.6 What was the total number of subjects in this study?   (1)

2.7 How were the subjects chosen for this study?   (1)

2.8 What method of sampling is this?   (1)

2.9 Describe **one** weakness in the way in which the diagnoses were made, explaining how it could have affected the results of the study.   (3)

2.8 Describe **two** controls that the psychiatrist should have included in this study, explaining clearly why each one is needed.   (6)

2.9 The psychiatrist believed that people with genetic disorders should be sterilised. Explain how this belief could have affected his findings in this study.   (4)

Methodology Questions

You and a friend have been asked to conduct a study into playground aggression. You will spend two lunch-hours observing the children in your nearby junior school playing in their school playground. Answer the following questions, making your suggestions as practical as possible.

2.1 What type of study is this? (1)

2.2 Briefly describe **three** types of behaviour which you would note down as showing aggression, and explain why you have chosen each one.

   i) ....
   ....
   .... (2)
   ii) ....
   ....
   .... (2)
   iii) ....
   ....
   .... (2)

2.3 Describe **two** difficulties which you might encounter using these measures of aggression. (4)

2.4 What do you understand by the term **validity**? (2)

2.5 Name **three** different kinds of validity. (3)

2.6 Choose **one** of the three types of behaviour that you described in question 2.2, and state which type of validity it has. Give a reason for your answer. (3)

2.7 Explain what is meant by the **social-learning** explanation for aggressive behaviour. (3)

2.8 Briefly describe **one** other explanation that has been put forward to explain aggressive behaviour. (3)

3

Brain and Behaviour

'. . . the actions of the brain are quite unlike those of any other organ, because they determine the behaviour of one man towards his fellows.'
Blakemore (1983)

Plate 3

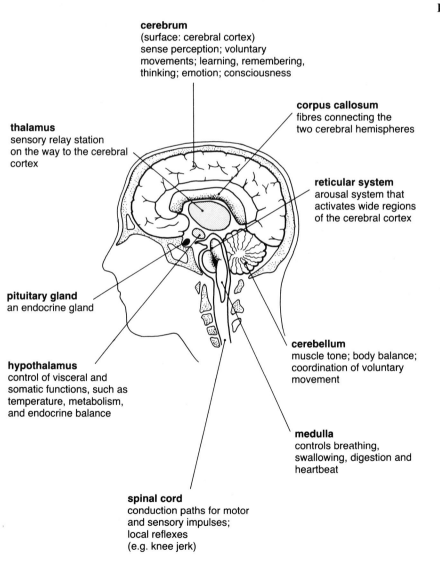

cerebrum
(surface: cerebral cortex)
sense perception; voluntary
movements; learning, remembering,
thinking; emotion; consciousness

corpus callosum
fibres connecting the
two cerebral hemispheres

thalamus
sensory relay station
on the way to the cerebral
cortex

reticular system
arousal system that
activates wide regions
of the cerebral cortex

pituitary gland
an endocrine gland

cerebellum
muscle tone; body balance;
coordination of voluntary
movement

hypothalamus
control of visceral and
somatic functions, such as
temperature, metabolism,
and endocrine balance

medulla
controls breathing,
swallowing, digestion and
heartbeat

spinal cord
conduction paths for motor
and sensory impulses;
local reflexes
(e.g. knee jerk)

Readings on 'Brain and Behaviour'

Our knowledge of the role of the brain in human behaviour is far from complete. The growth of technology during the twentieth century has, however, helped to clarify several theories and, in some cases, emphasised the genius of many early researchers who had reached the same conclusions without the help of such 'tools'. The great Spanish neuro-anatomist Cajal (1852–1934) described the way that information travels to and from the brain via the nerve cells or **neurones**, and how the junctions of these cells (named **synapses**) are traversed with the help of chemicals (**neurotransmitters**). It is via this flexible system of **neural transmission** that information travels rapidly to and from the brain.

In our brief introduction into the workings of the brain and the observable effects on behaviour we shall concentrate on three main areas of interest:

1 **The Central Nervous System (CNS)**: brain functions and ways of monitoring the brain.

2 **The Autonomic Nervous System (ANS)**: how the brain links with the hormonal and glandular system – especially in relation to stress.

3 **Drugs**: the effect of common and medically prescribed drugs on behaviour and drug-related problems.

All information comes to us through our sense organs. The main sense organs, namely the eyes, ears, nose, touch and taste receptors, are specialised to receive this. For example, receptors in the eye and ear are sensitive to light rays and sound waves respectively; these are converted into electrical impulses and transmitted through pathways to the brain.

Valuable information on the brain and the specialised areas responsible for such functions has been gained from patients with brain damage. By observing changes in behaviour after such damage, researchers have been able to determine the probable sites of many physical and cognitive behaviours. Some such **brain functions** are introduced in Reading 3.1.

Reading 3.1   Brain Functions

All the information picked up by our sense organs is eventually transmitted, by way of the brain's many pathways, to the cerebral cortex.

The cortex has specialised areas that receive the sensory messages for vision and hearing, also a long strip that receives messages of bodily sensations from the feet (at the top) to the head (at the bottom). In these specialised areas the messages are analysed and interpreted. The brain decides which messages are important and what they mean. The sounds of speech – which are of particular importance because language plays such a large role in human behaviour – have an area of their own especially concerned with understanding the meaning of words and sentences.

The importance of the cerebral cortex in registering and processing sensory information becomes dramatically clear in cases of harm to any of these portions of the brain (Williams, 1979). Depending on the location and extent of injury to the back part of the cortex responsible for vision, for example, an individual might suffer varying degrees of blindness, even though the eye and its own muscles and nerves remain perfectly intact. If the area for understanding speech is injured, an individual might no longer be able to interpret what is being said, even though all parts of the ear are perfectly healthy and the sounds of the words spoken are clearly heard. In such cases, the afflicted persons literally cannot get the words 'through their heads.'

J. Kagan et al (1984) *Psychology: An Introduction* (5th edn)
Harcourt Brace Jovanovich

1 What is the cerebral cortex and where is it situated?   (2)

2 Which parts of the brain are specialised for receiving the following sensory messages?
   a) vision
   b) hearing
   c) body sensations
   d) motor skills.   (4)

3 Explain the possible effects of damage to the left visual cortex.   (4)

4 Discuss, with evidence, the functions of **two** brain structures.   (8)

TERMS TO DEFINE

cortex   excitatory and inhibitory synapses
sensory/motor/connector neurones

However, these areas are not separate and many of our complex behaviours involve many such sites. It is sensible to think of these areas as being strongly involved in that particular behaviour, and not necessarily the only area responsible for it. Damage to the speech areas of the brain, often caused by cerebral haemorrhage, or stroke damage, demonstrates this interconnection between brain areas. This is seen in Reading 3.2 **Language Areas.**

Reading 3.2   Language Areas

In the 1960s, a French neurosurgeon, Pierre-Paul Broca, suggested that injuries to a small subdivision of the frontal region of the left hemisphere of the human brain will result in a person's having great difficulty speaking in sentences. The term expressive aphasia describes such a result, as the patient has difficulty with verbal expression even though comprehension of both written and spoken language is unaffected. Broca's conclusion has since been abundantly confirmed with methods other than the study of patients with injuries to this zone, called Broca's area. (Geschwind, 1979). One is to apply electric currents to the zone in the brain of a person who is undergoing neural surgery, and who has been instructed to count before the currents are applied. When that is done, the patient's rate of counting will slow, and eventually the counting will stop. This occurs no matter how strongly the surgeon might urge the patient to continue. When the current is cut off, however, the patient can speak once again and will say that he or she had to quit counting because 'I got mixed up and couldn't think.'

A few years following Broca's discovery, Carl Wernicke, a German investigator, described another syndrome in patients with injuries to the left hemisphere's temporal lobe. In 1874 Wernicke reported that these patients had severe impairments of verbal comprehension. Thus, although they weren't deaf, they could not understand the meaning of a spoken message, thereby showing receptive aphasias. However, if they were literate, they could follow simple written instructions and, in general, could express themselves reasonably well whenever they needed to speak.

D. Hothersall (1985) *Psychology* Merrill

1 Label the following areas on the diagram below:
   a) Broca's area   (2)
   b) Wernicke's area.   (2)

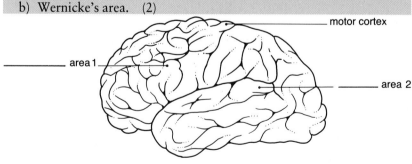

2 Describe in your own words the functions of the two named areas. (4)

3 Critically discuss **one** study of brain damage to the language area. (4)

4 What are split-brain studies? What have they told us about the brain? (8)

TERMS TO DEFINE

aphasia   cerebral dominance   split-brain studies

The two cerebral hemispheres of the brain are joined by a mass of nerve fibres (the **corpus callosum**), which enable information to pass between the two halves. In rare cases of severe epilepsy these fibres have been cut, thus reducing the extent of random firing of nerve cells (which results in an epileptic fit/seizure). This treatment, although relieving the epilepsy, does result in the two hemispheres becoming functionally separate (they act as separate brains). Studies of such **split-brain** patients have enabled researchers to investigate the functioning of the separate hemispheres.

Not all the information we have on the working of the brain has come from accidental damage to the brain. Several techniques have been developed to investigate the activity of the brain. The electroencephalogram, commonly termed **EEG**, by means of **electrode** contacts on the outside of the skull, picks up the underlying brain activity. This is just one of many recent methods of **monitoring the brain** which are discussed in Reading 3.3.

Reading 3.3   Monitoring the Brain

Brain waves can be detected by electrodes attached to a person's forehead or skull. Examination of the EEG patterns allows doctors to determine whether an individual's brain waves indicate brain tumours or epilepsy, and psychologists can use EEG readings to learn about dreams, sleep, and other states of consciousness.

Although brain waves provide us with reflections of the activity of the brain, they do not provide direct information about specific brain structures. In recent years researchers have been developing new techniques for monitoring the activity of specific brain areas. For example, microelectrodes can be implanted in an animal's brain to record the firing patterns of individual neurons as the animal engages in different behaviours. With humans, new techniques make it possible to monitor the activity of specific portions of the brain from outside the skull. In one such procedure a radioactive substance is injected into the brain's blood supply. The amount of blood flowing to different parts of the brain can be precisely measured as the subjects perform different activities.

This *blood-flow measurement* provides a good indicator of the functioning of these parts of the brain, because the more activity in any part of the brain – that is, the more frequently its nerve cells are firing – the more blood it needs to provide oxygen to support the activity (Lassen, Ingvar, and Skinhøj, 1978).

Another new technique, called *positron-emission tomography* (or PET), monitors the activity of the sugar glucose in different parts of the working brain; the more active a part of the brain, the more glucose is used in that area.

Z. Rubin and E.B. Mc Neil (1981) *Psychology: Being Human* (3rd edn)
Harper Row

1 Are the following statements true or false?
   a) implanted micro-elecrodes measure general brain activity
   b) the more frequently nerve cells fire, the more oxygen is used
   c) the more active the brain, the more glucose is used.   (3)

2 Describe **two** techniques used in studying the brain.   (4)

3 Give **two** examples of situations in which EEG recordings might prove useful.   (4)

4 Describe and discuss **one** study on the brain which has used implanted micro-electrodes.   (6)

TERMS TO DEFINE

EEG   micro-electrodes   PET

The development of micro-electrode recording has led to a great deal of research into different **states of consciousness**. Research in **sleep laboratories**, where electrodes can measure brain activity during the night, has shown that sleep is not just the brain slowing down for the night. Several different **sleep** patterns have been noted and these are discussed in Reading 3.4.

Reading 3.4   Sleep

Most of the night is spent in what is called ordinary sleep. As can be seen in the illustration below, the brain's activity during ordinary sleep differs considerably from the pattern during waking hours, and the muscles of the body are considerably more relaxed. Four stages of ordinary sleep, ranging from light to very deep, can be distinguished from tracings of brain and muscle activity. We move back and forth among these four stages during the night. Most people have three periods of the deepest sleep, the first starting within an hour after dropping off, the last ending after about three or four hours.

	wakefulness	ordinary sleep	paradoxical sleep
brain waves			
muscle activity			

About a quarter of the night is spent in paradoxical sleep – which gets its name from the fact that the brain's activity is very similar to the waking state but the bodily muscles are almost totally relaxed. When subjects who are in paradoxical sleep are awakened, about 80 to 85 per cent of them report they have been dreaming (Berger, 1969). In fact during paradoxical sleep the eyes dart quickly about as if following a series of visual images. Therefore this stage is also known as REM sleep – REM standing for the rapid eye movement that can be observed.

J. Kagan et al (1984) *Psychology: An Introduction* (5th edn)
Harcourt Brace Jovanovich

1 Describe **one** difference in brain patterns noted between ordinary sleep and wakefulness. (2)

2 a) What is paradoxical sleep? (1)
  b) Describe **two** characteristics of paradoxical sleep. (4)

3 Describe the normal pattern of brain activity during the course of the night. (4)

4 Discuss **two** psychological explanations of the functions of dreams. (8)

TERMS TO DEFINE

alpha/delta waves   consciousness   REM sleep

In addition to recording the activity of the brain, electrodes can also be used to stimulate areas of the brain and the corresponding behaviour observed. Some interesting research using this technique was reported by James Olds in Canada. Olds was interested in an area near the hypothalamus in the centre of the brain, an area known to be involved in sleep and arousal. An electrode had been implanted into the brain of a rat. The rat was free to wander around an enclosed area. Whenever the animal entered one corner an electric current was sent, via the electrode, to the brain. Olds expected that the rat would begin to avoid the area (remember the conditioning experiments on **learned associations** in Chapter Two), but over the series of experiments he found that this type of electric stimulation could be rewarding or pleasurable when sent to this particular area of the brain. Using a Skinner box, (see Chapter Two), he found that rats would learn to push the lever for the reinforcement of stimulation, just as Skinner's rats had done for the reinforcement of food. These experiments using **brain stimulation** are discussed in more detail in Reading 3.5.

The brain is supplied with thousands of blood vessels which carry nutrients to the neurones. We are becoming increasingly aware of the importance of diet on the development and functioning of the body, so we should not be surprised to find that the brain and nervous system can be adversely affected by lack of adequate nutrition. In 1988 Dave Benton

Reading 3.5 Brain Stimulation

Olds connected the electric current to the lever so that every time the rat pressed the lever current was directed to the spot in the brain that Olds had found earlier. The results were phenomenal. With electrodes implanted in certain locations in the hypothalamus, the rat pressed the lever constantly. In the initial study (Olds and Milner, 1954) individual rats pushed the lever more than 700 times an hour. In subsequent studies some rats pressed up to 5000 times an hour for 24 consecutive hours, rested, then returned for more. They would even walk across an electrified grid floor, which shocked them, to get to the lever.

This research began a series of studies mapping various regions of pleasure and punishment in the brain. Stimulation very close to the 'pleasure' areas can have a punishing effect. One press in some of these places is enough to make a rat avoid the lever thereafter. Other sites seem to yield both reward and punishment. Bower and Miller (1958) trained rats to press one lever to turn on brain stimulation and another lever to then turn it off. It appears from their tests that prolonged brain stimulation might be aversive.

The rewarding effect of brain stimulation is strong. In one experiment (Routtenberg and Lindy, 1965) rats could press either of two levers: one delivered brain stimulation, the other food. The rats were allowed to press the levers for only one hour each day. Some spent so much time pursuing brain stimulation that they starved to death. In another experiment, however, when both food and brain stimulation were freely available, rats ate, slept, and performed other activities as well as pressed for brain stimulation (Valenstein and Beer, 1964). One theory of why brain stimulation can be so persistently pleasurable is that it provides both drive, or motivation, and reward (Deutsch and Howarth, 1963; Gallistel, 1973). Normally a reward such as food will satiate and thus reduce hunger. If, as seems the case in brain stimulation, the stimulus provides both reward and motivation, then satiation will never occur.

H.L. Roediger et al (1984) *Psychology* Little, Brown and Co

1 a) Where is the hypothalamus situated?   (2)
  b) Describe **two** functions of the hypothalamus.   (2)

2 In your own words describe the findings of the Olds and Milner study.   (4)

3 Finish the following sentences:
  a) Prolonged brain stimulation may be . . . . .
  b) Brain stimulation may be pleasurable because it provides both . . . . and . . . . .   (2)

4 Critically evaluate the use of animals in determining human behaviour.   (8)

TERMS TO DEFINE

comparative studies   ethics   sub-cortical areas

from Swansea University appeared on television in the UK, reporting on some interesting research on the possible effects of diet on intellectual performance in children. Many children today are living on a diet described as 'junk food' – food lacking many of the essential vitamins. The response from the public was an initial rush to the chemist for vitamin supplements, which apparently exhausted supplies in some areas of Britain! Perhaps it might have been wiser (and cheaper) to have changed their diet to include these vitamins! Benton's research is among many investigating the effects of **malnutrition and brain development,** which are discussed in Reading 3.6.

Reading 3.6   Malnutrition and the Brain

One effect of malnutrition is to reduce the number of brain cells in the cerebellum, the portion of the brain responsible for fine motor control and coordination. Another effect is on the quality of nerve cells: axons in malnourished animals shrink in diameter in many parts of the brain. Finally, malnutrition has an enormous impact on the synapses – the connection between nerves – in the brain. Researchers have found reductions of up to 40 per cent in the number of synapses in the cerebral cortexes of under-nourished animals. Malnutrition may well have similar effects on humans. It is not surprising that tests on undernourished children show them to be retarded in many physical and intellectual skills.

Researchers have pinpointed the mechanisms for some specific nutritional effects on brain activity. For example, foods rich in lecithin, such as soybeans, eggs, and liver, can increase the amount of *acetylcholine*, a transmitter substance in the brain. This chemical seems to be involved in memory, sleep disturbances, and motor coordination. Similarly, the consumption of carbohydrates may affect the levels of *serotonin*, a transmitter substance that apparently plays a role in temperature regulation and sensory perception.

Z. Rubin and E.B. Mc Neil (1981) *Psychology: Being Human*
Harper Row

1 Where is the cerebellum and what are its functions?   (2)

2 Describe **two** effects of malnutrition on the brain.   (4)

3 Link up the following sentences correctly:

eggs and liver can   affect serotonin levels
carbohydrates can   be involved with acetylcholine
sleep disturbance can   increase acetylcholine   (3)

4 Discuss, with evidence, the role of neurotransmitters in the nervous system.   (6)

TERMS TO DEFINE

axons   neurotransmitter substances   synapses

So far we have been mainly concerned with the activity of the central nervous system in behaviour; however, the CNS seldom works in isolation. The autonomic nervous system has an important part to play by stimulating production of hormones or chemicals needed for action.

Psychologists have tried to resolve the question '*What is an emotion?*' since this was voiced by William James in 1884. Emotion can be seen as a subjective experience involving body responses, especially the autonomic nervous system. We are aware when something good or bad is occurring and our facial expressions may register these cognitions. Such responses to various emotions can be seen, even in children, as we can see in Activity 3.1.

Activity 3.1

Interview a group of children and ask them what they mean by such emotional words as: fear, jealousy, anger, love, excitement. Repeat the exercise with a group of a different age and note any similarities and differences. What factors could bias this comparison?

When an individual is placed in what is seen to be a potentially threatening situation the body reacts, with the help of the ANS, with what has been named the **fight or flight** response (Cannon, 1920).

Today's threats and stresses are different from those of our ancestors and preparation for fighting or running away is often inappropriate. Research into **stress** has 'snowballed' in recent years. Many situations can be seen to be stressful and these vary between individuals and between situations. Any situation which results in anxiety, frustration or conflict can result in the intense, prolonged emotion we associate with stress. Research by Hans Selye, initially with animals, demonstrated the damage which can result from **stress**, which is discussed in Reading 3.7.

Reading 3.7   Stress

Selye found that when an animal was injected with poison, its body automatically tried to defend itself. Most notably, its endocrine glands immediately sprang into action (as they also do in human emotional arousal). The adrenal glands in particular showed striking changes. They became enlarged and produced more adrenalin. They also discharged their stored-up supply of the hormones known as steroids, which make many contributions to the body's well-being. Because of this high level of activity of the adrenal glands, numerous physical changes occurred in the animals. For example, tissue was broken down into sugar to provide energy. The amount of salt normally found in the bloodstream was sharply reduced.

After a few days of continued exposure to stress-producing conditions, the animals seemed to adapt. The adrenal glands returned to normal size and began to renew their supply of steroids. The salt level in the blood rose to normal or even higher. Apparently the animals had adjusted to the situation and were perfectly normal.

Their recovery, however, was only temporary. After several weeks of continued pressure, the adrenal glands again became enlarged and lost their stores of steroids. The level of salt in the blood fell drastically. The kidneys, as a result of receiving an excess of hormones, underwent some complicated and damaging changes. Eventually the animals died, as if from exhaustion. They had been killed, so to speak, by an excess of the hormones they had produced in their own defence.

Another of Selye's important findings was that even during the period of apparent recovery, the animals were not so normal as they seemed. If a second source of stress was introduced during this period, the animals quickly died. In attempting to adapt to the original source of stress, apparently they had used their defences to the maximum and were helpless against a new form of pressure (Selye, 1956).

To describe the sequence of events that takes place during prolonged stress – the initial shock or alarm, the recovery or resistance period, and at last exhaustion and death – Selye coined the phrase General Adaptation Syndrome. (To physicians the word syndrome means the entire pattern of symptoms and events that characterise the course of a disease.)

J. Kagan et al (1984) *Psychology: An Introduction* (5th edn)
Harcourt Brace Jovanovich

1 Describe **two** changes noted by Selye when the animal was injected with poison.   (2)

2 a) What are steroids?   (2)
   b) Where are these produced?   (2)

3 Describe, in your own words, the reaction of the animal to prolonged stress.   (4)

4 Critically discuss **one** study, other than those reported above, which investigates stress.   (5)

TERMS TO DEFINE

alarm reaction   General Adaptation Syndrome   stress

FRED BASSET by GRAHAM

Fear lent me wings!

One factor which can help people deal with stress is that of developing adequate **coping behaviours**. Relaxation techniques are used for many anxiety-related disorders (see Chapter Six Reading 6.6 Systematic Desensitisation for a discussion of one such application). Another branch of research has been into the area of personality type and stress. Is there a stress-prone individual? Friedman and Rosenman (1974) found that people who exhibited a certain kind of behaviour, termed **Type A behaviour,** are more likely to be associated with coronary heart disease; whereas those with a Type B personality are more relaxed and less likely to be associated with such illness. This is discussed in Reading 3.8.

Reading 3.8 Type A Behaviour

This pattern – Type A – involves a constant drive to compete and achieve, and continual sense of urgency to get things done, together with hostile and aggressive reactions towards those who get in the way. Those with this pattern characteristically speak loudly and fast, tend to interrupt others and are impatient of hesitations and delays. Type B is essentially the opposite, a more relaxed and accepting attitude. This was based on a study of 3000 men in California who were studied over a period of eight years, and tested in a further study of 1500 men in Framingham, Massachusetts. It is important to note that being Type A increases the risk of a heart attack independently of other known factors such as smoking, high blood pressure, and raised blood cholesterol. Thus it is not that Type A behaviour makes people smoke more, for example. What it does do, it seems, is to activate the sympathetic nervous system frequently and strongly; the well-known 'Fight or Flight' syndrome. This has numerous effects. Heart rate and blood pressure increase; and the hormones adrenaline and noradrenaline are released into the blood stream. These in turn release fats into the blood which may help to clog the coronary arteries. Noradrenaline causes blood platelets to join together leading to blood clots which, if they occur in an artery which is already partly blocked, would constitute a thrombosis, with resulting heart failure. The evolutionary function of this, of course, is to ensure that external wounds stop bleeding rapidly. Noradrenaline also causes the heart to beat regularly; an excess may disturb the rhythm dangerously.

R. Raaheim and J. Radford (1984) *Your Introduction to Psychology* Sigma

1 In the Friedman and Rosenman study:
   a) how many participants were there   (1)
   b) how long were they studied?   (1)

2 Describe the behaviour associated with a Type A individual.   (2)

3 What are the effects of the 'fight or flight' syndrome on behaviour?   (4)

4 What techniques are recommended to reduce effects of stress?   (3)

TERMS TO DEFINE

adrenalin/noradrenalin   sympathetic nervous system   Type A behaviour

Stress control management programmes have been implemented in the USA, with a corresponding decline in stress-related disorders. Until recently this was not seen as a priority in the UK and such illnesses have increased. In recent years many researchers have tried to investigate potential **stressors** which threaten an individual's capability to cope, especially in the work situation. Further discussion on this area of research can be found in Chapter Eight especially Reading 8.5 Occupational Stress.

There is a widespread belief that overcrowding leads to psychological stress. Does the effect of density and crowding result in city dwellers being less likely to trust and help a stranger? Several researchers in the USA have found people in cities less likely to respond to requests for help from a passer-by than people in small towns. Perhaps you could test this hypothesis yourself as suggested in Activity 3.2.

Activity 3.2

Latané and Darley (1970) investigated the response of passers-by in different locations to the following requests:
'Excuse me, I wonder if you could . . .

1 tell me what time it is?'   (TIME)
2 tell me how to get to the nearest Post Office?'   (DIRECTION)
3 give me change for a quarter?' (in the UK substitute 20p)
                                                        (CHANGE)
4 tell me what your name is?'   (NAME)

You could perform a similar study. Choose a number of different locations. These will vary according to where you live. Examples are:

   a) in a city centre
   b) in a town centre
   c) in a suburban area
   d) in a village.

The results of the original study are given on p. 74 for comparison. Can you suggest any alternative explanations for the findings?

Type of Request	Amount of Density							
	Low		Medium		High		High	
	Small Town		Suburbs of Toronto		Inner City: Toronto		New York City*	
	% helping	Sample N	% helping	Sample N	% helping	Sample N	% helping	Sample N
1 Time	97[a]	92	95[a]	150	91[ab]	272	85[b]	92
2 Directions	97[a]	85	90[ab]	150	88[b]	276	85[b]	90
3 Change	84[a]	100	73[ab]	150	70[b]	279	73[ab]	90
4 Name	51[a]	65	39[a]	150	26[b]	246	29[b]	277

Note: Within each type of request those having different superscripts are significantly different by chi square ($p < .05$).

* New York City data from *The Unresponsive Bystander: Why Doesn't He Help?* by Bibb Latané and John M. Darley. Copyright 1970. Reprinted by permission of Prentice-Hall, Inc., Englewood Cliffs, New Jersey.

Source: From J.P. Rushton, "Urban density and sharing: Helping strangers in a Canadian city, suburb, and small town," *Psychological Reports*, 1978, 43, 987–990.

In times of stress many people turn to indirect ways of coping, sometimes with the help of drugs such as alcohol and tobacco which contains the drug nicotine. Such measures are termed **palliative**, in that they initially reduce the symptoms of stress. This is, however, temporary; and when the effects of the drug wear off the cause of the stress remains. These **common drugs**, as discussed in Reading 3.9, affect behaviour due to the biochemical effects they have on the brain.

Reading 3.9   Common Drugs

Cigarettes, for example, are a common source of nicotine, a drug that acts by blocking transmission in the sympathetic nervous system. Nicotine causes constriction in the peripheral blood vessels, elevates heart rate and blood pressure, and increases stomach activity. Perhaps for this reason smokers often find cigarettes after meals quite pleasurable.

Caffeine, in coffee, tea, and cola drinks, acts as a central nervous system stimulant. People who consume too much caffeine may experience tremors, rapid heartbeat, overactivity, restlessness, and nausea. Strangely enough, caffeine is the 'extra ingredient' in many common pain relievers, though its effects on pain are not clear.

Caffeine – like nicotine – is mildly addictive, a fact that has been discovered by millions of people who feel they can't function without beginning the day with a cup of coffee (or, for some people, a can of cola). Indeed, it has been suggested that if caffeine were a newly introduced drug, it would not be made available without a prescription (Timson, 1978).

Ethyl alcohol is consumed in huge quantities in beer, wine, and liquor. Alcohol abuse is the biggest drug problem in America today, in all age groups. Small doses cause dilation of the pupils, slight increases in blood pressure, and temporary elevation of blood sugar level. Larger doses interfere with fine discrimination, motor control, and self-restraint. Excessive doses can cause coma and death.

Z. Rubin and E.B. Mc Neil (1981) *Psychology: Being Human* (3rd edn)
Harper Row

1 What are the effects on the nervous system of:
   a) nicotine
   b) caffeine? (2)

2 '. . . . is the biggest drug problem in America today.'   (1)

3 What is meant by addiction? How does this occur?   (4)

4 Critically discuss the long-term use of alcohol to alleviate stress.   (6)

TERMS TO DEFINE

addiction   palliation   withdrawal

Psychoactive drugs are chemical substances which alter mood or behaviour by interfering with the functioning of the brain. People suffering from tension and anxiety may well be prescribed drugs such as tranquillisers. These are palliative methods subject to the same long-term effects as the common drugs. In the short-term they can prove helpful, by allowing the individual time to come to terms with the stressful situation; but there is some concern that we may turn to drugs for relief far too easily. Activity 3.3 might prove interesting in relation to this problem.

Activity 3.3

Conduct an informal survey among your friends and acquaintances to determine the extent of their use of non-prescribed medication for pain. How will you perform the survey? An unstructured interview or a questionnaire? Note the advantages and disadvantages of your chosen method. What differences did you find between people and the medication they use? What are the possible explanations for this?

Drug misuse and abuse has increased over the last ten years.

Although tobacco and alcohol kill more people than heroin and cocaine, the latter are classified as **hard drugs** and are considered more harmful. The effects of some of these drugs are discussed in Reading 3.10.

Reading 3.10   Hard Drugs

Heroin (sometimes known as 'H', smack, skag) and other opiates
Heroin is a white or speckled brown powder and is just one of a group of drugs known as 'opiates' which are made from the opium poppy.
Method of use – often smoked but can be sniffed or injected (injection maximises the effects).
Effects – can include a sense of well-being or euphoria. Overdose can result in unconsciousness and less frequently death. This is more likely if other drugs like alcohol or tranquillisers are used at the same time. Regular, frequent use means that 'tolerance' to the drug develops. The body gets used to the drug so to get the same effect the user needs to use more and more. Regular use can produce physical and psychological dependence. If a regular user stops taking the drug, 'withdrawal' symptoms include sweating, aches and chills.
Cocaine (sometimes known as coke, snow)
White, bitter-tasting powder made from the leaves of the coca plant.
Method of use – sniffed, smoked or injected.
Effects – has powerful stimulant properties. Feelings of excitement and well-being – sometimes replaced by anxiety or panic. Hunger and tiredness are reduced. Regular use can result in psychological dependence plus paranoia, restlessness, and confusion.
Amphetamines (sometimes known as speed, whizz, sulphate)
Manufactured powders commonly white or brown, but can be in pill or capsule form.
Method of use – sniffed, swallowed or injected.
Effects – similar to those of cocaine. Energy and confidence are increased. These effects can be replaced by anxiety and restlessness. Long-term regular use can lead to tolerance and psychological dependence as well as panic and paranoia.

Which Magazine July 1988

1 Psychoactive drugs are . . . . .   (2)

2 Describe the effects of:
  a) heroin
  b) cocaine. (4)

3 Explain what we mean by drug dependence and drug tolerance. (6)

4 How can psychologists help people who are drug dependent? Give examples of successful techniques which have been used. (8)

TERMS TO DEFINE

dependence   psychoactive   tolerance

Some mental disorders are considered more severe than others, and these often involve changes in thought and feeling which may result in a lack of contact with reality for the patient. Many are classified as **psychoses**. During the early twentieth century, treatment of such patients relied heavily on the use of drugs such as bromide and barbiturates. These drugs do not cure patients, and they have no effect on the cause of the disorders, the source of many of which remains unknown. They were useful, however, especially to overworked staff in mental hospitals, in sedating the patients and making them more manageable. From the middle of the century the discovery of anti-schizophrenic and anti-depressant drugs has allowed more selective control of symptoms, enabling many patients to live a more normal life. Recent concern has, however, been voiced on the continued use of such drugs, with the discovery of long-term medically induced, (or **iatrogenic**) disorders (see Chapter Six, especially Reading 6.9 Labelling and Reading 6.10 An Alternative to the Medical Model for further discussion on personality disorders).

Topic-related Essays

1   Discuss, with evidence, some of the ways in which the central nervous system and the autonomic nervous system interact to control behaviour.

2   What is stress? Discuss the physiological, psychological and situational factors which may influence stress.

3   'It is now widely accepted that drugs can be instruments of liberation rather than repression.' Critically discuss this statement.

This chapter has demonstrated the considerable importance of physiological factors in human behaviour. However, research on the behavioural effects of any drug shows that physiological and biochemical processes are influenced by the individual's understanding or **cognition** of the situation. The processes of **cognition** will be discussed further in Chapter Four.

SUGGESTIONS FOR FURTHER READING

Main texts
R.L. Atkinson et al (1987) *Introduction to Psychology* (9th edn) Harcourt
    Brace Jovanovich
N. Hayes (1988) *A First Course in Psychology* (2nd edn) Nelson
N. Hayes and S. Orrell (1987) *Psychology: an Introduction* Longman

Other useful texts
P. Evans (1988) *Motivation and Emotion* Routledge
J.M. Julien (1985) *A Primer of Drug Action* Freeman
J. Kagan et al (1984) *Psychology: an Introduction* (5th edn) Harcourt
    Brace Jovanovich
S. Rose (1984) *Not in our Genes* Penguin (critical review on the use of
    drugs in controlling behaviour)

Z. Rubin and E.B. McNeil (1985) *Psychology: Being Human* (4th edn)
   Harper Row
D.J. Sanger and D.E. Blackman (1984) *Aspects of Psychopharmacology*
   Methuen (more advanced text giving details on drugs and their use in
   the treatment of mental illness)

Stimulus Questions

A psychologist wanted to find out if people's feelings of emotion were
affected by the suggestion that they feel physiological arousal under
hypnosis. The flow diagram shows what she did.

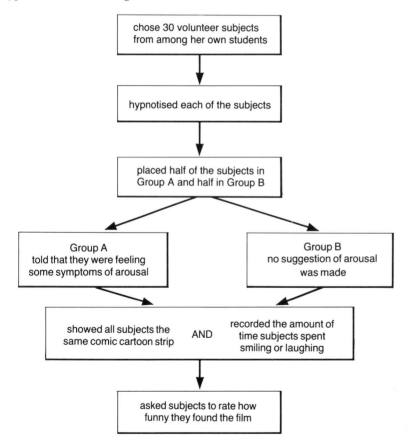

In rating the film, each subject was asked to use the scale: 1 = not
amusing, 2 = slightly amusing, 3 = amusing, 4 = very amusing.

The table below shows the results of the study.

	GROUP A	GROUP B
Mean time spent laughing or smiling	1 m 17 sec	1 m 19 sec
Median humour rating	3	1

3.1 How did the psychologist obtain the subjects for this study? (1)

3.2 How many subjects were in each group? (1)

3.3 What term is used to describe a group of subjects obtained for an experiment? (1)

3.4 Give and explain **one** criticism of the method used to obtain the subjects in this study. (3)

3.5 In what **two** ways did the psychologist measure her subjects' feelings? (2)

3.6 Do you think that the ways in which the subjects' feelings were measured were good ones? In each case give **one** reason for your answer. (4)

3.7 What is a median? (2)

3.8 Describe in your **own** words the outcome of this experiment. (3)

3.9 Suggest **one** reason why the two methods of measurement showed contrasting results. (2)

3.10 Why did the psychologist use hypnosis in this study? (2)

3.11 What ethical issues should be considered when conducting this kind of experiment? Give **two** examples. (4)

NEA Joint GCE/CSE Examination Paper 1 1987

Methodology Questions

You have been asked to conduct a structured interview study on people's sleeping habits. Working with a friend, you will be able to interview 20 people, for about 15 minutes at a time. Make your suggestions as practical as possible – describe a study that you yourself would be able to carry out if you were asked.

3.1 What is a structured interview? (2)

3.2 Describe how you would obtain the subjects for your study. (2)

3.3 What method of sampling is this? (1)

3.4 Give **three** aspects of the topic that you would be likely to ask questions about.

   i) ....

   ii) ....

   iii) .... (3)

3.5 What is the difference between an open and a closed question in an interview? (3)

3.6 Identify **two** areas of non-verbal communication which you would need to be careful about in your study. For each one, state what it is and how it could affect the interview findings.

   i) ....
   ....
   .... (3)

   ii) ....
   ....
   .... (3)

3.7 What is a leading question? (2)

3.8 Name and describe **one** way of making sure that the questions you ask in the study are not biased. Make sure that your description shows how you could carry this out. (4)

3.9 Suggest **one** way in which you could summarise your findings once you had completed the survey. (2)

4

Cognition

Plate 4

Readings on 'Cognition'

Cognition refers to mental processes being performed at a 'higher level' in our head. These higher level processes go on in the brain, and more specifically in the cortex. Such processes include our conscious thoughts and feelings, making plans and decisions and choosing what to say. To make these processes easier to distinguish and understand, they are often split into topic areas; although these are obviously artificial divisions considering that many of the activities often occur at the same time and are inter-related. We shall look at those activities displayed in Figure 4.1.

Perception	the selection, organisation and interpretation of sensory information
Attention	the focussing of awareness on specific targets
Memory	the coding, storage and retrieval of information
Learning	a relatively permanent change in knowledge, behaviour or understanding resulting from experience
Thinking and Problem Solving	mental restructuring of events and situations and making plans and decisions
Language	a system for expressing and understanding a large number of ideas using a limited set of grammatical rules

Figure 4.1 *Cognitive processes defined*

Perception is involved in the detection and interpretation of sensory stimuli. People become aware of their environment through their senses, which provide them with information about the world around them. **Sensation** refers to this reception of stimulation from the environment through the senses, and it is the beginning of the process of perception. It is the way in which the brain interprets this information which makes the distinction between sensation (the reception of information) and perception (the way in which we interpret this information). In this active process of perceiving, the brain can sometimes be confused. Some **visual illusions** can be seen as the result of such confusion. These are faulty perceptions whereby the brain distorts the incoming message and we misconceive the world around us, as discussed in Reading 4.1.

Reading 4.1   Visual Illusions

The process of perception, aided by the inborn characteristics of the nervous system, is the source of our first quick impressions of what is going on around us. The process is not perfect, and our first impressions are not always in accord with the facts. For example, you may have had the experience, when riding along a highway, of being sure you saw a dead dog at the side of the road – only to discover, as you got closer, that it was just a piece of rumpled cloth. Your perceptual process, in its effort to make sense out of the visual stimulation reaching your eyes, signalled dog when in fact there was no dog at all. Students of perception have shown that you can be fooled by many kinds of optical illusions, some of which are illustrated in Figure A.

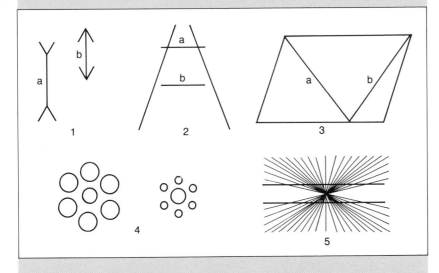

A *How do you perceive these drawings? Is line a or line b longer in No. 1? In No. 2? In No. 3? Which of the two inner circles in No. 4 is larger? In No. 5, are the horizontal lines straight or curved? After you have made your judgements, you can discover with a ruler that all the lines a and b are the same length and the two circles in No. 4 are the same size. The lines on No. 5 are parallel.*

Sometimes we perceive motion where none exists. A stationary spot of light, viewed in darkness without any frame of reference, may seem to move of its own accord. This phenomenon, known as the *autokinetic illusion*, used to plague pilots flying at night, who had trouble judging the position of a beacon light or another plane visible only by the lights on its wingtips and tail. The problem has been solved by lights that flash on and off, greatly reducing the chances of error.

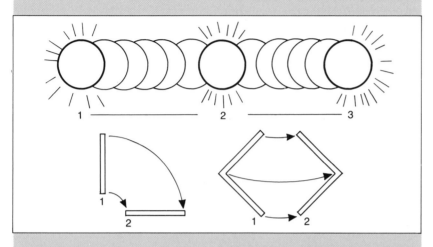

B *Stroboscopic motion.*

These are examples of the apparent motion produced by stationary objects. At the top, light 1, 2 and 3 are flashed briefly and in rapid succession. Nothing moves and in fact there is nothing in the spaces between the lights. But the viewer perceives the light as moving smoothly from position 1 to position 3, as indicated by the shaded circles. At the bottom, two slits of light shown in rapid succession appear to move as shown by the arrows. The bar at the left seems to flip over and move in three dimensions, as when the page of a book is turned.

Another visual illusion, called *stroboscopic motion*, is illustrated in Figure B. This one has been turned to advantage in motion pictures, which are actually a succession of still pictures flashed on the screen at the rate of about 24 a second, and in television, where still pictures are flashed at about 30 per second.

Perceptual illusions may also occur during what are called altered states of consciousness, like those produced by drugs and hypnosis, as will be discussed in the chapter supplement. Indeed people in altered states of consciousness sometimes believe they see objects that do not even exist.

J. Kagan et al (1984) *Psychology: An Introduction* Harcourt Brace Jovanovich

1 When a stationary light appears to move in a dark room it is known as the:
   a) waterfall effect
   b) altered state of consciousness
   c) autokinetic effect
   d) sleeper effect. (1)

2 What is meant by the 'stroboscopic effect'? (2)

3 What can produce 'altered states of consciousness'? How can such states affect perception? (2)

4 Describe **two** of the factors which may cause misperception of an object. (2)

5 Describe the ponzo illusion and give **one** possible explanation. (4)

TERMS TO DEFINE

perception   sensation   visual illusions

Why does the world look as it does? How do we identify shapes and patterns? These are some of the questions that cognitive psychologists have tried to answer. The Gestalt psychologists suggest that we are born with perceptual organisation which we use in order to make sense of the world. Some of these 'laws' are shown in Figure 4.2 (see also Reading 1.4 Gestalt Laws).

Figure 4.2

Proximity
Elements that are close together tend to be seen as forming part of the same figure against a background. In (i) you can see either horizontal rows or vertical columns with equal ease. When some of the dots are closer together, either horizontal rows emerge (as in (ii)); or vertical columns (as in (iii)).

```
O O O O      O O O O      O O  O O
O O O O      O O O O      O O  O O
O O O O                   O O  O O
O O O O      O O O O      O O  O O
             O O O O
   (i)          (ii)        (iii)
```

Similarity
Similar elements tend to be grouped together to appear as organised wholes; you tend to see columns rather than rows

Closure
One of the best known Gestalt laws is the way in which incomplete lines are filled in to produce 'good' figures like squares or circles

Continuation
Figures tend to stand out against a background when they are defined by an uninterrupted contour

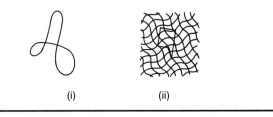

(i)   (ii)

Reading 4.2   Factors Affecting Perception

Strong emotion can distort normally accurate perception. A common experience is to imagine one sees in a crowd the person one is eagerly waiting to greet. One might put it that the recognition response has been triggered by a few cues, such as the approximate height and colour. Unusual conditions can likewise interfere. The two come together in the case of a desert mirage, where a heat haze takes on the appearance of desperately-needed water.

As human beings progressively extend their environment – the ocean depths, the upper atmosphere, outer space – it becomes important to know whether they can continue to function normally. Not all the investigations get published, but some do. For example, I.Y. Yakovleva, G.N. Kornilova, I.K. Tarasov and V.N. Alekseev, of the USSR, reported in 1982 the results of studying spatial perception and sense of balance in 26 cosmonauts before and after 30 spaceflights. Both were disrupted to some extent, though with considerable individual differences. The typical reactions included, for example, a decline in accuracy of perception of spatial co-ordinates, and a decrease in the sensitivity of the semi-circular canals, the organs in the inner ear that control the sense of balance.

Our environment is, of course, cultural as well as physical and psychological, and cultural differences too can change perceptions. Many textbooks quote, for example, the inability to comprehend drawings using perspective cues by people unfamiliar with our conventions. Whereas we see two animals of different sizes as being at different distances, they see one as really smaller than the other.

R. Raaheim and J. Radford (1984) *Your Introduction to Psychology* Sigma

1 What do we mean by emotion?   (1)

2 Describe **two** effects of space flight found by Yakovleva (1982).   (2)

3 Describe **one** other study which demonstrates the effect of emotion on perception.   (3)

4 Name **two** factors other than emotion which may influence perception. Give a possible explanation for **one** of them.   (8)

TERMS TO DEFINE

perceptual defence   perceptual set   subliminal perception

Several different **models** of pattern recognition have been developed to explain these processes. **Feature detection** models suggest a hierarchy of detectors which start by detecting simple features; more complex detectors pick up information from lines and angles, and finally the whole shape is detected further up the hierarchy. Support for such a view comes from the work of Hubel and Wiesel, which shows 'feature detectors' named simple, complex and hypercomplex cells. Such a system suggests that perception is dependent on the information coming in at the bottom of the system via the neurone receptors and working its way up to the top of the system (the brain). This has been described as **bottom-up** processing. However, evidence from other sources has demonstrated how the **factors affecting perception** (such as motivation, expectation and emotion) can affect our perception, as discussed in Reading 4.2.

Perception can thus be shown to be influenced by the interpretation of the incoming stimuli by cognitive processes and translation by the brain (at the top of the system); this allows us to use **expectancies** based on past experiences and learning to make sense of what we see. Such a model has been suggested by Neisser (1976). This approach has been labelled **top-down** processing.

Perception appears to be a combination of two systems, whereby expectations may guide the type of information the individual searches for (**top-down processing**) and information from the receptors modifies these expectations (**bottom-up processing**). **External** physical characteristics of the stimuli (such as intensity, size, and contrast) are important in perception, as are **internal** factors such as interests, needs and motives.

Perception is seen as an **active**, constructive process which is affected by many internal and external factors. It is also **selective**. It is impossible for us to respond to all the stimuli that are bombarding our senses at any one time. As you are reading this you may well have music or noise in the background; there may be a television operating in the same room, and the smell of cooking may be coming from the kitchen. These are a few possible stimuli which may be available to your senses, many of which you may not have been fully aware of as you were reading. You could become consciously aware of them by focussing your **attention** on them.

Attention refers to many different kinds of activity including:

1) concentrating on a mental task when trying to exclude other interfering stimuli (e.g. when taking an exam)

2) being prepared for further information (e.g. listening to an important announcement)

3) receiving several messages, or stimuli, and ignoring all but one (e.g. trying to follow a conversation at a noisy party).

Generally speaking, attention can be seen as '*a concentration of mental activity*' Matlin (1983), as you will discover in Activity 4.1.

Cherry (1953) reported on what has become known as the **cocktail**

Activity 4.1

How difficult is it for you to spread your attention over several tasks? Turn on the radio or put on a record and find a song with lyrics/words. Copy down the lyrics and at the same time recite the National Anthem. At the same time, with the hand you are not using to write, rub your stomach twice and pat it twice, alternating between the two activities. If you find you can do this, then think of some activity you can perform with your feet at the same time.

party phenomenon. This refers to a situation like a noisy party where you are concentrating on a conversation with a friend and block out the other noise. Sometimes other conversations are picked up especially if they involve you (e.g. if someone mentions your name). Perhaps the name of this process sounds somewhat dated and perhaps the **disco phenomenon** might be more appropriate today! Some might argue that nothing is heard above the noise of the music! However, the findings are still valid. Some of the techniques used in research on **selective attention** can be found in Reading 4.3.

Reading 4.3 Selective Attention

Cherry used two types of listening tests, which have become known as binaural and dichotic tests. They fall into two groups. Firstly, he presented two different messages to the subject through both ears. In the second group of experiments Cherry presented one spoken message to the subject's right ear and a different spoken message to his left ear.

The results of the first set of experiments tell us something about the subject's ability to separate the two messages which are presented to him as a 'babel'. Many tests were carried out using pairs of messages which varied in similarity, but the results consistently showed that the messages could be separated even when they were taken from adjacent paragraphs in the same book. However, the subjects reported great difficulty in separating the messages and often they would listen to the same section of the tape recording up to twenty times. It was possible to construct messages which could not be separated. If the messages consisted of strings of cliches then, even though they are spoken with continuity and natural emotional content, the subjects could not separate them.

The second set of tests proved to be in many ways the most fruitful. Two different prose messages were recorded, both by the same speaker. One of the messages was presented to the subject's right ear and the other to the left ear. The messages were presented via headphones. The subject's task was to repeat one of the messages as he heard it. This is now referred to as shadowing. The point of requiring a subject to shadow one of the messages is to make sure that his attention is directed towards it. This provides an experimental equivalent of the cocktail party situation where someone is listening to one conversation and ignoring others. Cherry was now able to determine exactly how much of the unattended (non-shadowed) message the subject could report. He found that they could always correctly identify it as speech, but they could not identify any words or phrases or even definitely identify the message as being English. A change of voice from male to female could be detected and a 400 cps pure tone was always reported. Reversed speech was thought to be normal by most subjects but was thought to have 'something queer about it' by others. This all seems quite straightforward really, the conclusion of course is that only the physical properties of the unattended message are 'heard' by the listener and the semantic content is completely lost.

J. Radford and E. Govier (1982) *A Textbook of Psychology* Sheldon

1 Differentiate between binaural and dichotic listening tasks.   (2)

2 One message can be presented through headphones to the right ear and another to the left. The listener may be asked to repeat one of the messages. This is known as:
   a) babel
   b) shadowing
   c) the cocktail party phenomenon
   d) reversed speech.   (1)

3 Give **one** characteristic of the unattended message which listeners can distinguish.   (1)

4 Describe **one** model of attention which tries to explain these studies.   (6)

TERMS TO DEFINE

bottleneck theories   masking   selective attention

The cognitive processes discussed so far are **active** rather than **passive**, in other words they are constantly changing and adapting to new stimuli as the individual searches for knowledge. This search is helped by information from earlier activities stored in the **memory**. Some researchers see the brain as having a limited capacity for processing information, although others argue that no limit has yet been found. Various models have been suggested which try to explain such processes as attention and memory (see Reading 10.8 Levels of Processing). Such models challenge the older view of a two-memory system with two memory stores (short-term memory known as **STM** and long-term memory known as **LTM**).

Several techniques for investigating memory have been developed, such as **free recall**, which is described in Reading 4.4.

Reading 4.4   Free Recall

The difference between serial learning and free recall is that, in free recall, the lists of words to be learnt are still presented in a predetermined order but the subjects are allowed to recall the items in any order they please: for instance, producing the last items first. In order to show whether items at the beginning or end of a list are more likely to be remembered better, the position of the items in the original presented list (30 items in this case) is plotted along the bottom of a graph, as shown below. Up the vertical axis are shown the average probabilities of subjects recalling each word correctly depending on its position in the original list.

You will notice that people tend to recall more items which were originally at the beginning and end of the presented list and less items from the middle of the list. This pattern is found very commonly in memory for lists of items and is known as the *serial position effect*.

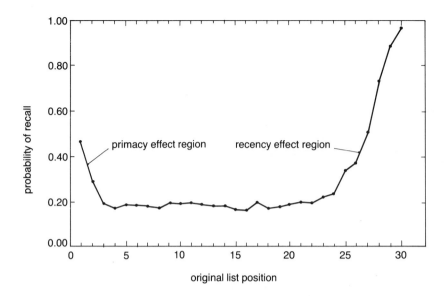

Recall for thirty word lists presented at one second per word

The serial position effect has been reinterpreted as two effects called the primacy effect and the recency effect. The *primacy effect* refers to the better recall of items at the beginning of a list and the *recency effect* refers to the better recall of the last three or four items at the end of the list.

J. Greene and C. Hicks (1984) *Basic Cognitive Processes* Open University Press

1 **Serial learning** involves .... whereas in **free recall** ..... (2)

2 The results of Murdock's (1962) free recall experiment are shown in the graph above. In this experiment what were the:
a) IV
b) DV? (2)

3 What was the probability of recall for items presented second in the list? (1)

4 Give a report of the findings in your own words. (4)

5 How do psychologists explain this effect? (4)

TERMS TO DEFINE

LTM   STM   working memory

Recently there has been a renewal of interest in the organisation of memory and how cognitive processing can affect what is remembered – just as it affects what is originally perceived (see Reading 10.6 Mnemonics in which techniques to improve memory are discussed). Bartlett (1932) displays this vividly with the use of the story 'The War of the Ghosts' as demonstrated in Activity 4.2.

Activity 4.2 'The War of the Ghosts'

Read the following story and five minutes later write down what you
remember. After you have done this answer the questions on page 92.

One night two young men from Egulac went down to the river to
hunt seals, and while they were there it became foggy and calm.
Then they heard war cries and they thought, 'Maybe this is a
war-party.' They escaped to the shore and hid behind a log. Now
canoes came up, and they heard the noise of paddles, and saw one
canoe coming up to them. There were five men in the canoe, and
they said: 'What do you think? We wish to take you along. We are
going up the river to make war on the people.'

One of the young men said: 'I have no arrows.' 'Arrows are in the
canoe,' they said. 'I will not go. I might be killed. My relatives do
not know where I have gone. But you,' he said, turning to the other,
'may go with them.' So one of the young men went, but the other
returned home. And the warriors went on up the river to a town on
the other side of Kalama. The people came down to the water, and
they began to fight, and many were killed. But presently the young
man heard one of the warriors say: 'Quick, let us go home: that
Indian has been hit.' Now he thought: 'Oh, they are ghosts.'

He did not feel sick, but they said he had been shot.

So the canoes went back to Egulac, and the young man went
ashore to his house, and made a fire. And he told everybody and
said: 'Behold I accompanied the ghosts, and we went to fight. Many
of our fellows were killed, and many of those who attacked us were
killed. They said I was hit, and I did not feel sick.'

He told it all, and then he became quiet. When the sun rose he fell
down. Something black came out of his mouth. His face became
contorted. The people jumped up and cried. He was dead.

From Bartlett (1932)

Some of the processes of memory appear to be below the level of
consciousness. Freud developed techniques for investigating unconscious
processes. In the early part of his career he was interested in the use of
hypnosis for such purposes. Sanders and Simmons (1983) have
investigated the use of hypnosis in eye-witness testimony. They found that
hypnosis could make subjects more susceptible to misleading implications
in the recall questions, and they recommended that hypnosis be used
cautiously – perhaps as a way of suggesting leads. Research into
eye-witness testimony demonstrates the effects of bias in memory, as can
be seen in Reading 4.5.

Memory research can be seen following the historical path of
psychology noted in Chapter One, with early research concentrating on
the behaviourist approach. From about the middle of the twentieth
century onwards the information processing model has promoted many
varying theories and experimental procedures.

Questions on 'The War of the Ghosts' from Activity 4.2
Bartlett found that the following characteristic errors were made:

1 details were omitted
2 details were added to 'reconstruct' the story (**reconstructive memory**).

Did you make similar errors? What other errors did you make? Compare notes with other people after reading the story.

Reading 4.5   Eye-witness Testimony

One particularly powerful source of bias in recognition is the clothing worn by the culprit and the suspect. This issue has been extensively explored in Australia by Donald Thomson, who became interested in the question following a legal case in which the clothing worn by a criminal was a very important factor in causing someone else wearing similar garb to be identified as the perpetrator of the crime. Thomson was able to show that context, in terms of the location of the crime or the clothing of the criminal, had an extremely powerful effect on whether the person would be recognised or not. He went on to show that this effect was still present even with highly sophisticated subjects who were alert to the possibility of bias.

Thomson became actively involved in presenting the case for the unreliability of eye-witness evidence, and on one occasion took part in a television discussion on the topic. Some time later he was picked up by the police, who refused to explain why they were arresting him. He assumed he was being unofficially harassed because of his strong views on eye-witness reliability. At the police station he was placed in a line-up; a woman, clearly very distraught, identified him, and he was then told he was being charged with rape. When he asked for details it became clear that the rape had been committed at the same time as he had been taking part in the television discussion. He said he had a perfectly good alibi with a large number of witnesses, including an official of the Australian Civil Rights Committee and an Assistant Commissioner of Police. To this the policeman taking his statement replied: 'Yes, and I suppose you've also got Jesus Christ and the Queen of England too!' It transpired that the woman had in fact been raped while watching the programme, and that Thomson was a victim of what is often termed *unconscious transference* whereby a witness correctly recognises a face as being that of someone seen before but incorrectly assigns that face to the crime.

Thomson also drew attention to another important aspect of identification, namely the role of knowledge other than memory for the target event. He cites a case in which an accused person, having been identified in a line-up, swapped identities with another man in the remand cell. The accused thoroughly briefed his substitute, and it was the substitute who was interviewed by the defence lawyer. In court, all the witnesses identified the substitute as the offender. After all, he was the person in the dock, wasn't he? When the ruse was revealed the accused was acquitted. The witnesses unquestioningly believed that the person produced in court by the police was the person picked out from the line-up.

A. Baddeley (1983) *Your Memory: A User's Guide* Penguin

1 Name **one** contextual effect which may bias eye-witness testimony.   (1)

2 Thomson was wrongly identified by an eye-witness to a crime due to:
   a) unconscious transference
   b) displacement
   c) the Oedipal conflict
   d) unofficial harassment.   (1)

3 Suggest **two** ways to reduce bias in a police line-up.   (4)

4 Describe another study apart from those presented which demonstrates the distortion of memory over time.   (5)

TERMS TO DEFINE

episodic memory   interference theory   semantic memory

Research on the process of **learning** can also be seen to be following the same trend. Several experiments have shown that animals take a more active role in learning than S–R learning alone can explain. Learning has been shown to be a complex process. Tolman (1930) distinguished a form of learning which is not always demonstrated at the time and may not show until the opportunity arises to use it, known as **latent learning**. He claimed that we construct internal **cognitive maps** (see Reading 10.6 to see how **mnemonics** make use of these). Harlow sees the learning process as a continuum from simple S–R learning to a more cognitive form whereby processes which are learned can be transferred in principle from one situation to another in the form of a **learning set** (as seen in Reading 4.6).

Reading 4.6   Learning Sets

If an animal can form a learning set it means that it can learn not just a problem, but the principle behind it and can steadily increase its learning speed when given a series of similar problems. Harlow has described the basic technique with primates.

A monkey is presented with a pair of dissimilar objects – a matchbox and an egg-cup, for example. The matchbox, no matter where it is placed, always covers a small food reward, the egg-cup never has a reward. After a number of trials the monkey picks up the matchbox straight away. Now the objects are changed, a child's building block is rewarded, a half-tennis-ball unrewarded. The monkey takes about the same time to learn this, again the objects are changed, and so on. After some dozens of such discrimination tests the monkey learns each discrimination much more rapidly, though viewed as an individual problem it is just as difficult as the first one. Eventually after 100 or so tests the monkey presented with a pair of objects lifts one; if it yields a reward he chooses it for all subsequent trials, if it is unrewarded he chooses the other (rewarded) object on the next and all succeeding trials. He has learnt the principle of the problem or, in Harlow's terminology, he has formed a 'learning set'.

This is one type of learning set based on successive trials of discrimination.

Perhaps a simpler version of the same type is the 'repeated reversal' problem. Here we train the animal to select object A in preference to object B. Once learnt, object B is now rewarded and A unrewarded; when this first reversal is learnt, the reward is again given with A, and so on. If the animal gets progressively quicker at learning each reversal this again implies it has learnt a principle.

A. Manning (1979) *An Introduction to Animal Behaviour* Arnold

1 What is meant by a 'learning set'? (2)

2 What did the animal learn in the 'repeated reversal' problem? (2)

3 Are the following statements true or false?
   a) Reinforcement can be defined as anything which increases the likelihood of an organism repeating a response.
   b) Köhler (1925) demonstrated apes solving problems using S–R learning.
   c) Harlow's monkeys learnt the principle of the problems, which is known as insight learning.
   d) Cognitive learning refers to mental aspects of learning. (4)

4 Describe **one** other study which demonstrates cognitive learning. (4)

TERMS TO DEFINE

insight learning   latent learning   learning set   sign learning

Problem solving is shown to be influenced by many varying factors, such as learning and experience. To understand a problem some kind of a mental representation must have been constructed. Interest in the kind of strategies we use for problem solving has led to the programming of computers to solve problems, but not all psychologists see **computer simulation** as comparable to human thought. Computers are strictly logical in approach, whereas human thinking is more complex and subject to more distortions and restrictions, such as **perceptual set** where previous experiences and learning can result in a state of preparedness for the stimulus to be seen in a particular way. However, computers have been influential in forcing psychologists to be more explicit in forming their theories of problem solving and also in testing them more rigorously.

One factor which has been shown to affect thinking is that of **functional fixedness**, as described in Reading 4.7.

Reading 4.7   Functional Fixedness

Think of an occasion in the past week in which you used some object in a new way. For example, you may have stirred your coffee with a pencil (assuming that you had no spoon and were quite desperate). People typically find it difficult to use common objects in new ways because of a factor called functional fixedness.

Functional fixedness means that the function we assign to objects tends to remain fixed or stable. If an object has one particular function for us (writing, for example), it is difficult to switch its function (to stirring, for example).

The classic study in functional fixedness, called Duncker's candle problem (Duncker, 1945), is shown below. Weisberg and Suls (1973) summarise studies that have been conducted on this problem. When people see the set-up illustrated below, most of them either try to tack the candle to the wall or use melted wax to try to glue it up. On the other hand, if the box of tacks is empty, people are much more likely to use it as part of the solution. Weisberg and Suls conducted six experiments in which various aspects of the set-up were varied, and they derived a flowchart model of subjects' performance on the task. A flowchart is a diagram with arrows used to connect a series of boxes, which represent different kinds of processing. A flowchart provides an overview of a computer simulation program. Thus, a person can understand the major steps in the programme without requiring an understanding of the computer language.

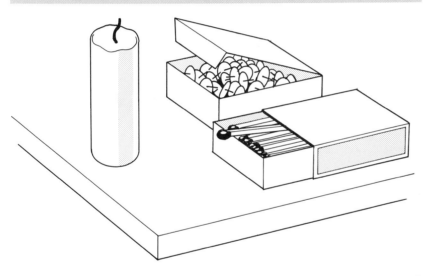

Imagine that you are in an empty room that contains only a table on which sit three items; a candle, a box of tacks, a box of matches. You must find a way to attach the candle to the wall of the room so that it burns properly. You may only use the three specified items in solving the problems. (The correct answer appears in the discussion of the experiment).

One aspect of their model, for example, is that subjects do not focus on the box at first. Instead, they consider the box only after they have found difficulties with other more direct solutions, such as tacking the candle to the wall. Weisberg and Suls recorded the protocols of subjects trying to solve the problem. Here is a typical protocol in which failures on the direct solutions lead to the correct, indirect solution:

Candle has to burn straight, so if I took a nail and put it through the candle and cardboard . . . (10 sec) . . . if I took several nails and made a row and set the candle on that. If I took the nails out of the box, nailed the box to the wall . . . .

The series of experiments confirmed that characteristics of the task, such as labelling the box as a separate object, makes it more likely that people will disregard functional fixedness and find new and creative uses for the box.

M. Matlin (1983) *Cognition* Holt Saunders

95

1 Which of the following refers to functional fixedness?
   a) using the same solution used in previous problems
   b) formulating the steps undertaken as the problem is tackled
   c) the inability to think of new uses for common objects.   (1)

2 Give **one** suggestion made by participants in the Duncker's candle problem prior to reaching the correct solution.   (1)

3 If you were presenting the candle problem to someone how could you help them to reduce functional fixedness?   (2)

4 Find **one** other example of functional fixedness.   (4)

5 Discuss **two** possible strategies used by people in problem solving.   (4)

TERMS TO DEFINE

computer simulation   heuristics   means-ends analysis

Problem solving involves finding a satisfactory way of reaching a goal, or solution; whereas **creativity** involves finding a solution that is unusual.

Several researchers have tried to investigate the relationship of thinking and creativity using tested measures of intelligence. Guilford made a distinction between two types of thinking: **convergent** thinking which requires the focussing of thought on one correct solution to the problem, and **divergent** thinking which involves branching out from one viewpoint to generate new ideas. Sometimes we need to look sideways at a problem (termed **lateral thinking** by Edward de Bono). Such **creativity** is discussed in Reading 4.8.

Reading 4.8   Creativity

The study of creativity arose from a general dissatisfaction with the concept of giftedness that was implicit in educational selection procedures, such as the 11-plus examination system in Great Britain. This examination, in one of its versions, had three separate papers – in English, in arithmetic, and in what was called 'intelligence'. This last paper was a conventional test of convergent thinking.

Writers such as Joy Guilford, who delivered his presidential address to the American Psychological Association on the subject of 'Creativity' in 1950, had begun to realise that there might be a whole realm of creative abilities which were not being tapped by traditional examination procedures. If these abilities were independent of convergent intelligence, and if they were important in children's development and education, their omission was presumably a serious one. Many of the child-centred, informal teaching methods that were being developed around this time put creative abilities in a very central position.

Jacob Getzels and Philip Jackson carried out a pioneering and controversial study in 1962 which looked at the relationship between intelligence and creativity in a sample of 533 Chicago school children. They identified a 'high creative' group who had high scores on what they called 'creativity tests' but low scores on IQ tests, and a 'high intelligence' group whose scores were biased in the opposite direction. Getzels and Jackson's provocative finding was that these two subgroups performed equally well on measures of educational success, which seemed to indicate that creative abilities were just as important as intelligence in school attainment.

Unfortunately, this study was riddled with problems of methodology and experimental design, and so the results are inconclusive. Nevertheless it served to stimulate an immense amount of further research, which has confirmed the importance of creative thinking abilities. Creativity has now become an established and respectable part of psychometrics, and divergent thinking tests are a recognised part of general ability tests (as in the British Ability Scales).

J. Berryman et al (1987) *Psychology and You* Methuen

1 What is meant by:
   a) convergent thinking
   b) divergent thinking?   (2)

2 Which statement is compatable with Getzels and Jackson's view of divergent thinkers?
   a) they will score high on an IQ test
   b) they will score low on an IQ test
   c) they will score low on creativity tests.   (1)

3 Describe **two** techniques used to encourage creativity.   (4)

4 What are the problems of testing creativity?   (5)

TERMS TO DEFINE

brainstorming   creativity   incubation   synectics

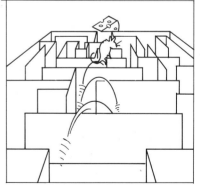

Several different types of test to investigate divergent thought (often seen to be equated with creativity) have been devised. Examples of such items can be found in Activity 4.3.

Activity 4.3 Creativity

Here are some items similar to those given by Guilford. See how you get on with them!

1   How many pictures of real objects can you make using a circle in a one-minute period?

2 See how many words you can find beginning with L and ending with N in a one-minute period.

3 Use the following four shapes to make a face, a lamp, and a tree. Each shape may be used as many times as necessary in forming the object. The sizes can be changed.

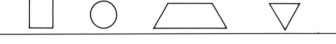

Research into **thinking** processes covers a vast area, overlapping many of the cognitive areas previously discussed. As noted in the introduction to this chapter, cognitive processes are all inter-related, and they do not exist in isolation.

Language can be seen as the expression of thought, in order to communicate. The relationship between language and thought has been the source of several conflicting theories. One view sees thinking to be dependent on language (Whorf 1956), so people speaking different languages, with different category terms, would have different thought patterns. The relationship between **language and thought** is discussed in Reading 4.9.

Reading 4.9   Language and Thought

The exact relationship between language and thought is uncertain and at least three views prevail. The first is that thought is dependent upon language; it is vocabulary and grammar that determine thought. For example, the Hopi Indians have exactly the same word for insect, aeroplane, and air pilot. However, we do not know whether using the same word means that the objects are seen, or thought of, in the same way.

The second view is the opposite, that is, that language is dependent upon thought. This view is seen clearly in Piaget's theory in which as the child's ability to think develops, so language is acquired to further the process of thought. Thus, for Piaget, a pre-linguistic child who sees an action and imitates it is already thinking; language, when it develops, is a tool to assist the process of thinking.

The third view, proposed by the Russian psychologist Lev Vygotsky, is that language and thought are independent. Thinking has the purpose of re-structuring a situation to give it meaning; language is used to communicate. Thus 'cat' has the meaning of a furry animal; to say 'I wish that all cats were friendly' is to communicate something about cats. However, the two abilities do have some degree of overlap: this overlap we call 'verbal thought'. There are, Vygotsky argues, aspects of language such as reciting a poem by heart which are not thinking; and areas of thinking such as imagery and mathematical symbols which are not language.

In total there is no ready answer to what constitutes 'thought'. Imagery, symbols and language provide some clues, but there is the complicated matter of 'thinking about thinking'. How do we do this? We know we are 'aware' of thinking, but how does the awareness work? The debate has been running since the time of Aristotle and there is no sign of a conclusion.

J. Berryman et al (1987) *Psychology and You* Methuen

1 How would you define thought?   (1)

2 Complete the table summarising the views presented:

Theory	Relationship between language and thought
Whorf	
Piaget	
Vygotsky	

(3)

3 What did Piaget mean by egocentric speech?   (2)

4 Compare and contrast Piaget's and Vygotsky's views on language and thought.   (6)

TERMS TO DEFINE

linguistic universals   linguistic relativity   psycholinguistics

The question of whether language is innate or learned has been discussed in Reading 2.2 Isolated Children. Similarly the controversy about whether language is exclusive to humans was investigated in Reading 2.3 Teaching Language to Apes.

One final area we shall look at briefly is that of **language development** which is discussed in Reading 4.10.

Reading 4.10   Language Development

Trevarthen (1974) studied babies from birth to six months with the aid of recording devices. He noted a particular kind of behaviour in babies as young as six weeks which he termed 'pre-speech'. This is a primitive attempt at speech by moving the lips and tongue, sometimes vocally, at other times soundlessly. He noted also that as early as two months, babies make soft, low vowel sounds in response to others. This responsive vocalisation may be the beginning of 'taking turns' as babies and adults do in conversation later on.

In a longitudinal study lasting 10 years, Roger Brown used naturalistic observation techniques to study the development of language in three children, Adam, Eve and Sarah. The children were visited in their homes and tape recordings made of conversations between child and mother. The tape recordings were later transcribed and analysed by Brown and colleagues. The following are among the insights obtained from Brown's work.

1   Early sentences produced by young children are short and incomplete grammatically. However, the words retained are 'telegraphic' in that they preserve the meaning of the message, while the smaller 'functor' words, which are not essential to the meaning, are left out, e.g. 'baby highchair', meaning 'baby is in the highchair'. Correct word order is invariably retained.

2   Children up to the age of four/five have difficulty in correctly expressing negation (I will not walk), past tenses (I shouted), plurals (give me the sweets).

3   Early sentences are much the same whatever language the child speaks. Whether the child is learning English, Russian or Chinese, she/he expresses the same variety of meanings, e.g. statements about location ('spoon table'), possession ('my doll') actions ('Mummy dance').'

Brown's innovatory approach to the study of language acquisition has produced a vast amount of data which has provided material for many further studies. However, the study has its limitations. Because of the nature and size of the sample, it is difficult to generalise findings to all children. Also, child speech was analysed from a typed transcript of the recordings. It was noted by Robinson (1981) that features of the language used, such as intonation, pitch and stress were not included, and the caretaker's utterances and the context in which the utterances were made were often left out.

Cazden (1965) found that a group of children whose utterances were commented upon on a regular basis over a period of three months showed more progress in language development than a similar group whose utterances were expanded upon and imitation of correct language encouraged.

A. Birch and T. Malim (1988) *Developmental Psychology*
Intertext

1 What is meant by 'pre-speech'?   (2)

2 Describe **two** differences that Brown found between the language of young children and adults.   (4)

3 Report Cazden's (1965) findings in your own words.   (4)

4 Discuss Brown's theory on the social aspects of language development.   (6)

TERMS TO DEFINE

LAD   surface/deep structure   telegraphic speech

Not only are cognitive processes active and inter-related but they do not work in a vacuum, they are also affected by other **external** factors. It is to these **social influences**, that we shall turn to in Chapter Five.

Topic-related Essays

1   Discuss the evidence that emotional and motivational factors affect our perception.

2   How successful is S–R learning in explaining all kinds of learning?

3   'A prime necessity in successful problem solving is being extremely flexible' (Eysenck, 1984). How can past experiences affect this flexibility?

SUGGESTIONS FOR FURTHER READING

Main texts
J. Berryman et al (1987) *Psychology and You* BPS: Methuen
N. Hayes (1988) *A First Course in Psychology* (2nd edn) Nelson
N. Hayes and S. Orrell (1987) *Psychology: An Introduction* Longman

Other useful texts
A.D. Baddeley (1983) *Your Memory: A User's Guide* Penguin
G. Cohen et al (1986) *Memory* Oxford University Press
J. and P. de Villiers (1978) *Early Language* Fontana
J. Greene (1986) *Language Understanding* Open University Press
J. Greene and C. Hicks (1984) *Basic Cognitive Processes* Open University Press (areas of research into cognitive processes explained clearly and briefly)
E.F. Loftus (1979) *Eye-witness Testimony* Cambridge, Mass: Harvard University Press (esp. memory of events)
M. Matlin (1983) *Cognition* Holt Saunders
R. Raaheim and J. Radford (1984) *Your Introduction to Psychology* Sigma (readable text with interesting reports on perception and memory)

Stimulus Questions

A psychologist wanted to undertake a case study of children's language, using his own two-year-old child as a subject. He decided to begin by writing down everything that the child said during a half-hour period each evening, and timing the sounds with a stopwatch. After three weeks, the psychologist found that it was impossible to keep to this timetable, so the session was changed to just once a week. The half-hour period usually took place just before the child was due to go to bed in the evening; but if the psychologist was busy at work it sometimes had to take place during the daytime at weekends.

The study lasted for thirteen months, during which time the child's use of language changed considerably. In particular, the child tended to come out with a greater range of words and much less apparently meaningless babbling, although throughout the period of observation it would sometimes seem to make sounds just for the sake of it.

Interestingly, the psychologist found that the total amount of time spent making vocal noises was less towards the end of the observation period than at the beginning of it; although when the notes were consulted there were fewer words at the beginning. The table below shows the mean amount of vocal sounds and the record of words made by the child, for the observation periods in the month concerned.

	Age 2yr 0m	Age 2yr 9m	Age 3yr 1m
vocalisation	18m 24s	16m 09s	11m 54s
no. of words (inc. repetition)	37	43	45
no. of different words used	11	25	53

4.1   What type of study is this?   (1)

4.2   How many subjects are there in the study?   (1)

4.3   What is a mean?   (2)

4.4   Describe in your own words the outcome of this study.   (3)

4.5   In what **three** ways did the psychologist measure language development in the child?   (3)

4.6   Give and explain **one** criticism of the way in which language development was measured in this study.   (3)

4.7   If you were conducting a similar study, describe **two** improvements that you would make in carrying out the study, and explain why you think that they would be a good idea.   (6)

4.8   Suggest an explanation for why the child made less vocal sounds overall as it grew older. What extra information could the psychologist have collected which would have supported your explanation?   (6)

Methodology Questions

Imagine that you have been asked to conduct an experiment to investigate the effects of expectation on how people perceive pictures. Answer the following questions as fully as you can, making your suggestions as practical as possible.

4.1 What exactly is an experiment? (2)

4.2 How would you choose the subjects for your experiment? (2)

4.3 What is this method of choosing subjects called? (1)

4.4 Write out your hypothesis for this study as clearly as you can. (2)

4.5 What is an independent variable? (2)

4.6 Explain clearly what the independent variable would be in the study that you are designing. (2)

4.7 How will you measure the outcome of your experiment? (2)

4.8 Describe **two** problems which could occur if you were not careful in designing your study, stating how they could affect the outcome of the study. (4)

4.9 Explain clearly how each of the problems that you have described could be controlled, assuming that you were carrying out the study in ideal conditions. (4)

4.10 How would you present the results of your study, in your experimental report? Describe **two** ways of presenting the results. (4)

5

Social Influences

'Social psychology has set as its goal the understanding, explanation and prediction of human social behaviour – certainly a broad and rich field of study.'

Deaux and Wrightsman (1984)

Plate 5

Readings on 'Social Influences'

Human beings are **social**. We live in groups and our behaviour is strongly influenced by other people. These social influences have been investigated in many varying research contexts. We shall examine some of the evidence from **three** large areas of research:

1 The social influence of groups

2 Social cognition

3 Attitudes and prejudice.

The **social influence of groups** has been shown to be involved in leading the individual to conform to the group **norms**. Norms are social expectations which are learned in the process of socialisation (see Chapter Seven: Human Development). **Conformity** is often referred to as yielding to group pressure and has been demonstrated experimentally by several researchers. Most introductory texts report the classic experiments of Sherif (1935) and Asch (1956) which show how group pressure can result in people going against their own judgement and conforming to the group. But why do people conform? In Reading 5.1 several factors affecting **conformity** have been identified.

The most superficial type of conformity has been identified as **compliance** (Kelman 1958). In this situation a direct request is made to the individual. When a salesperson is trying to sell us a product they may use what is known as the **foot-in-the-door** approach. This involves the purchaser being persuaded to comply with a small request. Once this is granted a larger request is often made. An example of this is given in Reading 5.2 **Compliance**.

Reading 5.1   Conformity

Soloman Asch carried out a famous experiment where people were asked to estimate the length of a line. Unknown to the subjects, the other people in the room who were also asked to estimate the length of the line were assistants (confederates) of the experimenter. In some of the trials, all these other people gave a wrong answer. Asch wanted to know how many of the subjects would conform to the majority opinion even when it was obviously incorrect. One of the variables he looked at was the number of assistants giving wrong answers, and whether subjects would be more likely to conform when the number of other people in the group was large. Below is a graph showing the percentage of conforming responses made by the subjects.

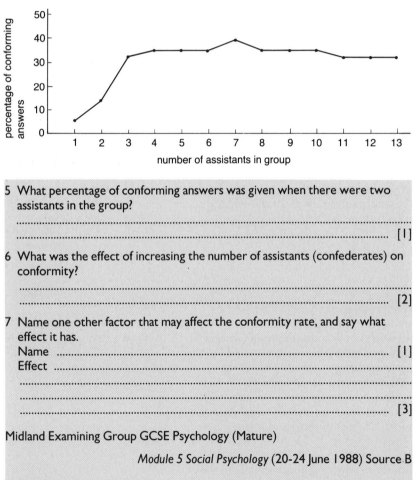

5   What percentage of conforming answers was given when there were two assistants in the group?

....

.... [1]

6   What was the effect of increasing the number of assistants (confederates) on conformity?

....

.... [2]

7   Name one other factor that may affect the conformity rate, and say what effect it has.

Name .... [1]

Effect ....

....

.... [3]

Midland Examining Group GCSE Psychology (Mature)

Module 5 Social Psychology (20-24 June 1988) Source B

TERMS TO DEFINE

anti-conformity   conformity   internalisation   non-conformity

Reading 5.2 Compliance

In one well-known experiment designed to test its effectiveness (Freedman and Fraser, 1966), a number of homemakers were called by a male experimenter who identified himself as a member of a consumer's group. At this time, he asked them to answer a few simple questions about the kinds of soaps they used at home. A few days later, the same individual called again and made a much larger request. This time, he asked if his organisation could send a five- or six-man crew to the subject's home to conduct a complete inventory of all the products he or she had on hand. It was explained that this survey would take about two hours. Further the men would require complete freedom to search through the entire house – including all closets, cabinets, and drawers. Despite the gigantic size of this request, fully 52.8% of the persons called agreed! In contrast, only 22.2% of those in a second group who were called only once and presented with the large request 'cold' agreed. Thus, it appeared that the strategy of starting with a small request and then moving to a large one was in fact effective.

Similar findings have been obtained in many other studies (e.g., Baron, 1973; Pliner et al., 1974). And more recent evidence (Snyder and Cunningham, 1975) seems to provide an explanation for the success of the 'foot-in-the-door' approach. It appears that once individuals have agreed to a small request from a stranger, they undergo a subtle change in their self-perceptions. They begin to see themselves as the kind of person who 'does that sort of thing' – that is, offers help to people who request it. Thus, when contacted again and presented with a much larger request, they agree in order to be consistent with their new self-image. Of course, other factors may play a role as well. Regardless of the precise reasons for its occurrence, though, the foot-in-the door effect seems to be a strong one.

R.A. Baron et al *Psychology: Understanding Behaviour* (2nd edn)
Holt, Rinehart and Winston

1 In the Freedman and Fraser (1966) experiment name:
   a) the Independent Variable
   b) the Dependent Variable.   (2)

2 What were the findings of this study?   (2)

3 How have psychologists explained this finding?   (3)

4 Find **one** research example, other than those presented, which demonstrates compliance.   (4)

TERMS TO DEFINE

compliance   obedience   persuasion   self-perception

Compliance occurs in situations involving a direct request, such as a teacher asking you to stay behind to discuss some outstanding coursework; whereas conformity occurs more indirectly. This could occur in a situation where your peer group have not handed in the above mentioned coursework and anyone doing so might be seen by them as a 'swot'. This situation could result in a conflict between the **obedience** expected by the school regarding homework and acceptance by the friendship group. Complying with the demands of an authority figure was investigated by Milgram (1963) in a series of controversial obedience experiments.

Our behaviour can be changed or modified by the presence of other people. There are several examples of **social facilitation**, whereby an audience can be seen to improve the performance of someone whose observed skills are well practised. Conversely, when skills are new or complex the performance usually deteriorates in front of an audience, and this is known as **social inhibition** (Zajonc 1965).

Activity 5.1

Social facilitation and inhibition can be observed in everyday life. You need to find **two** tasks: one must be a **simple** task and the other **difficult** (why?). Leave someone alone to complete the task, then have them observed by yourself (or a group). What difference does this make to their performance? If you were to perform this as a controlled experiment what modifications would you make to the procedure?

There are also occasions when the presence of a group can result in the individual being less likely to perform. Latané and Darley (1970) reported on how a bystander's reaction to emergencies can be changed by the presence of others. The readiness to go to the aid of someone in need of help has been termed **bystander intervention**. The report of one such case study can be found in Reading 9.1.

The way in which we interpret a situation has been shown to be critical to how we will act in the presence of others. For example, someone may reduce their effort when other people are engaged in the same task. Such **social loafing** is discussed in Reading 5.3.

Reading 5.3   Social Loafing

Marriott (1949) showed that factory workers in large groups produce less per individual than those in small groups. So, group working conditions may inhibit productivity increases in American industry. Social loafing may also explain in part the low productivity of Russian collective farms. There the workers 'move all over huge areas, working one field and one task one day, another field the next, having no sense of responsibility and no direct dependence on the results of their labour' (Smith, 1976). But each worker is also given an acre to till for private use, and although the private plots make up only 1 per cent of Russia's agricultural land, they produce 27 per cent of total output.

Not all collective enterprises fare badly. The Israeli kibbutz stands as a counterexample. Although these collective farms often have poor quality land, and the number of people working on them increased by only 31 per cent from 1949 to 1959, their production rose 360 per cent in the same period (Leon, 1969). The kibbutzim are much more productive than other Israeli farms and farms in other countries. Why does there seem to be no social loafing in the kibbutz?

The Israeli kibbutz and the Russian collective farm, or kolkhoz, differ in a great number of ways. However, Latané and his colleagues have pinpointed one factor, the identifiability of the workers, that seems important. On the Russian farms, it is impossible to keep track of how hard individuals are working, while in the smaller kibbutz it is relatively easy. When people can be easily identified, they may feel more responsible for working hard; when they cannot be identified they may tend to slacken off. This suggests that social loafing is due to what Latané calls a *minimising strategy* by which people 'work only as hard as necessary to gain credit for a good performance or to avoid blame for a bad one.'

H.L. Roediger et al *Psychology* Little, Brown and Co

1 What is meant by social loafing? (3)

2 What key factor do Latané et al suggest explains the difference in productivity between the Russian and Israeli farms? (2)

3 Suggest **one** other factor which may be involved in social loafing. (1)

4 Describe, with evidence, how the presence of others may affect behaviour. (5)

TERMS TO DEFINE

bystander apathy   diffusion of responsibility   social facilitation

There is considerable evidence demonstrating that the environment (or situation) also plays a part in affecting our behaviour. Zimbardo (1969) and his students at Stanford University studied how behaviour can change to fit a **social role** associated with certain situations. Volunteer students were asked to play the roles of either prisoners or guards in a mock prison situation for a two-week period. They were randomly selected as either 'prisoners' or 'guards'. The effects of **depersonalisation** on the behaviour of these pseudo-prisoners and guards is reported in Reading 5.4.

Reading 5.4 Depersonalisation

Zimbardo designed his experiment in an attempt to study some of the conditions that lead to depersonalisation. He found out in a hurry that one primary factor was the behaviour of the guards. True, the prisoners had given up their identities and had become 'numbers.' But they were still human beings, despite the smocks they wore and the chains around their ankles. However, the guards rapidly began treating the prisoners as 'non-persons' who weren't really humans at all.

As far as 'depersonalisation' went, however, the reactions of the prisoners were probably just as important as the actions of the guards. Instead of protesting against their treatment, the prisoners began to act in depressed, institutionalised, dependent ways – exactly the role-behaviours shown by real-life prisoners and mental patients. And, as you might imagine, the more the prisoners acted like 'non-persons,' the more they were mistreated by the guards.

By the end of the sixth day, the situation had nearly gotten out of hand. The guards began modifying or changing the prison 'rules' and routines to make them increasingly more punitive, and even some of Zimbardo's students got so caught up in the spirit of things that they neglected to give the prisoners some of the privileges they had earned.

At this point, wisely, Zimbardo called a halt to the proceedings.

J.V. Mc Connell (1983) *Understanding Human Behaviour* (4th edn)
Holt, Rinehart and Winston

1 What was the purpose of Zimbardo's study?   (2)

2 What behaviour changes occurred in the:
a) 'prisoners'
b) 'guards   (2)

3 Why did Zimbardo stop the experiment earlier than originally planned?   (3)

4 Discuss ways in which our behaviour may be affected by the presence of others.   (10)

TERMS TO DEFINE

depersonalisation   norm   social role

Sensitivity to others can be conveyed without the need for language. In fact **non-verbal communication** (often termed **body language**), in the form of signals such as facial expressions, postures, non-verbal sounds, touch and even the way we dress, can be a powerful indicator of how we feel.

We are familiar with the phrase '*it isn't* **what** *you say but* **how** *you say it that matters*'. When there is a conflict between the verbal and non-verbal cues being picked up we tend to rely on the non-verbal cues (Argyle et al 1972). In the Zimbardo study the 'guards' wore reflecting sunglasses to prevent **eye contact,** one of the most important sources of information we have about other people.

Both **gaze** (looking), and mutual gaze or eye contact (when both people simultaneously look at each other), are involved in signalling interest in other people. They are also linked with status and dominance. As can be seen in Reading 5.5 **Gaze During Conversation**, this is critical in regulating the flow of speech.

Reading 5.5   Gaze During Conversation

It is found that glances are synchronised with speech in a special way. Kendon (1967) found that long glances were made, starting just before the end of an utterance, as shown by the graph, while the other person started to look away at this point.

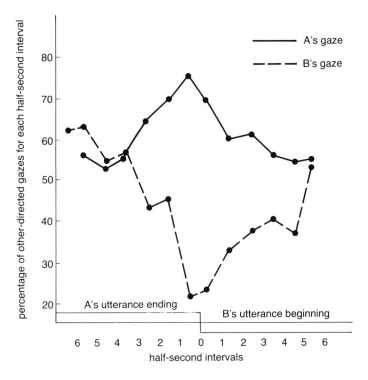

Direction of gaze at the beginning and end of long utterences.

The main reason why people look at the end of their utterances is that they need feedback on the other's response. This may be of various kinds. A wants to know whether B is still attending — his direction of gaze shows if he is asleep, or looking at someone else. A also wants to know how his last message was received — whether B understood, agreed, thought it was funny. At pauses in the middle of long speeches, A will look for continued permission to carry on speaking, and B will nod or grunt if he is agreeable to this.

In another experiment strong support was obtained for the hypothesis that looking is used to gain information on the other's response. Vision between A and B was interfered with in various ways, e.g. B wore (1) dark glasses, (2) a mask with only eyes showing, (3) was behind a one-way screen. In these conditions A was increasingly uncomfortable, was increasingly less clear about how B was reacting, and expressed a desire for more information about B's responses. The experiment shows that it is more useful to see the face than the eyes, though it was necessary to see the eyes themselves for signals about synchronising (Argyle, Lalljee and Cook, 1968).

111

In the Kendon study it was found that the terminal glance conveyed information to the other, that the speaker was about to stop speaking; if this glance were omitted, a long pause followed. In the one-way screen experiment there was much less gaze when subjects were asked to exchange monologues – where no signals for synchronising speech were required.

So gaze does three main jobs during conversation – it enables non-verbal reactions to be seen, it sends information, and it helps with synchronising of utterances.

M. Argyle (1979) *The Psychology of Interpersonal Behaviour* Penguin

1 a) When did Kendon (1967) find the speaker taking long looks in the conversation?   (1)
   b) How does he explain this?   (2)

2 Describe the pattern of gaze made by A shown in the graph over the period of B's speech.   (2)

3 Describe how Argyle et al (1968) demonstrated that gaze, or looking, was necessary for feedback.   (3)

4 Join up the sentences so that all three are correct:

gaze   unconsciously occurs when we find someone attractive
eye contact   occurs less when a topic is difficult
pupil dilation   increases with intimacy   (3)

5 Discuss, with evidence, two non-verbal cues (other than gaze and eye contact) which communicate information.   (8)

TERMS TO DEFINE

kinesics   non-verbal communication   paralanguage   proxemics

Perhaps you might find Activity 5.2 a rather revealing exercise in demonstrating the importance of **body space**.

Activity 5.2

The nearness of others (**proximity**) is culturally determined. Observe what happens in a public area such as a library, park etc. How close together do friends sit? How close together do strangers sit? If you were doing this as part of a controlled study, what factors would you need to take into account?

We use all the information available to understand the social situations in which we find ourselves. We can form impressions of other people based on very few details. **Halo effects** are an example of bias in impression formation. They refer to the tendency of people to assume that once people possess some good (or bad) characteristics, their other characteristics are also likely to be good (or bad). Asch (1946) demonstrated that even a list of adjectives (such as warm and cold) were thought to refer to what he described as **central** qualities, which could alter the description given. **Primacy** effects (such as when the adjectives are presented first) have been found to be important, so 'first impressions' do appear to matter!

When information presented is either positive (good) or negative (bad) the negative information appears to have more effect and is more resistant to change later. **First impressions** are discussed in Reading 5.6.

Reading 5.6   First Impressions

An unfavourable first impression appears to be more resistant to change than a favourable first impression. For example, in one study subjects were given a favourable or an unfavourable description of a person (Briscoe, Woodyard, and Shaw, 1967). After rating the person on an evaluative scale, the subjects received additional information, which was evaluatively opposite to the initial information. They then rated the person again on the same scale, and the difference between the two ratings was determined. The results showed that if the subjects received negative information about the person first and then positive information, their evaluative ratings changed less than when they received the favourable information first. In other words, a negative first impression was more resistant to change. However unfair it may seem, perceivers have a pervasive tendency to weight negative information more heavily in their impressions of others.

Why should we be so attuned to negative information about another person? There are several possible explanations, two of which will be mentioned briefly here. One possibility is that through our experience we have learned to be sensitive to information that implies a potential threat to our well-being. If you learn that a person is dishonest or has a violent temper, it is probably highly adaptive for you to pay special heed to that information. Such an orientation to avoid personal costs in their relationships with others may lead perceivers to give heavy weight to unfavourable information in the impression-formation process. A second explanation points to the differential 'informativeness' of negative and positive information about persons. Most people behave in a socially desirable manner most of the time. Consequently, most of the traits we perceive in a particular person should be desirable. Thus, learning something favourable about someone provides us with relatively little information about that person as a unique individual. In contrast, information about negative characteristics or behaviours provides some indication of how the person differs from most other people, and consequently provides a useful basis for making inferences about the person's personality. Information that is useful and informative in this sense would receive greater weight in the impression-formation process.

L. Berkowitz (1986) *A Survey of Social Psychology* (3rd edn)
Holt, Rinehart and Winston

1 Which statement is correct?
  a) a negative first impression is more resistant to change
  b) a positive first impression is more resistant to change. (1)

2 Give **one** explanation for this effect. (2)

3 What is meant by 'social desirability'? (2)

4 Describe **one** study, other than those presented, which demonstrates the effects of first impressions. (4)

5 Discuss the possible factors involved in determining the first impression that a person makes. (6)

TERMS TO DEFINE

halo effect   implicit personality theory   primacy/recency effects

How does someone arrive at an understanding of the behaviour of other people? The **attribution process** describes how we project motives on to others, to try and predict their behaviour and their future actions. Early research by Heider (1958) demonstrated that we tend to make a distinction between explanations of behaviour based on internal or **dispositional** attribution (such as personality) and external or **situational** attribution (such as social threat). As can be seen in Reading 5.7 such attributions are subject to **attribution error**.

Reading 5.7   Attribution Error

One of the major attribution tasks we face daily is deciding whether an observed behaviour reflects something unique about the person (his or her attitudes, personality characteristics, and so forth) or something about the situation in which we observe the person. If we infer that something about the person is primarily responsible for the behaviour (for instance, the athlete really loves the cereal), then our inference is called an internal or dispositional attribution ('disposition' here refers to a person's beliefs, attitudes, and personality characteristics). If, however, we conclude that an external cause is primarily responsible for the behaviour (for instance, money, strong social norms, threats), it is called an external or situational attribution.

The founder of modern attribution theory, Fritz Heider, noted that an individual's behaviour is so compelling to observers that they take it at face value and give insufficient weight to the circumstances surrounding it (1958). Recent research has confirmed Heider's speculation. We underestimate the situational causes of behaviour, jumping too easily to conclusions about the dispositions of the person. Another way of stating it is that we (in Western society, at any rate) have a schema of cause and effect in human behaviour that gives too much weight to the person and too little to the situation. One psychologist has termed this bias toward dispositional rather than situational attributions the *fundamental attribution error* (Ross, 1977).

In one of the first studies to reveal this bias, subjects were asked to listen to an individual giving a speech either favouring or opposing racial segregation. The subjects were explicitly informed that the individual was participating in an experiment and had been told which side of the issue to argue; the speaker had no choice. Despite this knowledge, when asked to estimate the individual's actual attitude toward racial segregation, subjects inferred that the individual held a position close to the one argued in the speech. In other words, the subjects made a dispositional attribution even though situational forces were fully sufficient to account for the behaviour (Jones and Harris, 1967). This effect is quite powerful. Even if the presentations are deliberately designed to be drab and unenthusiastic, and even if the speaker simply reads a transcribed version of the talk, speaking in a monotone and using no gestures, observers are still willing to attribute to the speaker the attitudes expressed (Schneider and Miller, 1975).

R.L. Atkinson, et al (1987) *Introduction to Psychology* (9th edn)
Harcourt Brace Jovanovich

1 a) Explain what is meant by:
       i)   internal attribution
       ii) external attribution.   (2)
    b) Give **one** example of each.   (2)

2 Are the following statements regarding the attribution process true or false?
    a) we underestimate situational effects
    b) we give more weight to the situation
    c) traits and motives are projected onto others to explain behaviour.   (3)

3 Briefly summarise the Jones and Harris (1967) study reported above.   (3)

4 Critically discuss **one** theory of attribution.   (8)

TERMS TO DEFINE

attribution process   fundamental attribution error

The way we feel and react towards events and people is not always consistent. We have seen how social factors play an important role. We often judge our opinions by comparing them with those of other people (refer to Reading 5.1 Conformity). Festinger (1957) suggested that when two of our attitudes are inconsistent and contradictory the state of tension so created has to be reduced. In such a situation we may seize upon evidence which is consistent with the decision we have made, even when this evidence is irrational and flimsy.

Such **cognitive dissonance** has been noted in relation to the accident at the Three Mile Island nuclear power plant in America in 1979. Radioactive material was accidentally released into the atmosphere and for several days the situation at the plant was unstable. The residents in the area had to decide whether they should leave or stay. The outcome is discussed in relation to the theory in Reading 5.8.

Reading 5.8   Cognitive Dissonance

As Elliot Aronson (1980) points out, cognitive dissonance theory would predict that people who lived in the immediate area of the plant would readily latch onto the NRC's reassurances, while those who lived just outside the immediate danger zone would be more sceptical and even hostile toward the NRC. After all, if you were a person who chose to live in the danger area, your cognition of having made a bad choice would be dissonant with your self-concept as a smart and prudent individual who cares about your family. Thus, you would be anxious to believe the reassurances. But if you were one of those who lived just outside the danger zone, your attitude might be quite different. As Aronson put it, 'These people are also worried and scared, though they are threatened less directly and have not been contaminated. They would be more able to express their scepticism and anger – indeed, it would be in their self-interest to do so, because they would be imperiled if the situation in the nuclear power plant deteriorated or if the crisis was more serious than what was being publicised'.

These dissonance theory predictions seemed to be borne out. A survey conducted shortly after the incident showed that people who lived within 15 miles of the plant were most likely to believe the information conveyed by the NRC, whereas those who lived outside the 15-mile zone were more likely to say that the information was totally useless. Anecdotal reports also support the conclusion that residents of the Three Mile Island area had a strong need to believe they were safe, whether or not they really were. While the national media were filled with reports of the NRC's incompetence and inadequacy, the people actually affected by the crisis greeted the National Regulatory Commission 'like cavalry riding to a nick-of-time rescue.'

Z. Rubin and E.B. Mc Neil (1981) *Psychology: Being Human* (3rd edn)
Harper Row

1 What predictions would cognitive dissonance theory make about the behaviour of the residents in the areas near the Three Mile Island plant?   (2)

2 Describe in your own words the outcome of the investigation.   (3)

3 a) What is meant by a survey?   (2)
   b) Give **two** advantages and **two** disadvantages connected with the use of surveys.   (4)

4 If you were planning a survey, what techniques would you use to ensure that bias was kept to a minimum?   (8)

TERMS TO DEFINE

attitude   cognitive dissonance   social comparison

Attitudes can develop on the basis of previous judgements made on individuals or situations. These pre-judgements or **prejudices** can be **positive**, whereby we see a group to be good, or **negative** where we evaluate them in a less favourable manner.

Activity 5.3

Read the following description of an unknown individual:

'Joy is a delightful little three-year-old. She has beautiful blonde hair and deep blue eyes. On Saturday she was playing with a neighbour's four-year-old boy. She threw a stone at him which cut his knee and he had to go to hospital.'

Imagine you were present and then rate the following statements and questions on a scale: Yes   1—2—3—4—5   No

Joy intended to hurt the boy.
She should be punished.
Is she likely to do it again?
Would you allow your child to play with her?
She is an intelligent girl.

After you have done this, read the comments at the top of page 118.

Prejudice usually refers to bias which can result in unfair negative attitudes shown towards members of a particular group. This can result in **discrimination**, which involves negative **actions** towards such groups. There are many types of prejudice such as **ageism** (against people of a different age to oneself), **sexism** (against gender) and **racism** (based on a belief that one race is inherently superior to another). Although surveys carried out in the USA indicate support for racial integration of schools and housing, studies of actual behaviour demonstrate that prejudice is still quite strong and exists in a more subtle form.

Topic-related Essays

1   'You never have a second chance to make a good impression.' Discuss.

2   Discuss cognitive dissonance in relation to attitude change.

3   What is prejudice? How can we try to reduce prejudice?

We have previously discussed how easily we build up **stereotypes** which apply to groups of people. Such stereotypes can result in false impressions of others. One suggested reason for the persistence of such views is **selective perception**, whereby we tend to focus on information that is consistent with our stereotypes and screen out or readjust information which is inconsistent with them. This can be seen in Reading 5.9.

Comments on Activity 5.3
Research has shown that good-looking people are rated higher on
measures such as intelligence, personality, status etc. Do you think
that you rated Joy less harshly because she was described as pretty?
Perhaps you could devise an experiment based on these findings?

Reading 5.9   Selective Perception

An experiment by Birt Duncan (1976) illustrates such selective perception.
White college students viewed a videotaped interaction between two other
students who were supposedly taking part in a discussion. After some initial
conversation, the students got into an argument that became more and more
heated until finally Student B shoved Student A. The subjects were later asked
for their impressions of the two students. When the shover was black and the
person he shoved was white, 70 per cent of the subjects classified the shove as
an instance of 'violent behaviour.' But when the shover was white and the
person he shoved was black, only 17 per cent of the subjects considered this
'violent behaviour,' while 42 per cent described it as either 'playing around' or
'dramatising.' Blacks are often viewed by whites as being prone to violence. As
Duncan's study demonstrates, selective perception can serve to maintain this
stereotype.

Without being fully aware of it, we all become skilled at perceiving only those
events that are consistent with our prejudices. After a while, we amass a pile of
evidence that assures us that our prejudices are justified. In addition, movies and
television often portray members of various groups in ways that conform to
popular stereotypes and, as a result, help to perpetuate them.

Z. Rubin and E.B. Mc Neill (1981) *Psychology: Being Human* (3rd edn)
Harper Row

1 In the Duncan (1976) experiment what was:
   a) the IV
   b) the DV?   (2)

2 Fill in the table below with appropriate percentages from the above
   research.

	Participants description of behaviour	
	'violent'	'playing around' 'dramatising'
black student pushing white		information not given in text
white student pushing black		

(3)

3 Can you find another research example which demonstrates prejudice? (4)

4 Discuss the possible reasons for prejudice. (6)

TERMS TO DEFINE

authoritarian personality   prejudice   scapegoat theory   selective perception

Stereotypes can be resistant to change and result in prejudice. Suggestions have been made as to how we can reduce prejudice. One factor found to be important is that people must have **equal status** in the situation. Aronson et al (1978) have developed a programme known as the **'jigsaw technique'**, in which children in a group are encouraged to work together for a common cause. In this interaction they not only learn to work together but also to respect each other as **equals**. This has been shown to be especially beneficial with young children whose attitudes have not fully developed. Several social psychologists have suggested that group conflicts can be reduced by successful co-operation. This was demonstrated in a classic study by Sherif and his colleagues in 1961 which demonstrated **reducing inter-group conflict**, the topic of our final reading in this chapter, Reading 5.10.

Reading 5.10   Reducing Inter-group Conflict

In a famous experiment, Sherif and colleagues at the University of Oklahoma (1961) showed how hostility decreases when rival groups work together to achieve a mutually desired goal. Preadolescent boys (about 11 to 12 years of age) at a summer camp at Robbers Cave, Oklahoma, were divided into two groups, the Rattlers and the Eagles, each group being at first unaware of the other's presence. Then when the teams discovered each other, they eagerly challenged each other to competitive sports. This was just what the investigators wanted, and a tournament was readily arranged. As expected, the competition quickly degenerated into open hostility between the groups. The boys engaged in name calling, fights, and destructive raids on the rival group's cabin.

Now was the time to reduce the conflict between the rival groups. The psychologists first examined the effects of merely bringing the groups into contact with each other. They arranged various meetings between the Rattlers and Eagles – in a common dining room, at a fireworks display, and at the movies – but as the researchers had anticipated, this contact didn't seem to help much. They then established superordinate goals – goals that were attractive to both groups but which neither one could achieve by itself – to see what would happen if the boys cooperated to reach their shared objectives. The experimenters created several apparent emergencies: an interruption of the camp's water supply, a shortage of money that required the groups to pool their funds, a stalled truck that could be started only if both groups pulled together on

119

a rope. As the boys worked together to master the difficulties facing them, the conflict between the Rattlers and Eagles decreased, and they even developed some liking for each other. In a later summary of the Robbers Cave experiment, Sherif (1966) noted that 'joint efforts in situations such as these did not immediately dispel hostility. But gradually, the series of activities requiring interdependent action reduced conflict. . . . As a consequence, the members of the two groups began to feel friendlier. . . . Now friendships developed, cutting across group lines.

L. Berkowitz (1986) *A Survey of Social Psychology* (3rd edn)
Holt, Rinehart and Winston

1 What conditions promoted the inter-group rivalry in the above study? (2)

2 Describe **two** ways in which the psychologists tried to bring the two groups together. (2)

3 What did the experimenters consider to be the most important factor that reduced inter-group conflict? (2)

4 Describe and outline the problems associated with a field experiment such as the one described above. (10)

TERMS TO DEFINE

ethnocentrism   group   group cohesiveness

Fortunately social influence can also be channelled into ways in which we can help our fellows, as shown by the appeals for help through the mass media for the starving in Africa by entertainers such as Bob Geldof. The research into the effects of social influence emphasises how people process the information they receive in relation to the setting in which they find themselves, and the people with whom they are in contact. However, research demonstrates that there are several **individual differences** which can distinguish us from other people and it is to these that we shall address ourselves in Chapter Six.

SUGGESTIONS FOR FURTHER READING

Main texts
J. Berryman et al (1987) *Psychology and You* BPS: Methuen
K. Deaux and L.S. Wrightsman (1988) *Social Psychology* (5th edn)
  Brooks/Cole
N. Hayes and S. Orrell (1987) *Psychology: an Introduction* Longman
Z. Rubin and E.B. McNeil (1985) *Psychology: Being Human* (4th edn)
  Harper Row

Other useful texts
L. Berkowitz (1986) *A Survey of Social Psychology* (3rd edn) Holt,
  Rinehart and Winston (esp. person perception, group conflict)

D.W. Bethlehem (1985) *A Social Psychology of Prejudice* Croom Helm
J.P. Forgas (1985) *Interpersonal Behaviour: the Psychology of Social Interaction* Pergamon (esp. person perception, attribution, and some goal related activities)
N. Hayes (1988) *A First Course in Psychology* (2nd edn) Nelson (conformity and obedience studies)
A. Taylor et al (1982) *Introducing Psychology* (2nd edn) Penguin (good section on NVC)

Stimulus Questions

A psychologist wished to investigate the effects which attributions made by people of higher status could have. The psychologist also wished the study to have ecological validity as far as possible. Accordingly, the following investigation was set up.

Four medical students were each asked to interview five diabetic patients attending a clinic, with a senior doctor present in the room. The students were told about a new product which had become available for the treatment of diabetes, and that they would be asked to assess privately whether each of the patients would be likely to benefit from the treatment. Before each patient was admitted to the consulting room, the senior doctor looked through their notes and commented on their case. The comments included either a situational attribution on why previous treatment hadn't been very successful (there were no backup or support services provided); or a dispositional attribution (that the patient hadn't bothered to do things properly).

At the end of each interview, the medical students were asked to rate the likelihood of success of the new treatment on a scale of 1 to 10; and also to tick those adjectives on a given list which they felt best described the patient that they had just seen. The outcome of the study was as follows:

	Modal adjective	Mean rating of success
Situational attribution	anxious	8.7
Dispositional attribution	inattentive	6.3

5.1 How many subjects were there in this study?   (1)

5.2 What type of study was this?   (1)

5.3 What does 'modal' mean?   (2)

5.4 What is 'ecological validity'?   (2)

5.5 Describe in your own words the outcome of this study.   (3)

5.6 Suggest **one** factor which could have biased the results of the study, and explain how it could have affected the results. (3)

5.7 Suggest **one** reason why the adjectives which the medical students chose were different for the two groups. (3)

5.8 Explain clearly what is meant by the terms: 'situational attribution' and 'dispositional attribution'. (4)

5.9 If you were conducting a similar study, describe **two** improvements that you would make in carrying out the study. Explain why you think that they would be a good idea. (6)

Methodology Questions

Imagine that you have been asked to carry out a survey of how styles of dress can influence people's attitudes to one another. Make your suggestions as practical as possible, such that the survey could be carried out in two afternoons by yourself and a friend.

5.1 What is meant by a 'survey'? (2)

5.2 State **two** ways of collecting information from your survey. (2)

5.3 Choose **one** of these methods of collecting information for your survey, and explain why you have chosen it. (2)

5.4 Describe how you would select the subjects for your survey. What is this method called? (3)

5.5 State your hypothesis for this survey, making it clear which styles of dress you would ask about. (3)

5.6 State where you would carry out your survey, and explain why you have made that particular choice. (3)

5.7 State **one** way in which you could try to make sure that your data would be reliable. (3)

5.8 Describe **two** problems that could occur in collecting the data for your survey. (4)

5.9 In writing a report of the survey, how would you present and summarise your data? (4)

NEA Joint GCE/CSE Examination Paper 1 1987

6

Individual Differences

'The number of specific ways in which people can differ is incalculable. Fortunately the human system is such that these specific differences among people tend to be interrelated, or correlated with one another, in a manner which makes possible the specification of more general dimensions of difference.'

Taylor et al (1982)

Plate 6

Scale measuring degree of internal-external control

I more strongly believe that:	Or
Promotions are earned through hard work and persistence	Making a lot of money is largely a matter of getting the right breaks
In my experience I have noticed that there is usually a direct connection between how hard I study and the grades I get	Many times the reactions of teachers seem haphazard to me
The number of divorces indicates that more and more people are not trying to make their marriages work	Marriage is largely a gamble
When I am right I can convince others	It is silly to think that one can really change another person's basic attitudes
In our society a man's future earning power is dependent upon his ability	Getting promoted is really a matter of being a little luckier than the next guy
If one knows how to deal with people they are really quite easily led	I have little influence over the way other people behave
In my case the grades I make are the results of my own efforts; luck has little or nothing to do with it	Sometimes I feel that I have little to do with the grades I get
People like me can change the course of world affairs if we make ourselves heard	It is only wishful thinking to believe that one can really influence what happens in society at large
I am the master of my fate	A great deal that happens to me is probably a matter of chance
Getting along with people is a skill that must be practised	It is almost impossible to figure out how to please some people

Readings on 'Individual Differences'

In previous chapters we have tended to look at characteristics shared by most people. However, most of us are aware that not everyone reacts in the same way. Why do some people react to a stimulus or situation differently to others? We talk about friends or acquaintances who are 'outgoing', 'shy' or 'intelligent'. These describe what we see as characteristics which vary between individuals. The study of groups to discover general laws is known as the **nomothetic** approach – we are comparing people with each other. Studying individuality and uniqueness involves an **idiographic** approach. Both of these approaches have been used in research into individual differences such as intelligence and personality.

Intelligence has proved to be an area of great interest in psychology. As noted in Chapter Two, most of the research on intelligence has proved controversial. There is little agreement among researchers on an accepted definition. Anastasi (1982) suggests that intelligence be regarded as '. . . *a descriptive rather than an explanatory concept. An IQ is an expression of an individual's ability level at a given point in time, in relation to the age norms.*'

Like many physical characteristics such as height, intelligence is considered to be **normally distributed**. This refers to the fact that when measurements are taken of such characteristics and plotted on a graph they usually make what is known as the **normal distribution** or 'bell-shaped' curve (see Figure 6.1).

Intelligence tests are designed and **standardised** so that scores on an intelligence/IQ test fit into this curve, with most scores around the mid-value (the mean score). This mean or average score is given as 100 for each

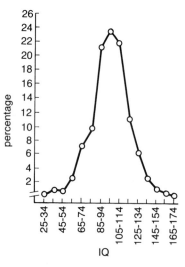

Figure 6.1 *A normal distribution curve of IQs*

Distribution of Stanford-Binret IQs for 2904 children and youths, ages 2–18. The slight bump on the left-hand tail represents those who are retarded as the result of specific genetic defects or birth injuries and are not part of the normal distribution. (after Terman and Merrill, 1937)

age level. The results of a population sample on an intelligence (or IQ) test should show most of the scores around 100, with few scores below 50 or above 150. In this way an individual's score can be seen in relation to other scores on the test. Activity 6.1 demonstrates this.

Activity 6.1

A group of 418 children had the following average scores on an IQ test:

5 had scores of 140	33 had scores of 70
19 had scores of 60	55 had scores of 80
20 had scores of 130	78 had scores of 110
30 had scores of 120	88 had scores of 90
90 had scores of 100	

Plot the scores on a graph. Do they form a bell-shaped curve?
What does the graph tell you about the group scores?

In **behavioural assessment**, as explained in Reading 6.1, tests are constructed and administered in accordance with set instructions or rules to try and eliminate bias.

Reading 6.1 Behavioural Assessment

The formal assessment of individual differences (as distinct from informal assessments, made both by psychologists and by laymen) is dependent upon the existence of adequate measuring devices, or tests, constructed and administered in accordance with rather stringent rules. The purpose behind these rules is to ensure that the measuring process is 'objective', in the sense that it is not biased by the personal judgement of the tester. In this chapter our concern is with psychological tests of ability and personality, but the rules apply also to any kind of behavioural measurement.

If the subject's performance on a test is to be free from the influence of the tester, it is important that testers should follow a standard procedure when using the test. To this end, manuals are provided which indicate precisely how the test should be administered and scored. It is of the greatest importance that testers should follow exactly the instructions given, for even small deviations can affect the subject's scores. In addition, manuals usually contain normative data, by which is meant details of the results of administering the test to large samples of subjects. The value of such data is that they enable the tester to interpret a particular individual's score in relation to specified populations of subjects.

However, the effect of the tester's personality can never be completely eliminated. This is because a testing situation is a social one, and the tester has to establish 'rapport' with his subjects: that is, he must secure the cooperation of the subjects and put them sufficiently at ease for them to produce something like their best performance. Individual testers clearly vary in the skill with which they can do this.

A. Taylor et al (1982) *Introducing Psychology* (2nd edn) Penguin

1 What is meant by:
  a) IQ
  b) psychometrics?   (4)

2 What is the average IQ score?   (2)

3 Why do testers follow the same procedure as set out in the test manual?   (1)

4 Name **one** reason why it is impossible to eliminate all possible bias from the tester.   (1)

5 Give **two** characteristics of a good test.   (4)

6 Describe **two** factors known to affect IQ scores.   (6)

TERMS TO DEFINE

assessment   intelligence tests

Several **theories of intelligence** have been developed to try and explain the underlying abilities of intelligence. One of the earliest attempts to explain intelligence came from Spearman in 1904. He distinguished between two types of intelligence: a general factor '**g**' which is applied to all situations and specific factors '**s**' which would be related to individual tasks. Spearman's theory and that of Cattell are discussed in Reading 6.2.

Reading 6.2   Theories of Intelligence

To Charles Spearman, the noted British psychologist, there were but two types of intelligence. He noted that, if you took 10 different intelligence tests, you would usually wind up with 10 different scores. True, the scores probably would be related to each other. But which one gives your real IQ? And why so many different scores? Spearman decided that each test item actually measured two factors. One he called general intelligence, or the 'g factor.' But each item also measured one or more specific types of mental ability, which he called the 's factors.' Thus different tests yield different scores because each test tends to emphasise 's' or 'g' to a different degree. However, the mix of 's' and 'g' factors for each test could still fit a bell-shaped curve.

Raymond Cattell agreed that there were two 'intellectual factors,' but disagreed with Spearman on what they were. Cattell claims you have fluid intelligence and crystallised intelligence. 'Fluid' intelligence is inherited, and involves such talents as the ability to think and reason.

'Crystallised' intelligence involves learned skills such as being able to add and subtract, and the size of your vocabulary. According to Cattell, your 'fluid' intelligence sets limits on your 'crystallised' abilities. If you aren't innately bright, all the training in the world won't help you get through school. However, if you have a high 'fluid' intelligence, and you grow up in a deprived and unstimulating environment, you won't acquire many skills. And you won't get a high score on most intelligence tests, either. From Cattell's point of view, if everyone grew up in the best of all possible environments, 'fluid' intelligence would be the major determinant of IQ – and test scores would then 'fit the curve' almost exactly.

J.V. McConnell (1983) *Understanding Human Behaviour* (4th edn)
Holt, Rinehart and Winston

1 What did Spearman mean by the 'g factor'?   (1)

2 According to Spearman why do different intelligence tests produce different scores for the same person?   (1)

3 What is meant by:
   a) fluid intelligence
   b) crystallised intelligence?   (2)

4 Explain how fluid and crystallised intelligence interact to determine the individual's behaviour.   (3)

5 What is meant by 'fit the curve'?   (4)

6 Describe **one** additional theory of intelligence to those presented, giving its strengths and weaknesses.   (5)

TERMS TO DEFINE

fluid/crystallised intelligence   'g factor'   IQ

Cattell's theory contradicts the innate view of intelligence. He sees ability as being determined by the **interaction** of innate ability and environmental factors. The origins of intelligence are discussed in Chapter Two, where evidence from twin and adoption studies is challenged (see Reading 2.9 Adoption and Twin Studies).

Several researchers have noted the effects of intellectual stimulation on IQ scores. On the basis of such findings several **intervention** programmes have been initiated to give extra cognitive experiences to children from what are seen to be impoverished homes. The findings from such programmes are far from conclusive, often with many initial gains dropping over a period of time. A report of one extensive intervention study on **compensatory education** can be found in Reading 6.3.

Reading 6.3   Compensatory Education

One of the major criticisms of intervention programmes generally is that they have been of too short a duration. A much more extensive and ambitious programme was undertaken by Heber and Garber (1970) who studied 40 newborn infants from the poorer areas of Milwaukee whose mothers had intelligence scores below 70. One-half of the children was assigned to an experimental group and the other half to a control group. Three months after birth, the children in the experimental group received an intervention programme which aimed at improving their motor, sensory, language and thinking skills. The programme lasted for several years and averaged about 35 hours a week. The intervention included maternal training (homemaking, child-rearing and vocational training). No special treatment was given to the children in the control group, but they took the same tests as the others.

Every 3 weeks children in the experimental and control groups were tested, and after 66 months the test scores of the experimental group averaged 124; the control group averaged 94. This difference of 30 points between the two groups is remarkable, the more so when they are compared with the differences of about 12 or 13 points which were reported in the shorter interventions. Nevertheless, several points should be noted:

(1) The small sample may be responsible for the production of an inflated mean.

(2) The reported increase in intelligence among children in the experimental group was no greater than that which might be anticipated on the basis of a genetic model.

(3) The method of matching experimental/control subjects was not accurate.

(4) The children were tested on the questions for which they had been prepared.

(5) Results are not yet available for those over 16 years of age.

R.B. Burns and C.B. Dobson (1984) *Introducing Psychology* MTP Press

1 What was the IQ of the mothers in the study?   (1)

2 What does this score mean?   (2)

3 Name **two** skills that the programme set out to improve.   (2)

4 In the study reported what was:
   a) the independent variable
   b) the dependent variable?   (4)

5 Report the results of the study in your own words.   (3)

6 Describe **one** study demonstrating the long-term impact of enrichment or deprivation.   (6)

TERMS TO DEFINE

compensatory education   intervention programme

Like intelligence, **personality** can be defined in many ways. Generally it is taken to refer to relatively permanent characteristics distinguishing one individual from another. Psychologists disagree as to which behaviour patterns are most important for characterising people and we find a variety of different approaches which attempt to identify the essential variables.

Trait theories of personality assume that we each possess dispositions to respond to stimuli in a certain way. For example, a person who is shy and withdrawn is likely to behave in a shy and withdrawn way in most situations. Such predispositions have been named **traits**. Someone rated high on a particular trait would be more likely to display certain characteristics in a wide variety of situations rather than someone rated low on the same trait. Such traits are usually measured by questionnaires, tests and observations. Eysenck believes that personality can be measured along such dimensions. He has described what he sees to be the underlying **type** of personality responsible for the traits which people display (see Figure 6.2).

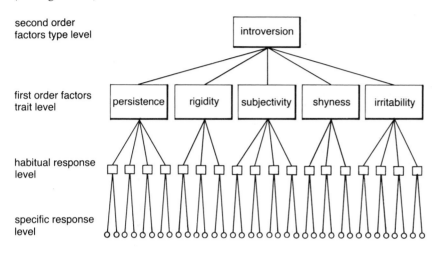

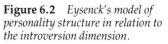

Figure 6.2 *Eysenck's model of personality structure in relation to the introversion dimension.*

In 1947 he identified two dimensions of **extraversion-introversion (E)** and **neuroticism-stability (N)**, which he supported with evidence from thousands of his patients. People high on extraversion were seen as sociable and outgoing, seeking exciting activities. He described them as restless, talkative, optimistic and cheerful. Introverts were seen as quiet, restrained and serious, somewhat inhibited and withdrawn, and interested in solitary activities. Individuals high on neuroticism were described as anxious, worrying, moody, subject to depression, and emotional; conversely a stable personality remained calm and unemotional in most situations. Perhaps you would like to investigate this scale yourself in Activity 6.2.

In later research he added a third dimension, known as **psychoticism (P)**. High scorers on this scale were seen as insensitive, hostile and aggressive. Eysenck has developed scales to measure these dimensions, with the P scale proving most controversial because it has not been found to be **robust** (replicable in a wide range of study populations in differing conditions). These underlying dimensions of **personality characteristics** are seen by Eysenck to be inherited, as can be seen in Reading 6.4.

If behaviour is learned then the process can be reversed and it can be unlearned. This behaviourist viewpoint has led to the development of several behavioural therapies based on both classical and operant conditioning to help patients change maladaptive behaviour. Operant techniques of **behaviour modification** have been developed which involve **shaping** behaviours (see Chapter Two especially Reading 2.6 Superstitious Behaviour to see how behaviour can be shaped using selective reinforcement). Classical conditioning techniques, such as **systematic desensitisation**, have been found helpful in the treatment of phobias (excessive fears), as can be seen in Reading 6.5.

Activity 6.2

This is an activity that you can try with a group of friends or members of your class group.

The first step involves rating the group on extraversion. This means deciding who you consider to be the least extravert, or outgoing member of the group. This individual will be rated, or ranked, as 1; the next least extravert is ranked as 2, and so on until you have ranked the whole group including yourself. The person ranked highest on extraversion will have the highest ranking. This part must be done independently with no discussion among the group.

You should now have several lists of ratings, collected from members of the group, with everyone's name and rank on each list. The next step involves putting the results into a matrix with everyone's name on both axes and the rank number from each judge. When the ranks are added, those rated high on extraversion will be shown to have the highest score and those considered introvert will have a low score, as shown in the example below:

	John	Alison	Jenny	Alan	Chris
John	2	1	5	4	3
Alison	1	2	4	5	3
Jenny	2	1	5	4	3
Alan	1	2	5	4	3
Chris	2	1	5	4	3
Total	8	7	24	21	15

Jenny is shown to be most extravert.
Alison is shown to be least extravert/most introvert.

If you are able to obtain copies of Eysenck's book *Know Your Own Personality*, then before transferring the ranks on to the matrix, and with no discussion in the group, you could all fill in the Extraversion Questionnaire and later compare the two measures. If you were to perform this as a correlation exercise, what steps would you take to eliminate bias?

Reading 6.4   Personality Characteristics

Eysenck is firm in his conviction that heredity is the primary determining factor in intelligence. He also postulates a strong role for heredity in extraversion-introversion, neuroticism, and psychoticism. He bases this position in part on the correlations he has demonstrated between these personality dimensions and behaviours that presumably reflect differences in ANS reactivity and cortical excitation, and in part on direct behaviour genetic studies (e.g. Young, Eaves, and Eysenck, 1980).

Despite this insistence on an inherited tendency to develop neurotic characteristics, Eysenck also maintains that neurotic behaviour – indeed, all behaviour – is learned. Moreover, neurosis does not develop out of (unconscious) conflict between instinctual forces and ego-defensive processes, as Freud argued. According to Eysenck, the core phenomenon in neurosis is a conditioned fear reaction. Such reactions are set in motion when on one or more occasions an initially neutral stimulus is paired with a physically or psychologically painful event. If the trauma is intense enough, and the person is particularly vulnerable – for example, by virtue of having an inherited tendency to neuroticism – only one such experience may be needed to establish an anxiety reaction of great strength and persistence.

Once they have been learned, conditioned fears or anxieties come to be elicited not only by the original object or event that triggered them but by other stimuli that either resemble the original ones or that just happen to be linked with the latter.

Every time the person encounters some such stimulus and makes further responses in an effort to avoid or reduce anxiety, Eysenck says, he or she may become conditioned to even more stimuli that just happen to be present. Thus, the person's propensity to respond with neurotic behaviour is expanded many times, and he or she may come to react with fear to stimuli that bear little or no resemblance to those involved in the original situation.

According to Eysenck, just as new stimuli that are in no way related to the original one(s) can become linked with the latter, so the person may develop ways of responding that have no real functional purpose but are simply behaviours that happened to be going on at the time the stimuli were encountered.

C.S. Hall and G. Lindzey (1985) *Introduction to Theories of Personality* Wiley

1 Which **three** personality dimensions does Eysenck identify?   (3)

2 a) According to Eysenck how does someone develop a fear reaction towards a stimulus?   (2)
   b) How is this linked with personality type?   (2)

3 a) What term is used to describe behaviour learned in one situation and transferred to another?   (2)
   b) Eysenck suggests that conditioned fears generalise to other stimuli. How does this occur?   (3)

4 Distinguish between neuroses and psychoses.   (4)

5 Critically discuss Eysenck's theory of personality.   (8)

TERMS TO DEFINE

extraversion   introversion   neurotic   personality type

Reading 6.5   Systematic Desensitisation

Experimentally, Pavlovian conditioning is achieved by pairing two stimuli without regard to the subject's behaviour. We can illustrate this procedure with Watson and Rayner's (1920) classic study of conditioned fear in a human infant (Little Albert). At the time of the study, Albert was eleven months old. Earlier, when he was presented with a white rat he showed no sign of fear. After seven pairings of the rat (conditioned stimulus) with a distressingly loud noise (unconditioned stimulus), Albert showed clear signs of fear when the white rat was presented alone. Watson and Rayner (1920) interpreted this result as a clear demonstration of the process by which fears of specific objects (phobias) are learned in everyday circumstances.

Experiments which have attempted to repeat Watson and Rayner's demonstration have met with varying success. Whatever the status of its empirical support Watson and Rayner's study has become an influential legend in the history of clinical psychology; that the development of emotional responses can be represented in terms of Pavlovian principles.

The most enduring and widespread applications of these principles have been those generated by J. Wolpe. Wolpe (1958) followed Mary Cover Jones' procedure by attempting to eliminate fear by associating feared stimuli with some activity or stimulus that was presumed to be pleasant. Wolpe considered that food, sexual activity, relaxation or, in the case of children, playing with attractive toys might all be used for the purpose of counter-conditioning. In practice, relaxation has been most commonly used with adult patients.

The method of treatment devised by Wolpe (now termed systematic desensitisation) involves three stages: relaxation training (Jacobson, 1938), construction of a list of hierarchy of feared items (anxiety hierarchies) and systematically pairing relaxation with items from the hierarchies. The treatment always begins with items low in the hierarchies which initially elicit only mild fear; more threatening material from higher up the hierarchies is only introduced when fear of the earlier items has been eliminated. Fear stimuli can either be presented in vivo, in representational form (e.g. pictures) or the patient can be asked to imagine the items while in the relaxed state.

G. Thomas and M.O. O'Callaghan in G. Davey (1981)
Applications of Conditioning Theory Methuen

1   In Watson and Raynor's study of 'Little Albert', how did Albert become afraid of the white rat?   (2)

2   Define what we mean by:
    a)   unconditioned stimulus
    b)   conditioned stimulus.   (4)

3   Wolpe developed a technique to counter-condition the patient so that they could unlearn their phobia. Name **two** activities he found useful.   (2)

4   a)   Describe the **three** stages of desensitisation.
    b)   In desensitisation how is the fear stimuli reintroduced to the patient?   (2)

5 Describe another technique based on classical conditioning which is
   used in behaviour therapy.   (4)

TERMS TO DEFINE

conditioning   phobia   systematic desensitisation

One of the most influential theories of personality to be used in therapy
is that of Freud (see Reading 1.5 Sigmund Freud). He stressed the
importance of **unconscious** processes in the formation of personality. The
first five years of life were thought by Freud to be of greatest importance
for later development. If such early stages were not 'navigated' successfully
then the child could become **fixated** at that level and this would determine
later personality characteristics (see Reading 7.3 The Oedipal Conflict for
details on the phallic stage).

Adult personality consisted of three parts: the id (containing primitive
impulses and urges), the ego (the realist part), and the superego
(containing ideas of conscience and duty). Freud saw the individual as
protecting the developing ego with a number of **defence mechanisms**, such
as **repression** and **denial**. **Psychoanalysis** (Freudian therapy) was designed
to give people **insight** into the source of their neurotic problems. Such
treatment is often lengthy, involving the patient and therapist in sessions
lasting over months or even years. The value and long-lasting effects of
psychotherapy have been challenged in recent years as can be seen in
Reading 6.6 **Does Psychotherapy Work?**

Reading 6.6   Does Psychotherapy Work?

In 1952, Hans Eysenck published a now-famous article apparently showing that
patients treated by psychotherapy were no better off than those who had not
undergone therapy. Eysenck argued that over a two-year period some 66 per
cent of neurotic problems cleared up spontaneously – even if the patient
received no therapy, a rate not surpassed by psychotherapy.

Indeed, some types of psychotherapy, and in particular psychoanalysis,
appeared to retard the patient's progress. Needless to say, Eysenck's review and
his conclusion were highly controversial and stirred up considerable interest in
research on the outcome of therapy.

After another decade and a half of research, Albert Bandura (1969) concluded
that Eysenck's estimates were generally accurate, except that they may have
been too generous to the insight-oriented therapies such as the psychoanalytic.
If behavioural measures are employed (e.g. a patient's ability to enter an
elevator, or wash hands thoroughly) instead of therapist ratings, the data 'yield
success rates that are substantially below the legendary two-thirds
improvement figure'.

Bandura based his conclusions on what have since become classic studies of
the relative effectiveness of different therapies for anxiety. Perhaps the most
famous was carried out by Gordon L. Paul (1966) and appropriately titled *Insight*

versus Desensitisation in Psychotherapy Two Years After Termination. Paul's 'patients' were ninety-six undergraduates who suffered from severe anxiety when they had to talk in front of others.

All accepted an offer of free treatment and were randomly assigned to one of several groups: *insight therapy*, in which five experienced insight-oriented psychotherapists worked individually with subjects for five hours over a six-week period; *behaviour therapy desensitisation*; an *attention-placebo* control group, in which subjects were supposedly given a tranquilliser; and a *no-treatment* control group.

After treatment, the subjects were required to talk in public. They were rated (1) by the amount of their own self-reported anxiety; (2) by the anxiety observed by others (e.g. trembling hands and quivering voice); and (3) by their sweating and pulse rates. The two groups that received treatment improved significantly as compared to the no-treatment control. But the placebo control group also improved, although its members had only been given faith and bicarbonate of soda. This clearly demonstrates a placebo effect in psychotherapy. People get better because they believe they will and because someone pays special attention to them. Of particular interest in the results, however, was the finding that desensitisation produced considerably more improvement than the placebo treatment, but insight treatment did not. These effects were still present on a follow-up two years later in which all the subjects were again questioned about their speech anxiety. Relative to the statements they had made two years earlier, improvement was shown by 85 per cent of the desensitisation subjects and by 50 per cent of both the insight and placebo subjects (Paul, 1967).

Improvement percentages for 'stage fright' after different treatments

	1 Self-Report Anxiety (per cent)	2 Behaviour Ratings (per cent)	3 Physiological Arousal (per cent)
Behavioural Desensitisation	100	100	87
Insight Therapy	53	60	53
No-treatment Placebo	47	73	47
No-treatment Control	7	24	28

Source: Adapted from G.L. Paul, *Insight versus desensitisation in psychotherapy: An experiment in anxiety reduction.* Stanford, Calif.: Stanford University Press, 1966.

H.L. Roediger et al (1984) *Psychology* Scott, Foresman and Co

1 What evidence did Eysenck use to demonstrate that psychotherapy was of no value? (1)

2 In Paul's investigation what was the:
 a) independent variable
 b) dependent variable? (4)

3 What were the results of the two treatment groups on:
  a) self-reported anxiety
  b) anxiety observed by others
  c) the follow-up two years later?   (3)

4 Repression was an ego-defence mechanism suggested by Freud.
   Describe **one** other defence mechanism.   (3)

5 Give **three** criticisms made against Freud's theory.   (6)

TERMS TO DEFINE

insight therapy   psychoanalysis   psychotherapy

Despite the criticisms over Freud's theory and the inadequacies levelled against its scientific foundations, many clinicians found that it provided them with a framework in which they could view their client's behaviour. Fonagy and Higgitt (1984) suggest that *'until another theory emerges which addresses the same range of experiences it is likely that a large number of clinicians will continue to treat Freud's ideas seriously despite their poor scientific status'*.

Humanistic approaches to personality see people as **unique**, demanding the opportunity to develop and express themselves creatively. This approach considers life as it is experienced by the **whole** person and the effects of current experiences. Each person sees the world in a completely individual manner, with no two people viewing things identically. This individual perspective is known as the **phenomenal field**. This can be seen in the description given by Shobin (1954) given below (see also Reading 1.9 Phenomenology).

Suppose that three men, a realtor, a farmer, and an artist, are standing on a hilltop looking at the panorama of uncultivated land spread out below them. To the realtor, the scene represents an opportunity to develop a new housing project. To the farmer, the view suggests a chance to obtain arable soil for growing grain. To the artist, the vista is the embodiment of natural beauty. On descending, the realtor makes inquiries about the cost of the land, the availability of municipal utility services, and the supply of construction labour in the vicinity. The farmer takes soil samples for testing. The artist gets his easel and returns to the hilltop to paint a picture. All three men have 'seen' the same thing, but each has responded in terms of a personal frame of reference, in terms of those aspects of the experience which were personally meaningful.

E.J. Shobin 'Theoretical Frames of Reference in Clinical Psychology' in L.A. Pennington & I.A. Berg (eds) (1954) *An Introduction to Clinical Psychology* (2nd edn) Ronald Press

Kelly (1955) provided an alternative to the psychoanalytic and behavioural schools. He saw man as a **scientist**, making hypotheses about the world, testing them, and if necessary revising and changing them dependent on the results. The individual's system of **personal constructs** are dimensions created to help make sense of the world. Kelly's **Personal Construct Theory** is discussed in Reading 6.7.

Reading 6.7 Personal Construct Theory

The American psychologist George Kelly proposed an elaborate theory of personal constructs in the 1950s which was some 20 years or more ahead of its time, anticipating many later developments in cognitive theorising, though Kelly himself would reject the term 'cognitive' as being too narrow to characterise the theory. Kelly's starting point is a view of the person as a scientist engaged in the task of interpreting and theorising about the world and using these theories to predict the future. Kelly's theory is rooted in the philosophical position of constructive alternativism which states that the world can be construed in infinitely varied ways. Individuals construe the world in terms of personal constructs which are bi-polar descriptions, these personal constructs being organised into systems. Thus a person may view his or her relationships with other people in terms of the bi-polar construct 'a relationship in which I am dominant' versus 'a relationship in which I am submissive'. Any one important construct will have implications for other constructs in the system. A relationship in which 'I am submissive', for example, might imply for that person 'an uncomfortable relationship'. The importance of constructs will vary for different individuals (constructs are personal) as will the implications of the construct within the system. For some people submissiveness may be associated with comfort and relaxation.

J. Berryman et al (1988) *Psychology and You* Methuen

1 'Kelly's starting point is a view of the person as . . . . engaged in the task of interpreting and theorising about the world.'   (1)

2 Describe, in your own words, what Kelly meant by 'personal constructs'.   (3)

3 George Kelly supports the phenomenological viewpoint. Describe the test he developed to examine such personal constructs.   (4)

4 Describe and discuss Kelly's Personal Construct Theory.   (8)

TERMS TO DEFINE

bi-polar constructs   personal constructs   Repertory Grid

You can investigate such constructs in Activity 6.3.

Rogers' Self Theory is based on the assumption that we each live in our own phenomenal field. Rogers believes that everyone has the capacity for self-understanding, and therefore clients suffering from neurosis do not need to be controlled or directed by the therapist. Instead the therapist must create a **therapeutic atmosphere** in which the clients can learn to accept themselves. Rogers noted several personal characteristics essential

Activity 6.3

This is an exercise which you can do to find out what are the main personal constructs that you use. When you have completed it, try comparing what you have said with other people's results. If you feel self-conscious about it, you can use codes to stand for the people that you are talking about, so that only you will understand who they are.

1 Name eight people who are important in your life:

A .... E ....

B .... F ....

C .... G ....

D .... H ....

Think about these people in groups of three at a time. From the following groups, work out a way in which any two of the three are similar, and different from the third. Once you have done this, describe it in the appropriate sentence:

(A,B,C) .... and .... are .... , but .... is ....

(D,E,F) .... and .... are .... , but .... is ....

(A,F,G) .... and .... are .... , but .... is ....

(B,D,H) .... and .... are .... , but .... is ....

(C,E,G) .... and .... are .... , but .... is ....

(H,B,F) .... and .... are .... , but .... is ....

(A,E,H) .... and .... are .... , but .... is ....

(D,G,C) .... and .... are .... , but .... is ....

N. Hayes and S. Orrell *Psychology: An Introduction* Longman

for therapists: empathy, genuineness and warmth. The development of the **self** is central to his theory. This is discussed in Reading 6.8.

Reading 6.8   Rogers' Self Theory

Rogers became aware of the importance of 'self' through his experience with clients in psychotherapy. Patients tended to describe their experience by reference to a 'self' and their problems often seemed to arise out of inconsistencies in their view of themselves – 'I don't understand how I could act that way' – 'I feel different from how I used to feel.'

The 'self' in Rogers' theory is the organised pattern of perceptions, feelings, attitudes and values which the individual believes are uniquely his own. They are the characteristics which define 'I' and 'me'. Thus the self is the central component of the total experience of the individual. An important additional concept in Rogers' theory is the 'ideal self' which is the person as he would like himself to be. The well-adjusted individual is regarded as having a fairly close correspondence between the self and the ideal-self.

The major activity of the total individual (which Rogers calls the 'organism') involves reaction with the field of experience in a way which satisfies its needs. The basic motive of the organism is to actualise, maintain and enhance itself. The tendency towards 'self-actualisation' gives meaning and direction to human activity. The trend is towards greater differentiation and integration, the individual becomes more independent and has more freedom of self-expression. Rogers is suggesting that the 'self' and the 'organism' are both involved in initiating and controlling behaviour. As long as the two systems are working in harmony and there is consistency between the self and the experience of the organism the individual remains 'congruent'. Where he experiences a discrepancy between his perceived self and his actual experience the individual will be in state of 'incongruence' which results in tension and maladjustment.

D. Peck and D. Whitlow (1975) *Approaches to Personality Theory* Methuen

"It says 'Think big'!"

1 In Rogerian theory what is meant by:
   a) self
   b) ideal self?   (2)

2 According to Rogers:
   a) what is the chief motivator   (1)
   b) what causes tension and anxiety resulting in 'incongruence'?   (1)

3 How does Rogerian 'client-centred' therapy attempt to help someone suffering from a neurosis?   (3)

4 Carl Rogers is a humanistic psychologist. What does this mean?   (4)

5 Discuss **two** criticisms made against Rogers' Self Theory.   (6)

TERMS TO DEFINE

empathy   humanistic   ideal self   self-actualisation

Personality disorders which originate from anxiety are usually described as **neuroses**. Such conditions usually result in abnormal behaviour patterns in the individual but the individual retains sufficient insight to realise that their thoughts, feelings and behaviour are not appropriate to the circumstances.

Disorders which result in the individual losing touch with reality are termed **psychoses**. Psychotic patients are often unaware that anything is wrong and yet their mental functioning is so distorted that they are unable to meet the demands of everyday life. One of the most common psychoses is **schizophrenia**, which does not mean 'split personality'. It means that the person's thinking has become separated from reality.

In our society there is a stigma associated with the label 'mentally ill', which affects not only the patient but also the people with whom they come into contact. Many feel that such **labelling** can result in a 'self-fulfilling prophecy' as discussed in Reading 6.9.

Topic-related Essays

1   Can intelligence be measured?

2   How much influence do situational factors have on the expression of personality characteristics?

3   'There can be no doubt about the general success of behaviour therapy.' Discuss.

Reading 6.9   Labelling

In a famous study 'On Being Sane in Insane Places,' Rosenhan (1973) examined the effects of being labelled schizophrenic. Over three years, Rosenhan arranged for twelve normal people to arrive at a psychiatric hospital under pseudonyms and to complain of hearing voices that kept saying 'empty,' 'hollow,' and 'thud.' The patients responded truthfully to all questions except for their names. On the basis of one reported symptom and without any confirmatory evidence, all were diagnosed as psychotic (either 'schizophrenic' or 'manic-depressive') and admitted for inpatient care. Hospitalisation ranged from three to fifty-two days and averaged nineteen, even though the pseudo-patients stopped manifesting symptoms and wanted to leave. When discharged, most were diagnosed 'schizophrenia-in remission,' which implies that they were still schizophrenic but did not show signs of the disorder at the time of release. In no instance did any hospital staff member detect that any of the pseudo-patients was quite sane. Labelling theorists argue from such evidence that terms such as 'schizophrenia' could become self-fulfilling prophecies.

Defenders of the view that mental illness is real and deserving of labels point to how difficult it is to change abnormal behaviour back to normal – an achievement that should be easy if it is just a matter of relabelling. They also point to cross-cultural studies which find the same evidence and pattern of abnormalities in such diverse cultural groupings as North American Eskimos and the Yoruba tribe of West Africa (Murphy, 1976). Eskimos and Yoruba could clearly distinguish between being in a religious 'trance' and being 'crazy.' In one the person was said to be in control of the altered state of consciousness, while in the other the altered state was said to be in control of the person. Furthermore, the number of Eskimos who manifested a schizophrenic-like syndrome of behaviour was 8.8 per 1000. This figure is directly comparable to incidence rates reported as early as the 1940s in places like rural Sweden.

H.L. Roediger et al (1984) *Psychology* Little, Brown and Co

1   Why did the psychiatrists place Rosenhan's 'pseudo' patients into hospital for treatment?   (1)

2   How long did these patients remain in hospital?   (1)

3 What is meant by 'self-fulfilling prophecies'?   (2)

4 Give **one** argument used to defend the view that mental illness exists and is not just labelling.   (1)

5 Explain what is meant by the medical model of abnormal behaviour.   (4)

TERMS TO DEFINE

abnormal   psychoses   schizophrenia

Szasz, a psychiatrist, is one of many theorists who object to mental abnormalities being described as mental **illness**. He finds such a **medical model** unacceptable and suggests that abnormal behaviour reflects **problems in living**, which are not comparable to physical disease. Several of the therapies which have been discussed previously, such as psychoanalytic, behavioural and humanistic, are all alternatives to the medical model. Many other alternatives have also been suggested and an **alternative to the medical model** is discussed in Reading 6.10.

Reading 6.10   An Alternative to the Medical Model

Existentialism places a strong emphasis on the individual's free will, and their right to choose their own alternatives or patterns of life. Although it may be subconscious, and disturbing for the patient, abnormal behaviour is seen as a choice which the patient has made – a retreat into illness as a way of escaping from an intolerable situation. The aim of therapy is to encourage the individual to learn to feel secure with the choices that they have made, and to act in ways that are in tune with their 'inner' self, so that they can be less of a victim of circumstances and more in control of their lives. Laing saw the psychiatric hospital as being the worst possible place for doing that, as patients have so little autonomy or control, and he advocated close, therapeutic communities as a more practical alternative. The most famous one of these is one which he founded himself, known as Kingsley Hall.

Laing's ideas had originated from work by Bateson (1956), who showed that some families seemed to be 'schizophregenic' – in other words, they seemed to produce schizophrenia in their family members, by placing them under continuous psychological pressure. Bateson identified the 'double-bind' – the situation where all courses of action were deemed wrong, and criticised or punished. Those family members who became schizophrenic, Bateson showed, tended to experience double-binds as a normal part of the family life. So schizophrenia was seen as being a comprehensible reaction to an intolerable life-situation, which was understandable in context.

Partly as a result of Laing's work, a new approach to therapy emerged, which sees the person in the context of their family. The idea behind family therapy is that often, the member of the family who is being 'difficult' or 'disturbed' is simply being used as a scapegoat for the tensions and problems of all the family members. By treating one person as 'ill' in this way, they don't need to face up to or admit their own feelings of anger, hostility or aggression towards other family members.

Family therapists see each family as a working system, with the behaviour of each member of the family affecting everyone else. They see families as being capable of adjusting to new circumstances, and sorting out their own problems once they can recognise what these are. This means that much of the work of a family therapist is concerned with teaching family members how to recognise unspoken messages and signals from each other, and how to provide feedback for one another, so that future misunderstandings can be avoided or dealt with in a less tense manner.

N. Hayes (1988) *A First Course in Psychology* (2nd edn) Nelson

1 Fill in the missing words:
   'Existentialism places a strong emphasis on . . . . , and their right to choose . . . . .' (2)

2 Give **one** reason why Laing found mental hospitals unsuitable for helping patients. (1)

3 What is meant by:
   a) 'schizophregenic'
   b) 'double-bind'? (2)

4 Explain, in your own words, what happens in family therapy. (4)

5 What is the medical model? Briefly discuss **two** alternative methods of treatment. (10)

TERMS TO DEFINE

double-bind   existentialism   family therapy   schizophregenic

This chapter has merely sampled some of the wide range of personality theories and therapy available. Many feel that there is a need for further research '*in order to find out more about all the mechanisms and processes which mediate individual differences and which interact with psychological treatments to foster psychological well-being*' (Fonagy and Higgitt 1984). How such processes occur in **human development** is investigated in Chapter Seven.

SUGGESTIONS FOR FURTHER READING

Main texts
J. Berryman et al (1987) *Psychology and You* Methuen (esp. personality and treatment in clinical psychology)
N. Hayes (1988) *A First Course in Psychology* (2nd edn) Nelson (informative chapter on abnormal behaviour)
N. Hayes and S. Orrell (1987) *Psychology: An Introduction* Longman

Other useful texts
S. Agras (1985) *Panic: Facing Fears, Phobias and Anxiety* Freeman
G. Davey (1981) *Applications of Conditioning Theory* Methuen (rather advanced text on behavioural techniques)
P. Fonagy and A. Higgitt (1984) *Personality Theory and Clinical Psychology* Methuen
C.S. Hall and G. Lindzey (1985) *Introduction to Theories of Personality* Wiley
P. Kline (1985) *An Introduction to Freudian Theory* Methuen
D. Shelley and D. Cohen (1986) *Testing Psychological Tests* Croom Helm

Stimulus Questions

A group of psychology students decided to conduct a study on early childhood memories, in order to see whether extraversion is learned or inherited. First, they asked 30 students aged between 19 and 22 to complete a questionnaire which would assess their level of extraversion. After that, the subjects were asked to answer questions about their childhood experiences, from when they were two until they were nine years old. The subjects were asked how many siblings (brothers and sisters) they had; approximately how many other children they played with regularly before they went to school; and how many 'out-of-school' friendships they used to have. They were also asked to rate themselves on how much they used to read during their early school years, on a scale which ranged from 0 = 'didn't read at all', to 10 = 'always had my nose in a book'.
When they examined the data, they found the following correlation coefficients:

a) Level of extraversion / number of 'out-of-school' friendships   + ·74
b) Level of extraversion / number of siblings   + ·49
c) Level of extraversion / pre-school friendships   + ·07
d) Level of extraversion / amount of reading   − ·79

The students concluded that extraversion came from childhood experiences rather than from inherited characteristics.

6.1 Which is the strongest correlation that the students found?   (1)

6.2 Which is the weakest correlation that the students found?   (1)

6.3 What does the term correlation mean?   (1)

6.4 Sketch out a small scattergram chart showing what the results of correlation (a) might look like.   (3)

6.5 Sketch out a small scattergram chart showing what the results of correlation (d) might look like.   (3)

6.6 What does a minus sign in front of a correlation coefficient mean? (1)

6.7 Suggest a possible explanation for correlation (c). (3)

6.8 Give and explain **one** reason why the conclusion that the students drew may not be valid. (3)

6.9 Give **one** criticism of the way in which the students obtained their measures of childhood experiences. (3)

6.10 Briefly describe **two** controls that the students should have included in their study, and explain why each was needed. (6)

Methodology Questions

You have been asked to conduct an investigation into the reliability of psychometric tests of creativity, in which you will compare two versions of the 'uses for a brick' test. In the first version – the standard test – subjects are asked to write down as many different uses for a brick as they can think of in five minutes; in the other version, they are given the same amount of time to write down different uses for a paperclip.

6.1 What is a psychometric test? (1)

6.2 What does reliability mean? (1)

6.3 What is the name given to this method of testing reliability? (1)

6.4 What are order effects? (2)

6.5 Describe and name the control that you would need to include to prevent order effects in this study. (3)

6.6 If you administered these two tests to 30 subjects, how might you go about analysing their results? (3)

6.7 What do you understand by the term validity? (1)

6.8 Name and briefly describe **three** different types of validity. (6)

6.9 All psychometric tests have to be standardised. What does that mean? (3)

6.10 Briefly describe how you might go about standardising the 'uses for a brick" test of creativity. (4)

7

Human Development

'Developmental psychology is the study of psychological changes that take place between birth and old age'

A. Birch and T. Malim (1988)

Plate 7

Readings on 'Human Development'

Developmental psychology looks at patterns and sequences of behaviour and how these are influenced by the passage of time and life experience. Developmental psychologists describe and analyse these patterns of behaviour over the whole life-span and identify factors or variables responsible for development. This requires looking at the characteristics of people of various ages to try and understand how they function. Such investigations look into the development of physical, cognitive, emotional and social characteristics.

Are characteristics inborn or are they shaped by environmental influences? As noted in Chapter Two, there are many conflicting viewpoints from the various schools of thought as to which are the important variables. Whilst there is no single theory of development acceptable to all, there are some views of psychological development which have proved to be highly influential. We shall look at three of these viewpoints:

1) social learning

2) psychoanalytic

3) cognitive-structural.

1 The social learning approach
This view stresses the role of **learning** in development. One of its supporters is Albert Bandura (born 1925), who investigated, among other factors, the influence of reinforcement and imitation in acquiring new knowledge and behaviour. Behaviour can be learned from observation,

with whole patterns learned without reinforcement at each stage, as was previously stated to be necessary by the behaviourists. When learning takes place by observing the behaviour of others and noting its consequences it is known as **vicarious learning**. Some of this **observational learning** is discussed in Reading 7.1.

Reading 7.1 Observational Learning

Bandura showed that children may learn the behaviour of a model without necessarily reproducing that behaviour. Three groups of children were shown a film of a model behaving aggressively; one group saw the model punished for the behaviour, one saw the model rewarded, and the third group observed neither reward or punishment. Subsequent observation of the children's behaviour revealed different levels of imitation. The 'model punished' group reproduced less aggressive behaviour than did the other two groups. Bandura concluded that vicarious punishment (experiencing the model's punishment as though it were administered to oneself) had influenced the children's learning of the aggressive behaviour. However, when the children were then offered rewards for imitating the model's behaviour, all three groups produced equally aggressive behaviour. It is therefore necessary to distinguish between acquisition of behaviour, and the performance of that behaviour.

Bandura and others went on to investigate what characteristics of a model were most likely to encourage imitation in children. Studies have shown that children are more likely to perform behaviour imitated from models who:

- are similar in some respects to themselves
- exhibit power and control over some desirable commodity
- are seen to be rewarded for their actions
- are warm and nurturant.

Bandura proposes that the ability to observe and then reproduce behaviour involves at least four skills:

1 observation of appropriate and distinctive features of the behaviour
2 retention of the critical features of the performance
3 adequate duplication of the model
4 justification of imitation in terms of internal, external or vicarious rewards.

These processes are evident, he contends, in all manner of modelling, from the imitation of single acts to the reproduction of complex social behaviour.

A. Birch and T. Malim (1988) *Developmental Psychology* Intertext

1 What do we mean by imitation? (2)

2 Describe **two** characteristics of models which are likely to encourage imitation in children. (2)

3 In the first Bandura experiment:
   a) What hypothesis was tested? (2)
   b) What was the independent variable? (2)
   c) Which group was the control group? (1)
   d) What is the purpose of the control group? (2)

4 Some children imitate more than others. Describe, in your own words, **two** skills necessary before children can reproduce observed behaviour. (2)

5 How do imitation and identification differ? Give **one** example of each type of behaviour. (8)

TERMS TO DEFINE

imitation modelling vicarious learning

Another area of interest for the social learning theorists is that of **sex-role** development. These theorists argue that sex-roles are learned and therefore subject to change by later experience. Such a view is not shared by all psychologists and an opposing view is presented by the psychoanalytic school which will be discussed later.

What determines the sex-role that a child plays? The child can be seen to be looking for guidance on the behaviour of men and women from everyday life. In our culture television and books are readily available to most children, and it is acknowledged that children watch a great deal of television. Murray (1980) estimated this to be about 3–6 hours a day on average, although some might consider this to be a conservative estimate. Children in some situations spend more time in front of a television than they do in school or at play! Thus it would appear that television would be an important source of information on the child's concept of appropriate sex-role behaviour. Activity 7.1 could prove enlightening on the sex-roles portrayed on television.

Activity 7.1

Advertisements portray very strong sex stereotypes. Watch and analyse the advertisements on at least 10 television programmes chosen from a wide range of events e.g. sport, comedy, 'soap operas'. Note whether the characters are male or female. What about the 'voice overs'? List the activity they are involved in. You could use the following categories:

a) aggression   d) constructive/productive behaviour
b) nurturance   e) physically active behaviour.
c) conformity

Make sure that you define your terms accurately, and write up the report clearly (you should find Chapter Nine: Planning Psychological Research helpful).

Books also seem to show males and females in certain **stereotyped** roles. How accurate is this picture? Several researchers have shown how children's reading books tend to have few female characters, with those

147

which are included being shown as weaker, more dependent and less competent than the male characters (Saario et al 1973). These stereotyped views of **sex-roles** are described in Reading 7.2.

Reading 7.2   Sex-roles

In one reading book, for example (O'Donnell, 1966), a little girl is shown having fallen off her roller skates. The caption said, " 'She cannot skate,' said Mark. 'I can help her. I want to help her. Look at her, Mother. Just look at her. She is just a girl. She gives up.' "

Fortunately, blatant examples like this have disappeared from children's reading books, partly as a result of the efforts of parent groups. But on TV, women (and men) are still portrayed highly stereotypically. Not long ago Jane Trahey (1979) went through an issue of *TV Guide* and picked out the descriptions of the female characters: heartbroken housekeeper, misguided housewife, restless housewife, student-victim, old flame, invalid wife, do-good nun, natural mother, rich society deb, nurse, and stage-struck singer. In the same issue, the male roles were described as venerable physician, country-music veteran, private eye, lawyer, teacher, and handsome dentist.

A continuous exposure to these stereotyped males and females does seem to affect a child's vision of men and women and their roles. Terry Frueh and Paul McGhee (1975) found that elementary-school children who watched more than 25 hours of TV a week had much more 'traditional' views of sex roles than did children who watched less than 10 hours a week. Even more persuasive is an experiment by Emily Davidson (Davidson, Yasuna, and Tower, 1979), who found that 5- and 6-year-old children who were shown highly sex-stereotyped cartoons gave more stereotyped answers to questions about the qualities of men and women than did children who had seen cartoons depicting men and women in more equal roles.

H. Bee (1985) *The Developing Child* Harper Row

1 What do we mean by:
   a) sex-role b) stereotype?   (4)

2 What picture of the little girl is created in the reading book quoted by O'Donnell (1966)?   (2)

3 Give a stereotyped description of each sex as portrayed on TV.   (2)

4 What difference in sex-role views did Frueh and McGhee find in children who watched a lot of television compared with those who did not?   (3)

5 Distinguish between sex identity and gender identity.   (2)

6 Discuss, with examples, the social learning view of sex-role identity.   (10)

TERMS TO DEFINE

gender sex-role stereotype

2 The psychoanalytic approach

This view emphasises the role of **instinctual** urges and the importance of experiences in early childhood for later development. The origins of this view come from the writings of Freud (see Reading 1.5 Sigmund Freud).

The child is seen to be driven by sexual urges, known as the **libido.** Personality is formed as the child progresses through a number of stages, each of which is linked with sexual excitement in different parts of the body. Each stage has to be 'navigated' successfully for normal development. Any anxiety or trauma can result in the child becoming **fixated** at any stage. This will result in problems which will probably surface later in life. One stage which has caused much controversy is the **phallic** stage which occurs between 4–6 years. According to Freud, the sex-role develops during this period in the child's life and is determined by **psychosexual** relationships at that time. At this time the child becomes aware of the sexual characteristics of the parents. Freud suggests that this can result in a period of jealousy and fear for the child resulting in what he named the **Oedipal conflict** which is briefly described in Reading 7.3.

Reading 7.3   The Oedipal Conflict

The young boy begins to desire his mother, often his most constant companion and the one who has satisfied earlier needs for oral pleasure. He is now mature enough to see that the mother-father relationship is characterised by the same tenderness that he enjoys in the mother-son pair. He becomes intensely jealous of the fact that his father shares his mother's bed because he has reached the age where he feels genital excitement. The mother sees the boy's new-found interest in his own genitals, along with an interest in hers as well. Some mothers gently turn their sons from these preoccupations, but others scold and blame them as 'naughty boys'.

Whichever course of action is followed by the mother, the child senses a rebuff from the object of his love (mother) as well as a threat from his rival (father). According to Freud, the boy studies his rival only to discover, to his dismay, that father has a bigger penis as well as being taller and stronger. Moreover, this bigger and more successful lover appears annoyed at signs of the awakening sexual interest in his son. Father tells his son to stop being a mummy's boy, to stop clinging to mum's apron strings. Freud believes that the boy fears that his father will punish him – or even castrate him – for his 'naughty desires'.

Freud believes that boys resolve this painful and frightening dilemma by identifying with the father. The boy notes that they are both male, that someday he too will be a father, and that his father actively encourages him in 'manly' pursuits. Identification with the father (the imagined aggressor) is the means by which young boys outgrow dependence on their mothers and come to seek masculine activities and interests outside the family. Part and parcel of the identification is the acquiring of an ego ideal, that moral standard that the father has set.

K. Sylva and I. Lunt (1984) *Child Development: A First Course*
Basil Blackwell

1 What is sex-role identification?   (2)

2 Which is the odd one out?
   a) anal
   b) phallic
   c) senile
   d) oral   (1)

3 According to Freud why does the boy become:
   a) jealous of his father?   (2)
   b) frightened of his father?   (2)

4 How does Freud explain the girl's sex-role development?   (4)

5 Explain how the ego and the superego develop, and describe their
   different functions in the personality.   (8)

TERMS TO DEFINE

identification   Oedipal/Electra conflict   superego

Freud suggests that moral development is the last part of the personality to evolve during the Oedipal conflict and is shown by the acquisition of the **superego** whereby the child takes on the moral standards of the parents, together with the norms of society. The superego includes the conscience which is a source of guilt feelings and the **ego ideal** which is a source of feelings of pride and self-satisfaction. The superego was seen by Freud as an internal judge of our moral behaviour.

Our understanding of abnormal behaviour and its treatment has been influenced by Freud's ideas on these **unconscious** urges and how they can result in adults **regressing** to child-like behaviour (see Reading 6.7 Does Psychotherapy Work? for a discussion of the value of such therapy).

Awareness of the early years and the effects on later development have been investigated by many post-Freudians and other researchers. The effects of the attachment bond between mother and child, and possible detrimental effects due to lack of **bonding** have been investigated by several researchers including John Bowlby (1951). His investigations led him to suggest that an intimate relationship between mother and child in the early years was essential for normal development. Lack of bonding at this early stage would result in later personality disorders (his descriptions included '*affectionless psychopaths*'). This research has, however, not been without its critics, as can be seen in Reading 7.4 (see also Reading 8.4 Working Mothers for further discussion on this topic and also Reading 2.1 Critical and Sensitive Periods for some of the related animal research).

Reading 7.4   Bonding

The capacity to care and feel deeply about others may be potentially available to every child, but (according to Bowlby) unless it is elicited and sustained without any break in the first two and a half years of life it will atrophy and the child's ability to form personal relationships will be severely affected. Unbroken mother love, in other words, is vital during this period; any amount of subsequent love cannot make up for earlier deficiencies.

Yet so far few systematic studies have unequivocally supported this contention. Examining children institutionally reared for the first few years of their lives and then adopted, Barbara Tizard was unable to find any evidence of gross pathology in their social behaviour. They showed some tendency to be over-friendly with strangers, but the great majority had no difficulty in forming normal ties of affection with their adoptive parents – even well after the supposed critical period for forming relationships. For that matter Bowlby himself failed to find confirmation of long-term effects: in a sample of pre-adolescent children who had been hospitalised by tuberculosis for lengthy periods in the first two years of their lives, he found no obvious sign that the capacity for relationships was in any way inferior to that of similar non-separated children.

Once again we see that early childhood experiences, even when they span the so-called crucial first few years, do not necessarily produce irreversible effects. But what if the deprivation is not limited to the early years, what if it continues so that the child never has the opportunity to form a bond with a mother-figure? Both Harlow's work with monkeys and the miscellaneous clinical experience of social workers and psychiatrists suggest that such circumstances may well cripple for life an individual's capacity to love. Bowlby's 'affectionless character', in other words, is an individual who cannot give love to others because he has never known love throughout childhood, early or late.

R. Schaffer (1977) *Mothering* Open Books

1 Define: a) deprivation
b) privation. (4)

2 Which period of the child's life did Bowlby see to be most important if the child is to form good relationships in later life? (2)

3 According to Bowlby, which person is of vital importance to the child at this early stage? (1)

4 Report, in your own words, Tizard's findings on children reared in institutions. (3)

5 Find these **two** studies:
a) a study supporting Bowlby's findings (4)
b) a study which shows other variables which may be responsible for the pathological behaviour. (4)

TERMS TO DEFINE

bonding   maternal deprivation   privation

3 The cognitive-structural approach

A great influence on developmental psychology has been the research of Jean Piaget (1896–1980). Piaget investigated how children develop their thinking and reasoning. He suggested that thinking passes through regular stages from birth to adolescence with each stage **qualitatively** different from those preceding or following.

Each stage is a structured whole and is an essential preparation for the next, into which it is integrated. The order of progression through the stages is the same for every child, although the age at which the transfer occurs will vary, dependent on the **interaction** of genetic factors and environmental experience. The stages (with approximate ages) are:

1 sensori-motor   (0–2 years)

2 pre-operational   (2–7 years)

3 concrete-operational   (7–11 years)

4 formal operations   (11 years–maturity)

The thinking process of a young infant at the sensori-motor stage is not the same as that of a pre-school child. Each stage creates a view of the world for the child which will structure thinking at that time. According to Piaget, intellectual development is active, involving the central processes of **organisation** and **adaptation** of ideas. In this way we build up an internalised representation of the world, or **schema**, achieved by the interplay of two processes: **assimilation and accommodation,** as can be seen in Reading 7.5 about watching people dance.

Reading 7.5   Assimilation and Accommodation

It is easy to spot very poor dancers, who don't adapt their movements to the music at all. They always do the same old step at the same old pace, so they miss the beat. But it's harder to differentiate the good dancers. Some people dance well because they assimilate well. They don't need to adjust, or accommodate, their usual dancing style very much because it fits almost any music and almost every beat. If their partner says, 'I don't know that dance,' they reply. 'Don't worry, just follow me.' They are good leaders, but if you watch them long enough you realise they aren't creative, just skilled.

By contrast, other people dance well because they accommodate well. They quickly change their movements to adjust to their partner, to the music, to the current fad. They are good followers and more enjoyable to watch, but they don't seem to have a style of their own.

The best dancers of all assimilate and accommodate. Sometimes they lead; sometimes they follow. Sometimes they do traditional dances; sometimes they invent new ones. They change steps smoothly, no matter what the dance. The particular steps they choose depend on the music, their partner, what's 'in' their mood, their energy, and even the space on the floor. When you watch a pair of these dancers, you can't tell who is leading because they move as one, adapting to each other and to the music. They are flexible and creative dancers, just as, according to Piaget, the most intelligent people are flexible and creative thinkers.

K.S. Berger (1980) *The Developing Person*
Worth

1 'The best dancers of all assimilate and accommodate.' Describe **two** characteristics of such dancers. (2)

2 Distingish between assimilation and accommodation. (4)

3 Complete the sentence:
A schema refers to . . . .
   a) writing a plan of action
   b) an internal representation of a physical or mental action
   c) the process whereby concepts and actions are modified to fit new situations. (2)

4 What are the key features, or 'landmarks' of children's thinking at each of Piaget's stages of development? What did Piaget see as determining the speed at which children progress through these stages? (8)

TERMS TO DEFINE

accommodation   adaptation   assimilation   schema

Piaget described the child entering the pre-operational stage as **egocentric,** by which he meant that the child cannot separate itself from the environment and tends to view the world from a central, self-centred position. This restricts the view to only one dimension, that seen by the child, as illustrated by the 'mountains task' set by Piaget whereby the child had to give the view seen by someone in a different position. According to Piaget this is not possible for a child at this stage of development. The child is unable to see that when objects change shape or size the object is the same as before the transformation. He is able only to see in one dimension.

By the time that the child has reached the stage of **concrete operations,** the **conservation** of properties begins to occur and the child begins to perform the complex sequence of **operations** mentally. Some of these demonstrations are illustrated in Figure 7.1 and the possibility of **teaching conservation** is discussed in Reading 7.6.

Reading 7.6   Teaching Conservation

One would think that any intelligent child who has spent hours pouring water in and out of various containers and making balls and snakes and whatnot from Play-Doh would understand such obvious concepts as conservation of liquids or matter. However, most parents, teachers, and psychologists who have duplicated Piaget's experiments have found that Piaget knew what he was talking about. Today's children sometimes show logical thinking earlier than Piaget's subjects, but the difference is not as great as one might expect. Philip Cowan reports the experience of one psychologist, the father of a 5-year-old.

The father had apparently made repeated attempts to drill the child on the conservation of water problem. One day the father proudly demonstrated the child's skill. On the first two trials, the boy said, 'There's more water in this glass; it's higher.' The father's face fell. Given a third try, his son said, 'Oh, it's the same, it's still the same amount of water.' The father beamed proudly, while the son added in a tiny whisper, 'But it really isn't.' (Cowan, 1978)

The child's insistence on maintaining his preoperational perception despite his father's instruction is typical of a child who has not yet developed concrete operational thought. However, special instruction may speed the progress of children in the transitional period, from 5 to 7 (Inhelder et al., 1974). According to one report, even 4-year-olds sometimes learn conservation after careful instruction, including demonstrations, descriptions of what occurred, and an opportunity for the children themselves to perform the experiments, with the experimenter telling them how well they are doing (Denney et al., 1977).

The fact that instruction can hasten the onset of concrete reasoning does not make Piaget's basic ideas invalid. He has always insisted that he was interested in the sequence of stages rather than the exact ages at which each stage appeared. Cross-cultural research verifies that the sequence is almost always the same, although the ages at which particular concepts are mastered depends somewhat on the experience of the child and the emphasis of the culture.

K.S. Berger (1980) *The Developing Person* Worth

1 What is meant by 'conservation'? (2)

2 Describe **one** task which demonstrates the child's lack of conservation. (3)

3 Describe:
   a) 'preoperational perception'
   b) 'concrete operational thought'. (4)

4 Cowan (1978) reports on a psychologist teaching his child to conserve. Report his findings in your own words. (4)

5 Discuss **two** criticisms made against Piaget's work. (8)

TERMS TO DEFINE

centration   conservation   egocentric   irreversibility

At this point the child begins to see from perspectives other than its own and becomes less egocentric. Having **concrete** objects available for manipulation aids the understanding at this stage, as the child cannot think abstractly. It is not until the stage of formal operations that the child can manipulate problems mentally and draw conclusions from purely abstract data.

Child psychology was greatly influenced by Piaget, with the child portrayed as an **active** seeker of knowledge and stimulation. The influence of Piaget's theory can also be seen in education, especially in the primary school. Most of his theory has been supported by studies world-wide, although some aspects have been subjected to criticism. Many researchers suggest that Piaget may have underestimated the children's ability due to the difficulty of the actual task he gave to the children. He may have overestimated the language and memory skills of young children.

Figure 7.1 *Piagetian conservation tasks.*

Experiment 1 **Conservation of substance**

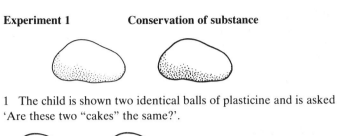

1   The child is shown two identical balls of plasticine and is asked 'Are these two "cakes" the same?'.

2   The experimenter rolls out one ball of plasticine into a sausage shape. The child is asked 'Does the sausage have the same amount of plasticine as the "cake"?'.

Experiment 2 **Conservation of volume**

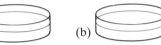

1   The child is shown a short, 'fat' beaker (a) containing milk and is asked to pour milk from a jug into a second identical beaker (b) until it has the same amount of milk as the first beaker. The child agrees that the amount of milk in each beaker is identical.

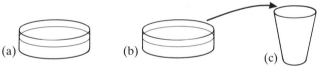

2   The child is then shown a tall 'thin' beaker and is asked to pour the contents of one of the original beakers into it. The child is then asked 'Is there the same in (c) as there is in (a)?'.

Experiment 3 **Conservation of number**

1   The child is shown counters placed in two identical rows (A and B) The child agrees that the two rows have the same number of counters.

2   The experimenter 'bunches up' the counters in row B. The child is asked 'Do the two rows still contain the same number of counters?'.

Donaldson (1978) and her colleagues showed that children under the age of five years were capable of more sophisticated thought when the task procedure was modified. Despite all criticisms Piaget made a very influential contribution to our knowledge of the child's intellectual development, and recent research continues to modify his views.

Piaget's developmental stages have also been applied to the **play** of children, which has been shown to progress in a similar manner, as can be seen in Reading 7.7.

The cognitive-structuralist view has been applied in areas other than intellectual development. One such area is that of moral development. How do children develop concepts of 'right' and 'wrong'? How do these change with age?

Reading 7.7   Play

This first of Piaget's stages is the sensori-motor period, from 0–2 years, in which the child is mainly concerned with physical development and learning to make sense of the information which it is receiving through its senses. So the kind of play which the child engages in during this time reflects that: it is play in which the child is practising skills. These are mainly physical skills, such as manipulating objects, or climbing on furniture; but the child will also be practising and exploring sounds, tastes, and other features of the environment. Piaget referred to this as mastery play, because he saw the overall purpose of such play as the child learning to 'master' its environment, so that it could control its actions and operate effectively within its world.

The second of Piaget's stages is the pre-operational period, from 2–7 yrs (approximately), in which the child is learning basic information about the world and how it works. During this time, Piaget said, the child mainly engages in symbolic, or make-believe play. This type of play involves children acting out imaginary situations, like playing at being different people that they have encountered, or making up stories and acting them out. Objects are sometimes used to represent something else – so for instance, a hairbrush might be used to represent a pet hedgehog, or something else that the child has encountered.

The third stage, the concrete operational period (from about 7–11 yrs), involves the child developing rule-bound play. This is play in which there are definite rules, some of which are learned from other children, as in playground games like marbles or hopscotch; and some of which are learned from adults or older children, like card games or organised sports. According to Piaget, this form of play marks the development of full social participation on the part of the child. The previous forms of play were all fairly individualistic, involving only a slight amount of co-operation on the part of the child, but rule-bound play involves the recognition of general social concepts like 'fairness' and taking turns.

N. Hayes (1988) *A First Course in Psychology* (2nd edn) Nelson

1   Fill in the following chart:

stage of development	play activity engaged in
1 sensori-motor	
2	symbolic/make-believe
3	rule-bound

(3)

2   Give **one** example of a play activity you would expect of a child exhibiting:
  a)   symbolic play
  b)   rule-bound play.   (2)

3   a)   What research method could you use to investigate play behaviour?   (2)
  b)   Give **one** limitation of this method.   (2)

4   Explain, with **one** example, what is meant by parallel play.   (4)

5 You are involved with a playgroup and wish to stimulate cognitive development in children. Which play activities will you choose? What value have play activities which do not promote such development? Which of these activities would you include in your playgroup? Explain your choices.   (8)

TERMS TO DEFINE

mastery/symbolic/rule-bound play   play

Piaget investigated children's attitudes towards rules in a game of marbles and also their answers to whether a situation presented in a story was right or wrong. Piaget saw the child developing morally through stages. In the first stage the child is influenced by what is allowed by adults; obedience is 'right' and disobedience is 'wrong'. This is the period of **moral realism** or **heteronomous morality**, when the child's egocentricity does not allow understanding of the viewpoint of others. In the next stage, parents would be disobeyed if the child saw the solution to be 'unfair'. In the final stage the reasons behind rules and regulations are assessed to decide if they are morally valid. This is the stage of **moral relativism** or **autonomous morality,** where intentions and consequences are considered, a level not always attained by all people.

Kohlberg (1969, 1973) has further developed Piaget's theory relating to **moral development**. He suggests that there are three stages but with these stages subdivided into an early and later part. His theory is illustrated in Figure 7.2 and discussed in Reading 7.8.

At this point it might be worth reflecting on the different interpretations put forward by the three schools of thought (social learning, psychoanalytic, cognitive-structuralist) on how we develop a moral conscience. See if you can complete Activity 7.2.

Activity 7.2

See if you can fill in the following chart showing the origins of moral reasoning as depicted by the three schools discussed:

psychological model	origin of moral conscience	permanent (P) or changeable (C)
social learning		
psychoanalytic		
cognitive-structural		

Each age level has tasks to be solved with various crises and conflicts. The growing child has to balance what he or she wants with the demands of society. Gradually the child tries to express independence at home and

Level 1: Pre- Conventional	*Stage 1 (Punishment and Obedience Orientation)* What is right and wrong is determined by what is punishable and what is not – if stealing is wrong it is because authority figures say so and because they will punish stealing ('might makes right'). So moral action is essentially the avoidance of punishment, things are not right or wrong, good or bad, in themselves.
	Stage 2 (Instrumental-Relativist Orientation) What is right and wrong, good and bad, is now determined by what brings reward and what people want (rather than the more negative avoidance of punishment). Other people's needs and wants come into the picture but only in a reciprocal sense ('You scratch my back, I'll scratch yours').
Level 2: Conventional	*Stage 3 (Interpersonal Concordance or 'Good boy–nice girl' Orientation)* Good behaviour is whatever pleases others, and being moral is being 'a good person in your own eyes and those of others'. There is emphasis on conformity to stereotyped images of 'majority' or 'natural' behaviour – what the majority thinks is right is right by definition. Intentions begin to be taken into account too. But primarily, behaving morally is pleasing and helping others and doing what they approve of.
	Stage 4 ('Law and Order' Orientation) Being good now comes to mean 'doing one's duty' – showing respect for authority and maintaining the social order (status quo) for its own sake. Concern for the common good has gone beyond the stage 3 concern for the good of the family – society protects the rights of individuals and so society must be protected by the individual. Laws are automatically and unquestioningly accepted and obeyed.
Level 3: Post- Conventional	*Stage 5 (Social Contract-Legalistic Orientation)* Apart from what is constitutionally or democratically agreed upon, what is right is a matter of personal 'values' and 'opinions'. Consequently, there is emphasis on the 'legal point of view' – since laws are established by mutual agreement, they can be changed by the same democratic process. Although laws and rules should be respected, since they protect the rights of the individual as well as those of society as a whole, individual rights can sometimes supersede these laws if they become too destructive or restrictive. The law should *not* be obeyed at all costs, e.g. life is more 'sacred' than any principle, legal or otherwise.
	Stage 6 (Universal-Ethical Principle Orientation) Moral action is determined by our inner conscience and may or may not be in accord with public opinion or society's laws. What is right or wrong is based upon self-chosen, ethical principles which we arrive at through individual reflection – they are not laid down by society as such. The principles are abstract and universal, such as Justice, Equality, the sacredness of human life and respect for the dignity of human beings as individuals, and only by acting in accordance with them do we ultimately attain full responsibility for our actions.

Figure 7.2 *Kohlberg's levels and stages of moral development*

Reading 7.8   Moral Development

Building upon Piaget's work, Kohlberg (1969, 1976) attempted to produce a more detailed and comprehensive account of moral development. Like Piaget, Kohlberg focused on an individual's reasoning when presented with a series of moral dilemmas in the form of short stories. Kohlberg's 'moral stories' have been presented to thousands of people of all ages, intelligence levels and socio-economic backgrounds.

Kohlberg sees moral development as occurring at three levels, each of which contains two distinct stages. He states that these stages are fixed and that everyone passes through them in the same order, starting at the lowest level. The end product of progression through these stages is a mature and reasoned sense of justice.

While the ages at which people attain different levels varies, subjects' responses to Kohlberg's moral dilemmas indicate that, in general, children in middle childhood are pre-conventional (level 1), younger adolescents (13–16 years) are at the conventional level (level 2), and about half of older adolescents (16–20 years) attain the principled level (level 3). Cross-cultural studies have revealed that the same sequence of stages exists in certain other cultures (Kohlberg 1969).

Many studies have provided supporting evidence of the links between children's moral reasoning and their stage of cognitive development. However, Kohlberg's theory has also generated much controversy. Debate centres on the main tenets of Kohlberg's theory:

1 moral reasoning is linked to cognitive development
2 the stage sequence is the same for everyone
and on the relationship between Kohlberg's stages and moral behaviour.

A. Birch and T. Malim (1988) *Developmental Psychology* Intertext

1 At what approximate age would a child be at Kohlberg's:
   a) pre-conventional level
   b) conventional level?   (2)

2 How did Kohlberg investigate moral reasoning?   (2)

3 Draw up a comparison chart of Piaget and Kohlberg's stages of moral development.   (8)

TERMS TO DEFINE

morals

later at school. New demands and expectations emerge at this time. The social skills emerging in the newborn are tested in a wider setting throughout life (see Chapter Eight for discussion of some of these).

Adolescence is a period which has promoted interest from many sources. Adults often appear to expect this to be a period of '*storm and stress*'. Many researchers feel that such a description is unfounded. Bandura (1964) found, after discussion with adolescents and their parents, that there was little sign of such disharmony. Most of the adolescents interviewed adopted their parents' standards of conduct and did not see their parents as 'enemies'. There is little evidence of a **generation gap**. However, there is evidence of the period of adolescence often proving to be one of swings of mood and emotion. Unlike many primitive societies we do not officially mark the transfer from childhood to adulthood, or do we? Activity 7.3 may shed light on this question.

Activity 7.3

How do your family mark the passage from childhood to adulthood:

a) formally (such as a special celebration)
b) informally (such as not needing a babysitter)?

Adolescence can be a time of great sensitivity. It is a time of comparison and criticism, when young people discover abilities and sometimes find themselves lacking what they desire. Television has been shown to be influential in shaping the adolescent's concept of self (see also Reading 2.8 Television and Violence). In our western culture physical attractiveness is valued and 'beautiful' bodies are used to sell many products. Adolescents seem to be particularly vulnerable, because it is a time of great awareness of the **body image**, or concept of one's physical self, and most adolescents refer to what is known as the **body ideal**. This can be seen depicted in advertisements, films and television in the shape of slim, shapely women and tall, muscular men. As seen in Reading 7.9, physique is valued by both sexes and many adolescents spend hours in front of a mirror and spend a great deal of money on clothes and cosmetics to improve their **body image in adolescence**.

Reading 7.9   Body Image in Adolescence

Whereas most adults have learned to accept the discrepancy between the cultural ideal and their own appearance, few adolescents are satisfied with their looks. One nationwide study of young people between 12 and 17 years old found that 49.8 per cent of the boys surveyed wanted to be taller, and 48.4 per cent of the girls wanted to be thinner. A scant majority of the boys (55 per cent) were reasonably satisfied with their build. While most of the girls (60 per cent) were not satisfied (Scanlan, 1975).

Other studies show that girls are dissatisfied with more parts of their bodies than boys are. Both sexes, for example, are likely to be concerned about facial features, complexion, and weight, and boys worry about the size of their penis in much the same way girls worry about the size of their breasts. But girls are much more likely to worry about the size and shape of their buttocks, legs, knees, and feet as well (Clifford, 1971).

The adolescent's concern over appearance is more than vanity – it is a recognition of the role physical attractiveness plays in gaining the admiration of the opposite sex. Hass (1979) found that the characteristics that boys sought in girls were, in order, good looks, good body, friendliness, and intelligence; girls wanted boys to be intelligent, good looking, have a good body, and be good conversationalists.

K.S. Berger *The Developing Person* Worth

1 What is meant by:
   a) adolescence
   b) body ideal
   c) self-concept? (6)

2 Scanlon (1975) found many adolescents to be dissatisfied with their appearance. What changes were desired by:
   a) girls
   b) boys? (2)

3 According to Hass (1979), what characteristics of the opposite sex were found desirable by:
   a) boys
   b) girls? (2)

4 Erikson described the period of adolescence as a stage of *identity vs role confusion*. Explain what he meant. (4)

5 Outline briefly what is meant by self-concept and suggest **two** of the main factors which may influence this. (8)

TERMS TO DEFINE

adolescence   body image   generation gap   self-esteem

You will find that many developmental theorists concentrate on the early childhood years of development, a period of rapid growth and change. In fact many theories of development concentrate on child development and stop when the child becomes adult. The theories of Freud and Piaget are two such examples. Few theorists cover the whole life span of development, although many agree that we do continue developing after adolescence.

One theorist whose theory progressed across the whole life span is Erik Erikson. He describes life as having a series of eight conflicts which have to be resolved. Although he was influenced by Freud, he saw the conflicts as being more **social** in origin than the sexual battle seen by Freud. Erikson saw problems developing and a change of personality for anyone who does not resolve each crisis satisfactorily.

In our culture we have a rather rigid social structure whereby the elderly **retire** from paid employment, usually about the age of 60–65 years. This is often compulsory and consequently many people hold the belief that this is an age of decline in abilities. In fact current research is showing this to be a

---

Topic-related Essays

1   What do you consider to be the most important contribution made by Freud to our understanding of development? Give evidence to support this view.

2   'Piaget underestimated the young child's intellectual ability.' Discuss.

3   What are the major methods used to investigate infant development? Illustrate the contribution and drawbacks of each by reference to relevant research.

---

myth, one which many of the elderly have questioned for some time. Most of us know elderly relatives, friends and neighbours who are alert, active and productive. Are these the exception? Current research demonstrates that most ageing people are capable of demonstrating cognitive skills equal to those of younger groups. Research into **age changes in skills,** as discussed in Reading 7.10, supports the view that the healthy elderly not only maintain their performance in many areas of competence but bring with them bonus points such as experience and conscientiousness.

Reading 7.10   Age Changes in Skills

Of course the physical changes of age produce some decline in abilities; but unless there is actual brain damage it is quite possible to maintain peak performance in selected fields.

A very similar conclusion comes from a quite different study by Seymour Giniger, Angelo Dispenzieri and Joseph Eisenberg of the City University of New York. They investigated a total of 455 workers in a factory in the New York garment industry. This industry has a wide variety of jobs within it, which differ in the extent to which they require speed and skill. Older theories of ageing have tended to assume that although skills may be maintained, speed of performance declines. In this investigation, jobs were first classified as mainly speed-oriented or mainly skill-oriented. Information was taken from the factory's records as to absenteeism and productivity, defined as average hourly piece-rate wages. 'Older' and 'younger' were taken as over or under forty-five.

It was supposed that older workers in speed jobs would do less than others. This was not so. Older workers fairly consistently did better than younger ones: they earned more, were absent less, had fewer accidents and had less turnover (leaving the factory), both on speed and skill jobs. However, there are several points to consider. It appeared that it was length of experience, rather than simply age as such, that was the important factor. Further, it may be that the demands of these particular jobs, in this industry, were not too great for the older workers; in another industry they might be. Again, it may be that as workers get older, those who find the job becoming too difficult tend to leave; the more able survivors remain. And it may also be that older workers regard hard work as more of a virtue than do younger ones.

R. Raaheim and J. Radford (1984) *Your Introduction to Psychology* Sigma

1 What is the traditional view of the skills of the elderly?   (1)

2 In the study by Giniger et al:
   a) What was the sample size?   (1)
   b) How were the jobs classified?   (1)
   c) Give **two** examples of how the older workers were better than the younger ones.   (2)

3 Give **two** alternative explanations of the findings.   (2)

4 Discuss the evidence supporting the claim that old age is a time of physical and psychological decline.   (8)

TERMS TO DEFINE

performance   skill

Perhaps as Rabbit (1977) suggests we should be studying the adaptation of the individual to decrements in performance rather than just studying the decrements!

We have looked briefly at research covering all stages of the life span. The student who wishes to know more on the topics discussed will find that several excellent texts are available (some of which are noted in Suggestions for Further Reading below). Some of the important **life-events** which occur over this life span are discussed in Chapter Eight.

SUGGESTIONS FOR FURTHER READING

Main texts
A. Birch and T. Malim (1988) *Developmental Psychology* Intertext
N. Hayes and S. Orrell (1987) *Psychology: A First Course* Longman

Other useful texts
H. Bee (1985) *The Developing Child* Harper Row (good section on the effects of television on behaviour)
K.S. Berger (1980) *The Developing Person* Worth
A.M. Clarke and A.D.B. Clarke (1976) *Early Experience: Myth and Evidence* Open Books (reports on studies reflecting the resilience of young children to adverse early experiences)
D. Cohen (1987) *Play* Croom Helm
M. Donaldson (1978) *Children's Minds* Fontana (research demonstrating how Piaget may have underestimated children's ability)
N. Hayes (1988) *A First Course in Psychology* (2nd edn) Nelson (good chapter on play)
M. Rutter (1981) *Maternal Deprivation Reassessed* (2nd edn) Penguin
K. Sylva and I. Lunt (1984) *Child Development: A First Course* Basil Blackwell

Stimulus Questions

A psychologist wanted to develop a technique for investigating how children play with objects. By contacting local playgroups and nurseries, he was able to study 25 children aged between fourteen months and two years, and another 20 children aged between two years three months and three years nine months.

The children were asked to perform a series of play actions using toys which the psychologist provided. The toys which the children were asked to use were classified as either 'appropriate' or 'inappropriate'. Two of the tasks that the children were asked to perform were:

i) feeding a toy horse, either from a toy bucket or a toy car, and
ii) putting a small teddy bear to bed in either a small cradle or in a cup.

The psychologist noted how readily the children performed the actions, using a scale as follows:

5 = enthusiastically; 4 = fairly readily; 3 = calmly, without objecting; 2 = slowly or hesitantly; 1 = objecting but still doing it; 0 = refusing to play.

The results obtained from the study were as follows:

Mean Scores:	Younger Children	Older Children
Feeding horse appropriately	3·8	3·9
Feeding horse inappropriately	2·7	1·4
Putting teddy to bed appropriately	4·7	4·3
Putting teddy to bed inappropriately	3·6	2·1

7.1 What was the sample size in this study? (1)

7.2 What did a child have to do in the 'feeding horse inappropriately' condition? (1)

7.3 What type of statistic is a mean? (2)

7.4 Describe briefly how a mean is calculated. (3)

7.5 Many psychologists would say that mean scores should not have been used in this study. Explain why a mean might be the wrong type of statistic to use. (3)

7.6 Suggest an alternative type of statistic which the psychologist could have used. (2)

7.7 In general, how did the younger children react when they were asked to put the teddy to bed in the small cradle? (2)

7.8 What general difference between the younger and older children can be noticed from the table of results? (2)

7.9 The psychologist thought that these results showed how older

children were not as good at pretending as younger ones. Suggest a
different explanation which could be given for these findings.   (3)

7.10 Give **two** criticisms of this study, and for each one, suggest a
way in which it could have been improved.   (6)

Methodology Questions

Imagine that you have been asked to conduct an observational study into
the non-verbal aspects of children's play. The particular area that you have
decided to look at is proxemics – the distances which children keep
between themselves and others when they are playing. You will be
conducting the study on two weekday afternoons, with a friend. Answer
the following questions, making your suggestions as practical as possible:

7.1 Describe very briefly where you will carry out your
observations.   (1)

7.2 Who are the subjects of your study likely to be?   (1)

7.3 What type of a sample is this?   (1)

7.4 How many instances of non-verbal behaviour will you aim to
record?   (1)

7.5 Describe **one** advantage and **one** disadvantage of the place that
you have chosen.   (4)

7.6 How will you classify the personal distances that you see?   (2)

7.7 Describe **three** different kinds of play that you would expect to
see in your observational setting.   (3)

7.8 For each type of play that you have just described, guess what
personal distances you would expect (in metres).   (3)

7.9 Draw up a sample table which could show the results of the
study. (You can invent some results to put in it if you like.)   (3)

7.10 When you write up your report on the study, you will be
expected to suggest how it could have been improved. Describe **two**
improvements that a professional researcher might make to this
study.   (6)

8

Life-Events

'Another way of looking at adult development and adjustment is to examine the way in which people confront and deal with important life-events.'

D. Brodzinsky et al (1986)

Readings on 'Life-Events'

A **life-event** can be seen as any experience which is recognised as significant and alters the behavioural life pattern of the individual. Many of these events are common to most adults in our society, such as starting a first job or getting married; whereas others, such as unemployment, may be experienced by certain groups only. All such events, even happy positive ones, are potentially stressful and require adaptation on the part of the individual.

Research by Thomas Holmes and his colleagues (Holmes and Rahe, 1967; Holmes and Masuda, 1973) has demonstrated the effects of such life events on health; the greater the number and severity of these events, the greater the level of stress. Holmes and Rahe (1967) devised a questionnaire, the **Social Readjustment Rating Scale**, on which **life-change units** are totalled for all events affecting the individual over the previous year. These units reflect the adaptation and coping required for each event (as can be seen in Figure 8.1).

During youth and early adulthood people begin to adopt many more social roles, such as student, worker, spouse and parent, with great individual differences in the timing of these. Society has expectations in regard to role adoption and has a system of positive and negative sanctions on the individual for meeting, or failing to meet, these expectations.

With the rise of technology and the demand for greater education, people whose life-events are 'out of sequence' are now more readily accepted. However, as can be seen in Reading 8.1 **Family Life Cycle**, family life can be seen to progress through a series of stages, each of which has tasks or conflicts which provide a challenge for family members and demand new ways of coping. Duvall's model is investigated in Activity 8.1.

SOCIAL RE-ADJUSTMENT RATING SCALE
(From Holmes and Rahe, 1967)

Rank	Life-Event	Mean Value	Rank	Life-Event	Mean Value
1	Death of spouse	100	23	Son or daughter leaving home	29
2	Divorce	73	24	Trouble with in-laws	29
3	Marital separation	65	25	Outstanding personal achievement	28
4	Jail term	63	26	Wife begins or stops work	26
5	Death of close family member	63	27	Begin or end school	26
6	Personal injury or illness	53	28	Change in living conditions	25
7	Marriage	50*	29	Revision of personal habits	24
8	Dismissal from work	47	30	Trouble with boss	23
9	Marital reconciliation	45	31	Change in work hours or conditions	20
10	Retirement	45	32	Change in residence	20
11	Change in health of family member	44	33	Change in schools	20
12	Pregnancy	40	34	Change in recreation	19
13	Sex difficulties	39	35	Change in church activities	19
14	Gain of new family member	39	36	Change in social activities	18
15	Business re-adjustment	39	37	Mortgage or loan less than £10,000	17
16	Change in financial state	38	38	Change in sleeping habits	16
17	Death of a close friend	37	39	Change in number of family gatherings	15
18	Change to different line of work	36	40	Change in eating habits	15
19	Change in number of arguments with spouse	35	41	Holiday	13
20	Mortgage over £10,000	31	42	Christmas	12
21	Foreclosure of mortgage or loan	30	43	Minor violations to the law	11
22	Change in responsibilities at work	29			

* Marriage was arbitrarily assigned a stress value of 50. No event was found
  to be any more than twice as stressful. Here the values are reduced
  proportionally and range up to 100.

An individual's level of stress is calculated in the following way.

1 The subject is asked to describe specific life-events experienced
   during a particular period of time, for example the past two years.

2 The appropriate stress value for each life-event is assigned to the
   person and a total stress index is arrived at by adding together
   all the stress values the person has received.

Figure 8.1

Reading 8.1   Family Life Cycle

The family life cycle begins, of course, with marriage; it ends with the process of
bereavement of the surviving spouse. Between these points are a series of
stages – the exact number of which varies according to the theorist – describing
different family structural patterns, role expectations, and life-events that
challenge family members and demand new patterns of coping from all of them.

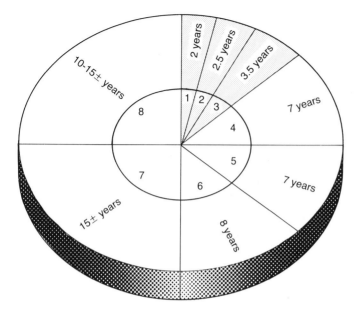

1   Married couples (without children)
2   Childbearing families (oldest child, birth–30 months)
3   Families with preschool children (oldest child, 30 months–6 years)
4   Families with schoolchildren (oldest child 6–13 years)
5   Families with teenagers (oldest child 13–20 years)
6   Families launching young adults (first child gone to last child leaving home)
7   Middle-aged parents (empty nest to retirement)
8   Aging family members (retirement to death of both spouses)

Evelyn Duvall (1977) has been a leading proponent of the family life-cycle perspective. In her model, she has described eight stages, with an approximate number of years for each stage, through which the typical family progresses. Since the average mother sends her youngest child to school when she is between 30 and 35, we can say that the early adult period generally corresponds to Stages 1 to 3 in Duvall's scheme. This varies for individual couples, of course. A couple who postpone having children may spend six or seven years, instead of the predicted two, in Stage 1, and this will affect the rest of the cycle; for example, the 'empty nest to retirement' stage will be shorter.

Although Duvall's model is useful for describing the progress of traditional families through the life cycle, it fails to take into account the considerable proportion of people who divorce or are widowed, who remarry, or who have a second family. Many of these people will spend some years as single parents or may bring up children not their own.

It is worth noting, too, that although we tend to picture families as young adults with young children (the kind of group attractively portrayed in advertisements), the amount of time people spend in the first three stages of family life is relatively small – no more than a dozen out of a total of perhaps 50 years (Duvall, 1977). Almost half of the family life cycle occurs after the children are gone. Thus, adjustments, such as how a person uses leisure time, worked out in the young-adult period are not necessarily appropriate for later periods.

170

Another limitation of Duvall's scheme is that it fails to acknowledge the overlap and interaction of family life cycles across generations. For example, a family composed of a young couple with preschool children would be classified as being in Stage 3 within Duvall's model. At the same time, however, these individuals remain part of a different family as children of their own middle-aged or aging parents, and thus can be classified as being in Stage 7 or 8 (depending on whether their parents are retired or not) with respect to their family-of-origin life cycle. Thus, the impact of life-cycle events on people must be viewed within the broader perspective of intergenerational relations – that is, the relations between members of a family from different generations. In other words, to understand the development and adjustment of the adult at any particular life-cycle phase, one must understand the 'fit' between the expectations and experiences a person has derived from the family of origin and those derived from his or her current nuclear family.

D. Brodzinsky et al (1986) *Lifespan Human Development* (3rd edn)
Holt, Rinehart and Winston

1 What is the family life cycle?   (2)

2 According to Duvall's (1977) model, for approximately how much time in the family life cycle do:
a) a married couple live together before the birth of the first child
b) parents have children at home?   (2)

3 Give **two** criticisms which have been made against Duvall's model.   (4)

4 Match each of the following crises suggested by Erikson with the adult stage during which it arises:
a) young adulthood   1) intimacy-isolation
b) middle age   2) integrity-despair
c) old age   3) generativity-stagnation   (3)

5 What is a family? What role does it play in the lives of parents and children?   (10)

TERMS TO DEFINE

family   intergenerational   lifestyle   marriage

Activity 8.1

If you would like to investigate Duvall's model, find a couple who have been married for a long time (such as your parents or better still your grandparents). Perhaps you could ask the people concerned how much time they spent in the eight stages (or as many stages as they have completed). How do your results compare with the Duvall model? Perhaps you could put your information into a pie-chart?

Reading 8.2   Life-Events

In young adulthood, the individual is confronted with a number of important life-events and developmental transitions. The more common ones include the development of intimacy relationships, leaving the nuclear family, marriage, pregnancy, birth of a child, divorce, entrance into the job market, change in financial status, change in social activities, and so on. Lowenthal, Thurnher, and Chiriboga (1975) found that although young adults generally report exposure to more life-events than middle-aged and older adults, they also report more positive stresses than the other two groups, whereas the latter report more negative ones. These researchers also found that the greatest stresses in the life of youth and young adults were in the areas of education, dating and marriage, and changes in residence. Lowenthal and his colleagues point out, however, that the mere occurrence of an event is not the critical factor in determining the impact of the event on the person. What appears to be more important is the person's perception of the event. For example, two individuals can be exposed to the same high level of stress and yet experience the event quite differently. These investigators found that individuals who are exposed to high stress and who perceive their lives as highly stressful are likely to feel 'overwhelmed.' In contrast, other adults, exposed to the same high levels of stress, but who perceive their lives as unstressful, are likely to feel 'challenged.' These findings suggest that the stress of life-events does not reside within the event per se, or within the individual, but is a mixture of the two (Lazarus and Launier, 1978).

D. Brodzinsky et al (1986) *Lifespan Human Development* (3rd edn)
Holt, Rinehart and Winston

1 '. . young adults generally report exposure to more life-events than middle-aged and older adults, they also report more . . . . stresses than the other two groups, whereas the latter report more . . . . ones.' (2)

2 Give **two** examples of situations in which questionnaires or surveys may be used. (4)

3 Circle the **positive** life-event:
   divorce   starting the first job   the death of a spouse   (2)

4 How is the individual's own evaluation of a life-event related to stress level? (4)

TERMS TO DEFINE

life-change units   role   Social Readjustment Rating Scale

All life-events are potentially stressful but, as can be seen in Reading 8.2 **Life-Events**, can be perceived differentially by individuals.

When two people marry many adjustments have to be made. They must learn to live together and co-ordinate their activities. For some couples these adjustments may take place before marriage, as many couples live together before deciding to marry. Although the sequencing is different the same issues must be resolved. In the past women have been shown to make greater role adjustments than men, which may result in less marital satisfaction for the wife than the husband (Barry, 1970). Bernard (1972) found that married women had more psychological problems than either married men or single women. Marriage appears to be good for the husband who gains more from the relationship when compared with single men. The **social support** gained from relationships is discussed in Reading 8.3.

Reading 8.3   Social Support

There are a number of different ways in which social support from relationships can work. The rather different kinds of benefit obtained from different relationships provide us with a useful guide. A general finding is that it is close relationships which are important. A small, helpful network is more useful than a larger, more diffuse one.

1 Intimate close attachments – caring, trust and empathy. These play an important role for young children. When mother is near they feel secure enough to explore strange environments. In later life a close attachment may provide similar benefits.

2 Confidants. The relationship with a confidant may be different from that already mentioned, though it often occurs with the same people. There is a lot of evidence that having a confiding relationship with a spouse or friend is good for mental and physical health. The process involved – disclosure and discussion of personal problems – may be akin to psychotherapy. This has been found to be the main reason that marriage is able to protect against stress.

3 Affirmation, giving confidence, increasing self-esteem, and the belief in ability to cope. Favourable evaluation from others may lead to the expectation of similar evaluation and confidence in getting our own way; belief in one's ability to cope results in confidence to tackle problems.

4 Tangible help. We shall see that help in minor, everyday matters is often provided by neighbours; major help by kin, help at work by workmates. This is the most direct kind of support.

5 Informational help. Social networks, as we have seen, are one of the main sources of information. Large and heterogeneous networks contain experts, or provide access to experts on a great variety of topics.

6 Social integration. Being accepted by a group of friends, being able to participate in regular social activities, may be a distinctive form of social support.

Some of these processes are more important than others. A recent study managed to separate the effects of different ones on mental and physical health. The most important were found to be the availability of a confidant, and the opportunity for positive evaluation of self by others.

M. Argyle and M. Henderson (1985) *The Anatomy of Relationships* Heinemann

1 Describe **two** ways in which close relationships benefit the individual.   (2)

2 What is meant by:
   a) confidant
   b) empathy?   (4)

3 Suggest **two** reasons why social support networks help to reduce stress.   (6)

4 In general women benefit more than men from social support. Discuss sex differences that you have noticed in the benefits of marriage to the partners.   (8)

TERMS TO DEFINE

confidant   social support

If a marriage breaks down then this not only affects the partners but also any children who may then spend part of their developing years in a single-parent household. There has also been research into the effects of divorce on family members and other life-events associated with family life (e.g. alternative family lifestyles, birth order effects, child abuse).

The social expectation of **roles** in marriage is now quite flexible. Most young couples have shared **conjugal roles**, with more husbands of working wives performing household tasks than husbands of non-working wives (Bahr, 1973). However, research also shows that husbands still spend less time on household tasks than wives, with women still generally responsible for most of the household tasks, meal preparation and child-rearing. When both partners work it demands careful balancing of marital and work roles, which become even more demanding when children arrive. More married mothers today are continuing to work outside the home and there are a large number of single mothers (divorced or never married) who are also employed. Use your psychological knowledge to tackle Activity 8.2.

Activity 8.2

A friend is considering returning to work after having a family. The youngest child is almost three years old and the other two children are at school. She asks your advice. Using the psychological knowledge you have available, draw up a list of suggestions that you could offer her to make this life-event more positive and less traumatic for her and her family.

Earlier research on the importance of **attachment** between infant and mother (see Chapter Seven especially Reading 7.4 Bonding, for a discussion of this topic), has been counterbalanced by research stressing the importance of a stimulating environment as well as a loving relationship in the early years. Some of the effects on the children of having **working mothers** can be found in Reading 8.4. The term working mother is usually taken to mean a mother who is in paid employment. However, any mother, especially one with pre-school children, will tell you that caring for children is hard work!

Reading 8.4 Working Mothers

Working mothers provide a variety of arrangements for their children's care. The majority leave their preschoolers at home to be cared for by a sitter or a relative while they work. The rest leave their young ones at someone else's home (to be cared for alone or with other children) or at day-care centres. Clearly, the effects of maternal employment on the child's development depend, to a large extent, on the quality of the substitute care. Research has focused on two broad areas: the general effects on children of having a working, versus a full-time, mother; and the effects of group child care versus those of individual child care.

Having a working mother appears to benefit girls more than it does boys. Daughters of working mothers tend to be more independent, better adjusted socially, and more likely to do well academically and aspire to a career than are daughters of mothers who are not employed (see Birnbaum, 1975; Gold, Andres, and Glorieux, 1979; Hoffman, 1980). Sons of working mothers are also more independent and better adjusted socially than are sons of nonworking mothers, but they do not do as well in school or on tests of cognitive ability (Banducci, 1967; Brown, 1970). How do we explain these findings? There are a number of possibilities. It may be that the loss of intellectual stimulation when the mother works has an adverse effect on both boys and girls. But the daughter's loss may be offset by other benefits, such as increased independence and the model of a mother who has a career outside of the home. Little boys whose mothers stay home during the preschool years tend to be more intellectually able as adolescents, but they are also more conforming, inhibited, and fearful. The nonworking mother may be so immersed in her role that she encourages dependency and has difficulty letting her son develop mature behaviour.

R.L. Atkinson et al (1987) *Introduction to Psychology* (9th edn)
Harcourt Brace Jovanovich

1 Describe **two** common arrangements made for young children while their mothers are at work. (2)

2 a) What are **two** benefits shown for girls with working mothers? (2)
   b) Describe **one** area in which boys with working mothers are shown not to do well. (1)
   c) What are **two** possible explanations of the above findings? (4)

3 Discuss **one** research study which investigates day-care systems for young children. (5)

4 Critically discuss the advantages and disadvantages of working mothers on the development of their children.   (8)

TERMS TO DEFINE
child-minder   nursery   playschool   work

With the growth of the female workforce, there has been a growing awareness of the possible effects of such work on the health and wellbeing of women. It has been hypothesised (Hall and Hall, 1980) that most women are expected to fulfil the role of both homemaker and career person at the same time. Although many men encourage their wives in their careers, few appear to take over traditional household chores to help them to cope. Also most work organisations do not accommodate the needs of women at work, especially those with families. The resulting pressure on women is enormous. Cooper (1981, 1983) suggests several ways in which these stressors could be alleviated, including more flexible working hours, working from home, refresher courses and adequate

'Remember when you went back to work and I decided to stay home and take care of the house, how we thought it wouldn't work out?'

maternity and paternity leave. Creche facilities can be a bonus for some lucky employees (and in a few cases some students!)

Women are not alone in finding work stressful. Actually entering the area of paid employment can produce a 'reality shock' for the young worker. The idealised image of the job, often taken from the media, and the actual rewards and demands can cause conflict. Even when the initial shock is over, they will still be subject to **occupational stress** which, as can be seen in Reading 8.5, varies for different occupations.

Reading 8.5   Occupational Stress

There is a belief that some occupations are sources of greater stress than others. An analysis of mortality due to arteriosclerotic heart disease, among U.S. males by occupational classification in the age range 20–64, shows that teachers fare better than lawyers, medical practitioners, estate agents, and insurance agents. However, general practitioners are more vulnerable to heart disease than are other physicians.

As to suicide rates, those connected with the enforcement of law had higher mortality rates than those who administer the law. Though surprisingly those who are exposed to life-threatening situations suffer less stress than those who are not. Among medical and related personnel, practitioners with above average suicide rates are dentists and psychiatrists.

Dentists are said to experience significant pressure from the demands of developing their practice. The dentist prone to stress tends to be anxiety prone and more easily upset when confronted with excessive administrative duties and when faced with too little work because of a preoccupation with building and sustaining the practice. Dentists with raised blood pressure perceived to some extent their image as inflictors of pain. They also experienced stress from their job interfering with their personal life.

It would be unwise to attribute stress, and its fatal consequences, only to professional and executive groups. There is a view that occupational stress is more likely to be found among blue-collar and routine white-collar workers. This is a view shared by the Chief Medical Officer of an Insurance Company in her address to a conference on managing stress. She maintained that the highest mortality rate from all causes was more likely to be found in socio-economic groups 3, 4 and 5.

In certain occupations – e.g. the police and fire service – the normal retirement age is 55. This might suggest that such occupations are stressful, and that it would be unfair to expect an employee to continue working until he or she reached the customary retirement age for most occupations (60 or 65). Of course it could also suggest that age and fitness are more critical factors for the successful operation of these services. Another occupational group in the emergency services – the ambulancemen – are said to be using the stress factor to secure a similar advantage to that enjoyed by the police and the fire service. An ambulanceman in Liverpool, who was fitted with an electro-cardiogram, experienced a significant increase in heart beat when he responded to an emergency call. The highest heart beat was recorded during two spells of stressful driving through heavy suburban and city traffic.

E.F. McKenna (1987) *Psychology in Business* Erlbaum

1 Name **two** occupations believed to be sources of great occupational stress. (2)

2 Connect the sentences correctly:
   Dentists and psychiatrists   have higher death rates than judges
   Policemen   suffer less heart disease than doctors
   Teachers   are more likely to commit suicide   (3)

3 Discuss **one** study other than those reported on the effects of occupational stress. (5)

4 Discuss some of the environmental variables which may prove stressful for the employee. What recommendations can psychologists make to reduce these effects? (10)

TERMS TO DEFINE

environmental   occupation   socio-economic

Individual differences in identifying a situation as stressful and in coping with stress have been identified (see Chapter Three, especially Reading 3.7 Stress and Reading 3.8 Type A Behaviour, for further discussion of this topic). A critical factor appears to be the individual's perception or understanding of the event. The potential stress of life events does not appear to lie in the events themselves or in the individual but rather in the interaction between the two.

One factor which has been shown to be relevant is whether the person feels that they have control over what is happening to them (known as **internal locus of control**). People who believe that what happens to them is outside their control are described as having an **external** locus of control. Kobasa (1979) found that executives with an internal locus of control handled their problems more directly and were less likely to suffer from stress-related illness.

More people today are deciding not to stay in jobs that they find boring or stressful and are making **career changes**. This is discussed further in Reading 8.6.

Reading 8.6   Career Changes

A small, but growing, percentage of middle-aged people, in response to the pressures of job obsolescence or job dissatisfaction, are making career changes. As one middle-ager said, 'I had the feeling I was getting nowhere. I struggled all my life to make money and be a successful business executive. But when I got there I realised it wasn't at all what I wanted. It became boring and meaningless, and that's when I decided to get out. I sold my business and got a master's degree in social work. Now I'm working in a counselling centre for college kids and have never been happier.' This type of career change is typical of many people going through mid-life crisis. There seems to be an overwhelming fear that time is running out – a now-or-never feeling for 'doing something important or meaningful.' Sometimes the change is made to pursue a dream that was put aside for a secure livelihood.

These mid-life feelings seem to be largely responsible for the phenomenon of second careers. More and more people in their thirties and forties are changing their lives and attempting to find more satisfaction in their work lives. Of course, not everyone is equally receptive to retraining and career change. Research indicates that the people who are most interested in such change are those who are concerned with the social-psychological aspect of jobs and who are strongly motivated to achieve but who see little chance of movement in their current job and consequently are less satisfied with what they are doing (Sheppard and Belitsky, 1966). In other words, they want to get ahead and/or do a good job, but they do not see much chance of accomplishing their goals in their current position.

Of course, other factors contribute to the growing trend of second careers. There is increasing acceptance of job-hoppers and career changers – it is no longer considered a sign of flightiness or immaturity to move from one job or one vocation to another. Another factor is the higher standard of living that has made it possible for potential career changers to take time out and live on their assets during the critical period of transition and readjustment. More people, therefore, feel the freedom and security to carry out a career change. The feminist movement is also responsible for career changes. Many homemakers are pursuing careers because of economic need and a desire to participate in the wider society outside of the family (Sheehy, 1976).

D. Brodzinsky et al (1986) *Lifespan Human Development* Holt,
Rinehart and Winston

1 What do you understand by 'mid-life crisis'?   (2)

2 Describe **two** factors which may contribute to people deciding to embark on a second career.   (2)

3 Discuss **one** problem which may be encountered by a middle-aged worker who decides to change careers.   (4)

4 What psychological changes related to ageing might cause problems for retraining older workers? Describe, with at least **one** research example, how psychologists may overcome such problems.   (10)

TERMS TO DEFINE

age discrimination   job satisfaction   mid-life crisis

With the rapid growth of technology many jobs are becoming obsolete and some people are having to make career changes they had not intended. Inevitably, at such a time, there are many who find that movement in the job market is restricted and that employment is not available. This is one life-event which can prove very stressful and result in health and personality problems, which in turn can extend the period of unemployment. The importance of maintaining **self-esteem** during **unemployment** is discussed in Reading 8.7.

Reading 8.7   Unemployment

Loss of work may present a serious threat to the individual's self-esteem and promote attitudes towards self that make a return to normal working life difficult. Hartmann (1972) notes that a central assumption underlying the work of the industrial rehabilitation units in the UK is that rehabilitation positively influences attitudes towards self. Testing this assumption he constructed two scales, one to measure keenness for work and the other to assess a composite of attitudes which he labelled 'inadequacy', and which included feelings of inferiority, insecurity, loss of self-respect, and self-esteem. He found that an eight-week course at an industrial rehabilitation unit led to a reduction in feelings of inadequacy, thus supporting the assumption that rehabilitation may help to restore a person's self-confidence, improve the self-image, reduce anxiety and feelings of insecurity, etc. It was interesting to note, however, that Hartmann's study did not reveal any changes in the client's keenness for work.

Tiffany, Cowan, and Tiffany (1970) adopt a phenomenological stance and argue that the self-concept is a potent determiner of behaviour in so far as it influences the way people view the world. Schlien (1963), they feel, puts the point well when he states that the interpretation of self leads to a reactive interpretation of the external object.

For instance, if one feels strong, a boulder is a weapon to push into the treads of an armoured tank, if weak, the same boulder is a refuge to hide behind. If one feels sick and helpless, the nurse is a creature of mercy, appealed to for comfort. The same nurse may be seen as a temptress, to be sexually pursued, if the patient sees himself as well and sturdy. All experience is evaluated as friendly or dangerous, interesting or boring, possible, etc. depending not upon the nature of the experience so much as upon the self concept of the experiencer (cited in Tiffany, Cowan and Tiffany 1970:90).

Tiffany, Cowan, and Tiffany found that when they administered the Tennessee self-concept scale to thirty-one subjects with interrupted work histories which included long periods of unemployment, and also to a socio-economically comparable group who had been in steady employment for twelve months, there were marked differences in the profiles of the two groups. The profile of the unemployed group reflected their low level of self-esteem compared to the employed group. They saw themselves as undesirable, doubted their worth, often felt anxious, depressed, and unhappy, and had little faith or confidence in themselves. A state of affairs reflected in our discussion in Chapter 6.

Fineman (1979) presents a phenomenological model of stress which postulates that the meaning the individual places on particular potential stress stimuli and the affective reactions to them, depend on the individual view of self in relation to the demands which are characteristically made on him or her. Studying a group of unemployed managers he found that those who were highly stressed were less successful in locating employment than those who experienced only low levels of stress. His research indicated that high stress elicited less effective coping responses, such as avoidance and inactivity, whereas lower levels of stress tended to elicit more effective coping responses such as confrontation.

Fineman hypothesised that problems perceived as threatening to the self are potential stressors, that very low levels of self-esteem increase the individual's susceptibility for experiencing environmental demands as threatening and that low levels of self-esteem are associated with feelings of incompetence to deal with the environment. He also postulated a possible downward spiral in which the experience of stress could further erode feelings of competence and self-esteem. This model leads one to conclude that there is some substance behind the assumption, underlying the many programmes to help the unemployed, that improving self-esteem is an important intermediate goal. Fineman's model identifies a clear relationship between the individual's level of self-esteem and the ability to master problems, particularly problems associated with unemployment.

J. Hayes and P. Nutman (1981) *Understanding the Unemployed* Tavistock

1 What is:
   a) the self-concept
   b) phenomenology?   (2)

2 Note **two** differences in self-concept found by Tiffany et al (1970) between those in employment and those who are unemployed.   (2)

3 a) In your own words describe Fineman's model of stress.   (4)
   b) What are the implications for the unemployed if this model is correct?   (4)

4 Discuss Rogers' phenomenological theory of the development of the self-concept in relation to unemployment.

TERMS TO DEFINE

phenomenological   self-concept   unemployment

Unlike many of the previous life-events we have discussed, the **retirement** from employment signals an ending rather than a beginning. However, with many companies encouraging their employees to take early retirement we have a growing band of people who see retirement as the beginning of a new phase of life.

Atchley (1977) suggests that the retirement process involves seven phases, although not everyone progresses through all the stages nor necessarily in the order given. The stages include a pre-retirement period when little is done to prepare for retirement and the individual is active and enjoying work. As they approach retirement they enter a period when they begin to give up certain work obligations, perhaps to younger workers. Once retirement starts there is a 'honeymoon' period when many planned activities are carried out. This can be followed, in some instances, by a disenchantment phase when life is found to be less satisfying than expected. People who have retired usually progress through a period when they accept, reorientate and finally adjust. For those who do not adjust to extended leisure there may be a return to employment, perhaps in a part-time capacity. The final stage is a period which is identified as a time when, with illness or impending death, the role pattern changes. Some studies on **retirement** are discussed in Reading 8.8.

Reading 8.8   Retirement

Most studies show that as long as individuals maintain their health and have an adequate income, they find retirement a satisfying stage of life. Richard Barfield and James Morgan (1978) questioned a number of retired men and their wives on their feelings about retirement. Some of the most positive responses were: 'Enjoy every minute of it! Have the time at last to do just what I want or not do anything if I want that.' 'I like it! We enjoy life a lot more if we're out of the rat race.' The negative responses were usually related to poor health: 'Not much to think about – you got the black lung; you just sit and wait.' 'He feels helpless and lost. It gives him a sad feeling seeing the land lying vacant and not being able to plant something'.

Achieving satisfaction with retirement often requires considerable adjustment. Our society places its highest value on the work-oriented life, and it takes time to switch to a leisure-oriented life and still feel important. Judith Stevens-Long (1979) suggests that three conditions must be met before the retired can be completely comfortable with a leisure-centred life. First, they must have enough money to spend on leisure activities. Second, they must develop a new ethic, based on the belief that leisure is as important and valuable as work. Third, many people may have to learn to use their time in a new way. Just as vocational counselling provides people with information about the work they are best suited for, 'leisure education' might help people determine where to redirect their energy and how to restructure their time. Some people prefer 'true' leisure activities such as reading and golf; others pursue 'work' leisure in civic activities and volunteer work.

Z. Rubin and E.B. McNeil (1981) *Psychology: Being Human* (3rd edn)
Harper Row

1 Note **one** factor which is usually associated with a happy period of retirement.   (1)

2 Give **two** conditions which, according to Stevens-Long, must be met before a person can enjoy retirement.   (2)

3 What recommendations can psychologists make to prepare people for retirement?   (5)

4 Critically discuss the 'disengagement' theory of retirement.   (8)

TERMS TO DEFINE

compulsory retirement age   disengagement   leisure   retirement

Another negative life-event is when someone close to an individual dies. A death in the family can affect even the youngest members. Bowlby (1980) found that the loss of a parent in early childhood is associated with a higher percentage of depression and suicide in adulthood. Unlike adults, children who suffer ambivalent feelings after the death of someone close to them often find it difficult to come to terms with their anger.

A young person who loses a friend or lover can find themselves facing an event for which they are not prepared. This loss can prove to be quite traumatic for a young person who has not had to come to terms with mortality as the elderly have had to. A parent having to accept the mortality of their own child can find the grief difficult and healing can take some time. Many feel that this is the hardest grief to bear.

At whatever age it occurs, the death of a spouse is one of the most painful events for the surviving partner; hence this event has the highest stress value (100 units) on Rahe's scale (Figure 8.1). Holmes and Rahe suggest that a stress total of 150+ for any twelve-month period puts the individual into the high risk group for stress. You might find it interesting to investigate your own stress total as suggested in Activity 8.3.

Activity 8.3

Using the Social Readjustment Scale shown in Figure 8.1, make a list of important events which have occurred in your life over the last 12 months. Work out your total stress index. Make a note of how you reacted to each one. Did you find each event stressful? Have you suffered any health problems which could possibly be the result of the stress?

Bear in mind that this is only a guideline and finding that you have a high score does not necessarily mean you are going to suffer any ill effects. What it can do is make you more aware of the potential dangers and give you the opportunity (wherever possible) to change your lifestyle to reduce stress.

Do the same for an older member of your family (such as a grandparent). What difference in scores did you find? How do you explain this? Perhaps you can do this as a class exercise and compare the individual differences. Does any period of life appear more stressful than any other?

Parkes (1972) interviewed people who had lost their wife or husband at various intervals after the death. The three-stage pattern of grief that he found can be seen in Reading 8.9 **Bereavement**.

Reading 8.9 Bereavement

The first stage Parkes described was a period of numbness, that people felt when they first heard the news of their spouse's death. Often they would make comments like: 'It just doesn't seem real – I keep expecting to wake up soon.' This period would last for several hours, and in many cases for several days. It seems as though it does take time for such bad news to 'sink in'.

The second stage that people went through was a period which Parkes called 'pining'. One of the characteristics of this stage was a strong sense of the other person's absence, and a tendency to search for him or her in familiar places, or to look for their face in a crowd. Although many of Parkes' subjects were aware of how useless this behaviour was, they would still do it; often they would say: 'I just can't help myself – I keep expecting that they'll turn up.' Parkes found this to be strikingly similar to the searching behaviour that many animals show if they lose a mate, even though they may have seen the mate's dead body. He considers that this may be evidence of some kind of biological reaction, perhaps one that we inherit and share with other animals.

The third stage that Parkes outlines seemed to happen when the 'searching' had finished, and it was all too obvious that the missing person would not appear again. At this point the bereaved person would tend to become very depressed, and listless, and their grief would be felt most acutely. Parkes also pointed out that grief is not felt in the same way all the time, but comes and goes in 'pangs', or waves of intensity. He said that it reaches its peak, usually, about five to fourteen days after bereavement, although it may not ease off for some time. After a while, though, these pangs become less frequent, but can be easily triggered off by little things, like finding an old photograph.

N. Hayes (1988) *A First Course in Psychology* (2nd edn) Nelson

1 a) According to Parkes, what happens to an individual immediately after their partner dies? (2)
  b) What is a characteristic of the period of 'pining'? (1)
  c) When might depression occur? (1)

2 Describe **one** characteristic seen in the bereaved other than those noted above. (3)

3 Give **two** examples of ways in which we can help the bereaved. (4)

4 What do psychologists mean by:
  a) isolation
  b) desolation? (4)

TERMS TO DEFINE

bereavement   mortality   mourning

With improved medical facilities people are now living much longer and it is quite common for families to have a senior member aged over 80 years. In our society death is not usually discussed by the young; it is often considered 'too morbid' and parents are often reluctant to discuss it with their children. Even doctors sometimes avoid informing patients that they are dying. Psychologists are now becoming aware of the **socio-psychological** aspects of death for the patient and the family. We are becoming more knowledgeable about meeting the needs of people at this time. The growth of the **hospice**, with facilities designed for the terminally ill, tries to ensure that death occurs painlessly with peace and dignity, in a pleasant setting surrounded by loved ones. In Reading 8.10 we shall look at some of the socio-psychological research on **impending death**.

Reading 8.10   Impending Death

Death has become a socio-psychological, attitudinal experience as well as a physical event.

How do people cope, in a socio-psychological sense, with impending death? There are essentially three foci for their concern:

1 The pain, discomfort, disability, and social stigma of a terminal illness.
2 The reactions and emotions of others, particularly of close others or life partners.
3 The person's own reactions.

Kübler-Ross (1969) proposed that there were five stages of psychological adjustment to death:

1 Denial (it's a mistaken diagnosis).
2 Anger (why me?).
This can lead to envy of those still fit, resentment against them, and even to surprising verbal attacks on helpers, nurses, and friends.
3 Bargaining (dealing with Fate for more time).
Terminal patients often leave their body to medical science as part of an implicit bargain with Death for more time, and with medical staff for better care that may help them stay alive longer.
4 Depression, sadness, and crying.
5 Acceptance.

This is often characterised by silence, withdrawal, and a marked detachment from other people.

Some criticise this neat system on the grounds that the terminally ill more probably oscillate between the stages, rather than move steadily to each next one. Others note that some patients show all the stages at once or that the stages occur and re-occur. Whether these criticisms are valid, it makes sense to attend to the psychological dimension to dying and to concern ourselves with the psychological treatment of such patients as well as with their medical treatment.

S. Duck (1986) *Human Relationships* Sage

1 Name **one** normal problem for a person who is dying.   (1)

2 a) In your own words describe the five stages of psychological adjustment to death outlined by Kübler-Ross (1969).   (4)
   b) Give **one** criticism of this system.   (2)

3 What are hospices? What socio-psychological benefits can these provide for the terminally ill and their families?   (6)

TERMS TO DEFINE

hospice   terminally ill

You have now journeyed through some of the many life-events which can affect the way in which we behave. Obviously we have merely 'skimmed the surface' of all the research available. You can extend this view by following up Suggestions For Further Reading.

Topic-related Essays

1 What is meant by occupational stress? Discuss how the interaction of psychological and environmental factors may cause an individual to suffer stress reactions connected with their work.

2 Discuss the influence of some critical life events on adults.

3 '. . . . . a particular person's reaction to the death of a spouse depends on a number of factors' (Hothersall 1985). Discuss.

By now you may have become involved in your own research into psychology. In Chapter Nine we will introduce you to the various methods available to you and which should help you when planning psychological research.

SUGGESTIONS FOR FURTHER READING

Main text
D. Brodzinsky et al (1986) *Lifespan Human Development* (3rd edn) Holt, Rinehart and Winston

Other useful texts
M. Argyle and M. Henderson (1985) *The Anatomy of Relationships* Heinemann (esp. life events in the family)
H. Bee and S.K. Mitchell (1984) *The Developing Person* Harper Row
S. Duck (1986) *Human Relationships* Sage
H. Gardner (1982) *Developmental Psychology* (2nd edn) Little, Brown and Co (esp. birth order, peer group and adolescence)
N. Hayes (1988) *A First Course in Psychology* (2nd edn) Nelson (interesting chapter on environmental psychology)
Z. Rubin and E.B. McNeill (1985) *Psychology: Being Human* (4th edn) Harper Row

Stimulus Questions

A researcher wanted to investigate the relationship between stressful life-events and physical health. He handed out a questionnaire to 40 people attending a local medical centre on a mid-week morning, and to another 40 people attending a private fitness and sports centre at the same time. The questionnaires asked people about their current state of health, and also asked them to write down any particularly stressful life-events that had happened to them during the past year.

The researcher found that the group attending the medical centre reported almost twice as many stressful life-events as the group who were attending the fitness centre. The medical centre group also reported being significantly less physically healthy. The researcher concluded that stressful life-events could produce negative effects on people's health.

8.1 What type of study is this? (1)

8.2 How many subjects were there in the study? (1)

8.3 The researcher used a correlation test to analyse the results. What type of diagram could he have used to illustrate this? (1)

8.4 Why did the researcher make sure that the subjects were asked to complete their questionnaires at the same times in the week? (2)

8.5 What name is given to studies which look back at what has happened to people in the past? (1)

8.6 Describe **two** problems with the choice of subjects in the study. For each one, state clearly how it could have affected the results of the study. (6)

8.7 Can you suggest a better way of obtaining subjects? Describe clearly an alternative method that could have been used. (3)

8.8 What is a stressful life-event? (2)

8.9 What is wrong with simply asking people to list the stressful life-events that they can remember? (3)

8.10 Suggest an alternative method for finding out about someone's stressful life-events. (2)

8.11 State **one** alternative conclusion that the researcher could have drawn from the results of the study. (3)

Methodology Questions

Many people nowadays move from one career to a completely different one, or have several different types of occupations during the course of their working lives. Imagine that you have been asked to carry out a survey on attitudes to work and career changes. Answer the following questions as fully as you can, making sure that your suggestions are as practical as possible:

8.1 What is a survey? (1)

8.2 What would be the best age-range for the subjects of your study? Give a reason for your answer. (3)

8.3 Name and describe the sampling method that you would use to obtain the subjects for your study. (3)

8.4 Name and briefly describe **two** other sampling methods. (4)

8.5 Describe **one** method of attitude measurement which you have studied, and explain why it either would or would not be suitable for you to use in your survey. (3)

8.6 Write out **one** question that you would ask people in this survey. Remember that the question must be easy to understand and easy to score. (3)

8.7 In the final report, how would you present the information from this question? (e.g. table, graph, bar chart, pie-chart etc.) Give an example to illustrate your answer. (2)

8.8 Outline **two** problems that you might come across while carrying out your survey, and say what you could do about each one. (6)

9

Planning Psychological Research

> 'You cannot write an effective report of an experiment unless you understand the whys and wherefores of its design.'
> P. Harris (1986)

Plate 9

WHAT TYPE OF STUDY DO YOU WANT TO CONDUCT?

EXPERIMENTAL METHOD — CORRELATION — SURVEY — OBSERVATION

THIS EXPERIMENT HAS AN INADEQUATE LEVEL OF CONTROL. START AGAIN.

WHAT SORT OF DESIGN?

INDEPENDENT GROUPS — MATCHED PAIRS — REPEATED MEASURES

HAVE YOU ALLOCATED SUBJECTS TO CONDITIONS AT RANDOM?
No / Yes

SO, YOU'RE GOING TO WASTE ALL THAT TIME AND EFFORT AND MAYBE EVEN MONEY MATCHING SUBJECTS. WELL I CAN TELL YOU IT WON'T BE WORTH IT. IT WILL END IN TEARS. STILL, DON'T SAY YOU WEREN'T WARNED.

ARE YOU *SURE* YOU'VE NOT GOT ASYMMETRICAL ORDER EFFECTS? YOU'D BETTER DO A PILOT STUDY TO CHECK. AFTER ALL YOU DON'T WANT TO HAVE TO ~~FIDDLE~~ DO IT ALL AGAIN, DO YOU?

IS YOUR DATA INTERVAL SCALING OR ABOVE?
No

ARE THE POPULATIONS FROM WHICH YOUR SAMPLES ARE DRAWN NORMALLY DISTRIBUTED?
No / Yes

WHAT DO YOU MEAN YOU <u>THINK</u> SO? LOOK AT YOUR QUARTILES!!
No

HOW BIG IS YOUR SAMPLE?

HAVE YOU CONTROLLED FOR ORDER EFFECT? PRACTICE EFFECT?
No / Yes / No / Yes

LESS THAN 10 | BETWEEN 10 AND 900

ACTUALLY IT DOESN'T MATTER. BOTH OF THESE QUESTIONS HAVE NOTHING TO DO WITH EXPERIMENTAL DESIGN.

ARE YOU FOLLOWING ENVIRONMENTAL VARIABLES HELD CONSTANT? TEMPERATURE, NOISE, LIGHT, HUMIDITY, LEAD LEVELS, HYDROCARBON POLLUTION, CARBON MONOXIDE LEVELS, COLOUR OF NOTEPAPER.
No / Yes

DO YOU KNOW THAT IF YOU HAVE A SAMPLE SIZE OF MORE THAN 1000, A CORRELATION COEFFICIENT OF 0.1 WILL BE SIGNIFICANT AT THE 0.05 LEVEL? WHY DON'T YOU GO AWAY AND TRY FOR THE 1000?

I HAVE DIFFICULTY IN BELIEVING YOU
No

WELL DONE! GOT YOUR 1000 SUBJECTS HAVE YOU? NOW

HAVE YOU GOT A RANDOM SAMPLE?
No / Yes

HAVE YOU <u>COMPLETELY</u> ELIMINATED EXPERIMENTER EFFECTS?
No / Yes

LIAR!

Yes

REALLY?

WHO DO YOU THINK YOU ARE? PIAGET? A SOCIOLOGIST? IF INSULTS WON'T GET RID OF YOU AND YOU INSIST ON CONTINUING THE CHARADE . . .

P Sanders: a Handbook for Psychology Students

Readings on 'Planning Psychological Research'

There may come a time during your study of psychology when you will decide to investigate for yourself some of the psychological issues which you have encountered. This may be a course requirement, or perhaps interest and curiosity may motivate you. It can be quite a demanding task and involves a certain amount of background knowledge. We shall discuss three areas which are highly relevant to carrying out your own research:

1) choosing your method of study

2) designing the investigation

3) research problems.

Various methods have been developed by psychologists in order to investigate human behaviour objectively and systematically.

The method used by Freud as the basis of his research was the **case study**. This involved intensive investigations of his patients by analysing each case in great detail. This method has been used extensively by other researchers and examples of such case studies and the problems associated with them are examined in Reading 9.1.

Reading 9.1   Case Studies

Consider the following cases that actually occurred in New York City (Latané and Darley, 1970):

Kitty Genovese is set upon by a maniac as she returns home from work at 3 A.M. Thirty-eight of her neighbours in Kew Gardens come to their windows when she cries out in terror; none comes to her assistance even though her stalker takes over half an hour to murder her. No one even so much as calls the police. She dies.

Andrew Mormille is stabbed in the stomach as he rides the A train home in Manhattan. Eleven other riders watch the seventeen-year-old boy as he bleeds to death; none comes to his assistance even though his attackers have left the car. He dies.

An eighteen-year-old switchboard operator, alone in her office in the Bronx, is raped and beaten. Escaping momentarily, she runs naked and bleeding to the street, screaming for help. A crowd of forty passers by gathers and watches as, in broad daylight, the rapist tries to drag her back upstairs; no one interferes. Finally, two policemen happen by and arrest her assailant.

A researcher could choose one of these cases and try to find out as much about it as possible. The researcher could interview the witnesses who did not intervene to hear their reasons, could talk to the police, and so forth. But the information might be poor. First, since the event had already occurred, the researcher could not vary the situation and ask what effect different conditions might have had. Second, people's memories might not be accurate; they might be unaware of the reasons they did not intervene, or they might try to hide them. Third, even if useful information were obtained, how would the researcher know that it was true of all emergencies and not just of this one? A danger of case studies is that they might mislead investigators into believing that principles derived from one case apply to all cases. Do the principles Freud derived from observing neurotic Viennese patients apply to the personalities of all people?

For all these reasons, psychologists do not view the case study method as a technique for producing conclusive results. As with naturalistic observation, case studies are mainly useful as sources of ideas that should then be better researched. However, case studies may be the only research tool available for studying the effects on behaviour of unique events such as brain damage, tornadoes, floods, and other natural disasters.

H.L. Roediger et al (1984) *Psychology* Little, Brown and Co

1 a) In the Kitty Genovese murder how many neighbours went to their windows when they heard her screams? (1)
  b) How many went to her assistance? (1)

2 How does a researcher find out about reports of attacks such as those reported above? (2)

3 Describe **two** problems associated with this approach. (4)

4 Discuss the advantages/disadvantages of the case study method. (8)

TERMS TO DEFINE

case study   generalisation   idiographic approach

The case study is useful for investigating individual characteristics although it is open to bias from many sources such as those noted above. Case studies are just one of several methods which involve observing naturally occurring events. The researcher does not alter conditions in the situation but merely reports events. Interviews, surveys and naturalistic observation can prove useful methods in such situations and these can all contribute towards case studies.

Investigations sometimes involve a number of cases, noting the characteristics of each case, and discovering if these characteristics are related. This involves the use of the statistical technique of **correlation** as discussed in Reading 9.2.

Reading 9.2   Correlation

In a correlational study, the researcher tries to discover the relationship (or correlation) between two or more aspects of people's behaviour, attitudes, or background. Brown and Kulik's flashbulb memory study is an example of a correlational study – subjects' ratings of the personal importance of events were related to their flashbulb memories of those events. To take another example of a correlational study, suppose that you were interested in determining the relationship between people's training in psychology and their sensitivity to other people's feelings. You might go about such a study by choosing a sample of students, asking each one how many psychology courses he has taken, and finally giving them a test of interpersonal sensitivity. You would then be able to chart the relationship between your two measures. The diagram below presents one possible set of results from such a study, suggesting that the two measures (sometimes called variables) are in fact related to one another.

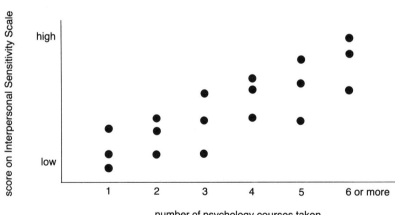

The results of a hypothetical study relating training in psychology to scores on a test of interpersonal sensitivity. Each dot represents one subject. The results show a high correlation between two variables.

As far as we know, this particular study has never been done, but it would certainly be an interesting one to do. Such a correlational study has its limitations, however. Although our hypothetical study demonstrates that training in psychology and interpersonal sensitivity are related to each other, it does not provide a clear test of hypotheses about cause and effect. One hypothesis would be that training in psychology increases people's sensitivity to others. But the causal link might go in the other direction: people who are sensitive to others may be especially interested in taking psychology classes. It is even possible that neither of the variables has any effect on the other and that both of them are caused by a third factor that we neglected to measure. For example, students who come from particular family backgrounds may be especially likely to be interpersonally sensitive and to take psychology, while people from other family backgrounds may tend to lack sensitivity and to avoid taking psychology. Similarly, in the flashbulb memory study, we can't be completely sure that the personal importance of events is what caused the flashbulb memories. Perhaps it worked the other way around, and the experiencing of flashbulb memories led the subjects to believe that the associated events must have been important. The moral of the story is that correlation does not imply causation. In other words, simply knowing that two variables are related does not in itself tell us what is causing what.

Z. Rubin and E.B. McNeil (1981) *Psychology: Being Human*
Harper Row

1 Describe **one** of the correlation studies reported above. (2)

2 a) Join up the following sentences correctly:
   negative correlation   means there is no linear relationship between the variables
   zero correlation   means that a high score on one variable is associated with a high score on another
   positive correlation   means that a high score on one variable is associated with a low score on another (3)

   b) Fill in the relationship shown at positions A and B on the diagram below:

−1	−0.5	0	+0.5	+1
A		no relationship		B

3 Explain the following correlation coefficients:
   a) -0.95 b) $+0.02$ c) $+0.97$ (3)

4 'Correlation does not imply causation.' Discuss. (6)

TERMS TO DEFINE

positive/negative correlation   scattergram   variables

Such results can be charted on a **scattergram** as suggested in Activity 9.1. Another method which can provide information on individuals is **psychometrics**. This refers to the development of tests which can be used to measure individual differences in such characteristics as intelligence and personality. Since Binet introduced one of the first acknowledged tests of

Activity 9.1

The table gives the height
and weight of a small sample of
six people.
Plot them on a scattergram.
What do they show?

S	height in cm	weight in kg
1	167	66
2	150	50
3	185	80
4	160	60
5	177	70
6	152	80

intelligence at the beginning of the twentieth century, such tests of intelligence and other abilities have 'mushroomed'. These tests are mainly used in clinical, educational and industrial settings. Along with personality tests they are often used in selection for educational courses and job suitability. In education they are frequently used to monitor a pupil's progress and diagnose individual areas of difficulty for the pupil, along with more recent techniques such as curriculum-referenced assessment.

Ability tests have often been at the centre of controversy (see Chapter Two for a discussion of the nature/nurture debate on intelligence). Some researchers suggest that they have often been used politically to justify the actions taken by a government (Gould, 1981). The use of psychometric tests also raises the issue of their **reliability and validity** which is discussed in Reading 9.3.

Reading 9.3   Reliability and Validity

In normal language, 'reliable' has two slightly different meanings. We say a thermometer is reliable if it works and provides, time after time, a correct reading of temperature. We also say a person is reliable if we can depend on him or her to turn up on time to do what they have promised to do. In testing terms, reliability is much closer to the first meaning. If a test is reliable subjects will turn up roughly equivalent scores whenever tested. Traditionally, the reliability of a test depends on two measures, its internal consistency and its test/re-test stability.

For a test to be internally consistent, the items that cover similar kinds of behaviour or attitudes should get similar answers. Imagine a test which includes questions like 'Do you enjoy going to parties?' and 'Do you dislike social meetings?' People who answer yes to the first ought to reply no to the second. A test becomes internally inconsistent if the pattern of replies is erratic. The second measure of reliability looks not at the coherence of items within a test, but at how likely people are to give the same kinds of scores at different times. Intelligence tests do throw up generally similar results when people retake them, though there is a tendency for people to do better the more IQ tests they take (Heim 1948) and for IQ to decline in old age, reflecting it has been said, a genuine decline in skill. In general, though, IQ tests reveal good test/re-test scores.

It is easy to confuse how reliable a test is with how valid it is. A test could be designed to judge the performance of ice cream vendors. If we use our wit to vet the Vendors of Ices Test (VIT) we might discover the following. Ice cream vendors who take the test at six-months intervals come up with fairly similar scores. The items on the test which are supposed to tap knowledge of ices and skill at communicating with the public are coherent. Each set of items forms a natural cluster so that vendors who say 'yes' to 'Do the public like to have a choice of flavours?' usually say 'no' to 'Do the public only buy chocolate?'. Despite this promising start, the Mega Ice Corporation notes that there is absolutely no relationship between performance on the VIT and how much ice cream each vendor sells. The VIT is reliable but not, alas, valid, and ought, of course, to be put on ice!

D. Shelley and D. Cohen (1986) *Testing Psychological Tests* Croom Helm

1 In testing terms what is meant by:
   a) reliability
   b) internally consistent?   (4)

2 Validity refers to . . . .   (2)

3 Give **one** advantage and **one** disadvantage associated with the use of psychometric tests.   (4)

4 Describe **one** psychometric test and discuss its possible uses, noting any potential associated sources of bias.

TERMS TO DEFINE

psychometrics   reliability   standardisation   validity

If we wish to investigate cause and effect then we must turn to the **experimental method** where we can exercise more control over the situation. Once we know what the subject of the investigation is to be, we need to state what prediction we are making; this is known as the **hypothesis**. For example, an experimental hypothesis might be that lack of sleep affects our performance on a test. To test this hypothesis, we could arrange for two groups, one of whom had slept normally prior to being tested, and the other who had been sleep-deprived and then tested. We could then compare the results of the test to see if a difference exists between the two sets of scores. In this way we have manipulated or changed certain events, situations or 'things'. These 'things' that we change are known as **variables** and are discussed in Reading 9.4.

Reading 9.4   Variables

Any idea or theory which makes certain provisional predictions is called a hypothesis, and the preliminary idea we have in our experimental work is termed – not surprisingly – the experimental hypothesis. Examples of experimental hypotheses are:

That a particular drug changes specified organic tissue
That diet influences intelligence
That facial appearance matters in inter-personal perception
That advertising policy affects beer sales
That environmental pollution is responsible for altering plant life
That study habits influence exam marks.

We have named particular things (organic tissue, intelligence, inter-personal perception, etc.) and stated our belief that each is influenced in some way by something else – the 'something elses' being a drug, diet and facial appearance, etc. All these 'things' and 'something elses' are called variables. The term 'variable', used in an experimental context, means anything which is free to vary, and in order to describe them in a quantitative way, they have to be expressed in appropriate units. Sometimes the units will be quite obvious, like inches, IQ scores, success rate on a task, pints of beer sold, etc., but at other times ingenuity will be called for. For instance how do we measure and express taste, attitudes, beliefs and motivation? Often we have to devise a rating scale specially for expressing a particular variable in an appropriate kind of unit. Such 'home-made' scales are often regarded as being less trustworthy than well-established units in common usage.

The kinds of units we use to quantify variables have an important bearing on the statistical test we will choose for data analysis.

The pairs of variables which occur in each experiment have separate names. The variable we manipulate is called the *independent variable*, and abbreviated to IV. The variable which we hypothesise will alter as a consequence of our manipulations is called the *dependent variable*, or DV. It is easy to remember which way round the IV and DV are. The dependent variable alters as a consequence of the value of the independent variable – its value is dependent upon this. The value of the independent variable is free to vary according to the whims of the experimenters. The IV's and DV's named in the hypotheses listed above are given in the table below.

Independent variable	Dependent variable
a particular drug	specific organic tissue
diet	intelligence
facial appearance	inter-personal perception
advertising policy	beer sales
environmental pollution	plant life
study habits	exam marks

Most variables can be either dependent or independent, within the context of a particular experiment. For instance, in the final example given above, it was hypothesised that students' study habits will affect their exam performance. However, it is also reasonable to wonder whether students' exam marks might actually lead them to seek to improve their study habits! Beer sales, given as a DV above, would become an IV in the context of studies concerning alcoholism, road accidents or sales of soft drinks.

F. Clegg (1984) *Simple Statistics* (2nd edn) Cambridge University Press

1 Variables, in an experimental context, are . . . .   (2)

2 Are the following statements **true** or **false**?
  a) the variable we manipulate is the dependent variable
  b) the variable which alters as a consequence of our manipulation is the dependent variable.   (2)

3 Give an experimental hypothesis, other than those given above, stating your independent and dependent variables.   (4)

4 What are confounding variables? Give **two** examples of how variables can be controlled.   (8)

TERMS TO DEFINE

experiment   experimental and null hypothesis
independent and dependent variables

Once the experimental hypothesis has been formulated, a decision is made about the **sample** of people that will be studied. If the results of the experiment are to be applied to the general human population, then the chosen sample must be **representative** of that total population. If the investigation is restricted to the behaviour of a target population, for example teenagers, then the sample must be fully representative of the teenage population.

The most popular method of **sampling** is **random** sampling whereby everyone theoretically has an equal chance of being selected, such as a random selection of teenagers. Sometimes the research demands that a certain **stratum** or a **quota** of the population are represented. For example, the researcher may wish to compare certain aspects of behaviour across the life span. To ensure that the sample includes a representative number of people from each age group these are specified in advance. In this way the sample can be seen to be representative of all ages. Some of the problems associated with sampling are discussed in Reading 9.5.

Reading 9.5   Sampling

The psychologist's choice of a sample of subjects is also likely to be dictated by convenience. By one count, fully 80 per cent of psychological research with humans has made use of college students as subjects (Schultz, 1969). This is not too surprising: because most psychological researchers work in colleges and universities, students – especially those taking psychology courses – provide their most readily available supply of subjects. The heavy reliance on college students as subjects presents certain problems, however. Because most college students are young, white, and middle class, it may not always be possible to generalise from the behaviour of college students to the behaviour of people from other segments of society. For example, a large number of studies have shown that people often devote a great deal of effort to making sure that their behaviour seems consistent to themselves and others. As a result of these studies, consistency has been viewed by many psychologists as a fundamental human motive.

But this conclusion needs to be taken with a grain of salt. In fact, the large majority of studies demonstrating the consistency motive were conducted with college students. It may well be the case that in the course of writing papers and giving class presentations students are taught that consistency is a virtue and inconsistency is a vice. As a result, college students may be especially likely to behave consistently in experiments. If the same experiments were done with people who are not college students, considerably less evidence for a 'fundamental human motive' of consistency might be found.

In fact, the degree to which the results of research can be generalised from one group of people to another depends in large measure on the particular problem being studied. Whereas basic processes of learning and memory may work in much the same way for almost all human beings, patterns of social behaviour are more likely to depend on people's social and cultural background. There is no easy answer to the problem of selecting subjects for psychological research. Being aware of this difficulty, you should ask yourself when reading about a psychological study: 'Who were the subjects? Are their responses typical of what my own would be? Do their findings apply to me?'

Z. Rubin and E.B. McNeil (1981) *Psychology: Being Human*
Harper Row

1 a) A large percentage of participants in psychological research are:
    i)   teachers
    ii) doctors
    iii) students. (1)
   b) Give **two** reasons why it is difficult to generalise from this sample. (4)

2 When could a sample of **one** person be useful? (2)

3 Describe **two** methods of selecting participants for an experiment. (4)

4 Discuss the problems of sampling and suggest ways in which researchers can improve their sampling techniques. (8)

TERMS TO DEFINE

population   random and quota sample   representative sample

It has been suggested that there is no such thing as the perfect sample (Shelley and Cohen 1986). This does not mean that studies with imperfect sampling are of no value. If the researcher is aware of the restricted sample employed, and is cautious in generalising about the results, they may still have value in giving partial insight into the problem investigated.

The selection of the sample group and the choice of **experimental design** are strongly associated. Basically there are three main designs:

1) **Repeated measures** where the same participants are involved in both experimental and control conditions

2) **Matched-subjects** where both experimental and control groups are matched on some variable relevant to the research, e.g. age, sex, ability

3) **Independent-subjects** whereby two groups are randomly allocated into either experimental or control conditions.

Once the experimental procedure starts there are possibilities of further bias. Participants involved in experiments have been shown to be open to suggestions as to what behaviour is expected. Such **demand characteristics** are discussed in Reading 9.6.

Reading 9.6   Demand Characteristics

Suppose that, one day, you participate as a subject in the following experiment. The researcher begins by announcing that the study is designed to examine certain aspects of problem solving. Your task is simple: to work on a series of problems so that your performance on different types can be compared. After providing these instructions, the experimenter leaves. Shortly thereafter, you hear a loud buzzing sound from the next room. You look up, but it soon stops, so you continue working on the problems. At this point, the experimenter sticks her head through the door and remarks: 'Don't pay any attention to that sound. I'm setting up some new equipment, and it's a bit noisy.' She leaves, and soon the sound starts again. You find it distracting, and it interferes with your work on the problems. Once again, though, it stops after a few moments. When it starts once again, you begin to get suspicious. Is it part of the study, you wonder? The experimenter did look nervous when she told you to ignore it, and it's a very unusual sound. After thinking things over for a while, you become convinced that the noise is part of the experiment. 'It's put there on purpose,' you say to yourself. 'The experimenter wants to see if it will stop me from finishing the problems.'

You are very pleased with yourself at having outguessed the researcher. But now, you face another question. What should you do about your knowledge? You think you know the true purpose of the study, and what the experimenter expects to find. But how should you now behave? Should you help her by confirming her predictions (i.e. doing poorly on the problems because of the noise)? Or should you try to confuse her by doing just the opposite?

Actually, regardless of which strategy you choose, the results of the study are no longer valid (Rosnow et al., 1973; Christensen, 1977). This is because they now stem from your beliefs about how you are expected to behave, not from the effects of the independent variable (the noise). In short, your behaviour is now being influenced by what psychologists term *demand characteristics*. Briefly, these are clues which reveal the purpose of an experiment or the hypothesis under study to subjects. Unfortunately, many sources of such information exist. For example, an experimenter can reveal her predictions to subjects through changes in the tone of her voice, or through changes in facial expressions. (Recall that the experimenter in the study discussed here looked nervous while giving certain instructions.) Similarly, such information may be provided by the instructions given, or even by parts of the study itself. Since the presence of such clues can render the results of an experiment meaningless, it is important for researchers to remove them. Fortunately, this can be accomplished in several different ways.

R.A. Baron et al (1980) *Psychology: Understanding Behaviour*
Holt, Rinehart and Winston

1 In the problem solving experiment reported above what was:
   a) the IV introduced to the participants
   b) the 'hidden' IV
   c) the DV?   (3)

2 Why were the results 'no longer valid'?   (2)

3 Describe **two** ways in which the experimenter may unintentionally reveal the purpose of the experiment to the participants.   (2)

4 How can researchers control the effects of demand characteristics?   (6)

TERMS TO DEFINE

confounding variables   demand characteristics
standardised instructions

There is a great deal of evidence from many sources which demonstrates that the experimenter may inadvertently produce the results expected. Rosenthal (1966) in a series of studies investigated such **experimenter expectancy effects** which are discussed in Reading 9.7.

Reading 9.7   Experimenter Expectancy Effects

Robert Rosenthal (1966) has conducted many studies that demonstrate the existence of such *experimenter expectancy effects*. In one study, ten advanced undergraduate and graduate students were recruited to serve as experimenters. Each experimenter was assigned a group of twenty students to serve as subjects. The experimenters were to show the subjects a series of photographs of people's faces. The subjects were to guess the degree of 'success' or 'failure' expressed in each face, on a scale that went from – 10 (extreme failure) to + 10 (extreme success). The experimenters were all given the same set of instructions about how to conduct the experiment and were told not to deviate from them. Finally, the experimenters were given an idea of the average ratings they could expect to obtain in the study, on the basis of previous research. Half were told that most people tended to rate the faces in the photos as quite successful; the other half were told that people tended to rate the faces as quite unsuccessful. After this briefing, the experimenters began their research. The results of the Rosenthal study were clearcut: the experimenters who were led to expect 'success' ratings in fact obtained much more 'successful' ratings from their subjects than did the experimenters who were led to expect failure ratings.
   How do experimenter expectancy effects work? The best guess is that

experimenters do not intentionally set out to shape their subjects' responses. Nevertheless, subtle nonverbal cues such as facial expressions and tone of voice can provide signals to the subject as to what sort of response is expected. And once they have picked up on these cues, subjects may unconsciously shift their responses in the direction that the experimenter seems to expect.

Z. Rubin and E.B. McNeil (1981) *Psychology: Being Human*
Harper Row

1 In the Rosenthal experiment reported above:
   a) Who were the participants?
   b) What was the hypothesis?
   c) What was the IV?   (3)

2 Report, in your own words, the results of the study.   (4)

3 Find **one** research example other than those discussed which demonstrates experimenter expectancy effects.   (6)

4 What reasons have been suggested to explain experimenter expectancy effects?   (6)

TERMS TO DEFINE

experimenter expectancy effects   self-fulfilling prophecy

Silverman (1977) noted that such co-operation may be due to the participants wishing to present themselves in a favourable light and not from a desire to confirm the experimenter's hypothesis. This desire to present themselves favourably may result in participants becoming worried or apprehensive about how they will be evaluated by the experimenter (Rosenberg 1969). Such **evaluation apprehension** has been shown to be prevalent in experimental research and Carlsmith, Ellsworth and Aronson (1976) found that the desire to be seen favourably was stronger than demand characteristics and expectancy effects.

It is essential that all other variables are held constant throughout the experiment, so that the experimenter can be satisfied that observed changes are due to the variables being manipulated (the **independent variables**). Otherwise it is possible that some other variables, such as the experimental effects discussed above, might have confounded the results.

Topic-related Essays

1 Critically evaluate methods used for investigating psychology.

2 What are the characteristics of the scientific method used by psychologists?

3 Discuss, with reference to studies, ethical problems in psychology.

You now have almost enough knowledge to embark on your own experimental work. Before you start you might find it useful to be taken through the report of a **psychology experiment** in Reading 9.8.

Reading 9.8   A Psychology Experiment

Twelve sets of identical twins aged 18 were selected. These subjects represent a very small sample from the fairly large population of adult identical twins aged 18 – or the larger population of all adult identical twins – or the even larger population of humans. The twins were asked to learn some poetry. From each pair of twins, one was chosen to join the group which was to do the learning under quiet conditions, while the other was put into the group which was to learn poetry under noisy conditions. By dividing our sample into two groups, and by giving them different treatments, we will (we hope) create two populations of scores. These scores are obtained after 10 minutes of learning, and they reflect the degree of material mastered. The stages of the experiment are shown below.

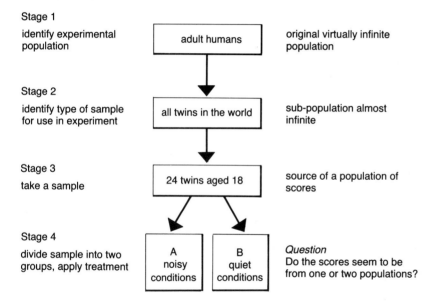

Stage 1
identify experimental population

adult humans

original virtually infinite population

Stage 2
identify type of sample for use in experiment

all twins in the world

sub-population almost infinite

Stage 3
take a sample

24 twins aged 18

source of a population of scores

Stage 4
divide sample into two groups, apply treatment

A
noisy conditions

B
quiet conditions

Question
Do the scores seem to be from one or two populations?

From an experimental point of view, the scores obtained in A and B can now be regarded as two populations. From a statistical point of view, we can't tell whether the numbers from A and B have come from two populations until we have carried out tests. If they seem to have come from one population, then we have to conclude that in applying our experimental treatment we did not create enough effect for the scores to be distinguishable. Our experiment did not 'work'. If, on the other hand, our scores are distinguishable, we can conclude that the experimental manipulations did have an effect.

Although we know what we did when we conducted the experiment, in terms of applying this or that treatment, we can't tell whether what we did had any effect until after we have looked at the results, and perhaps subjected them to statistical analysis. It is as if, when we conduct our analysis, we have to pretend that we don't really know what happened before.

If the learning ability scores appear to have come from two populations, A with noise and B without noise, then it can be concluded that noise does have a particular effect. However, taking the experiment as part of the broader context of psychological understanding, we would hope to generalise our findings from the twins actually used in the study to all humans. If we talk of 'learning' generally, as opposed to poetry learning, then we are making another generalisation, but this time in terms of the material being learnt.

F. Clegg (1984) *Simple Statistics* (2nd edn) Cambridge University Press

1 In the reported experiment identify:
   a) the experimental population
   b) the sample population.   (2)

2 a) Describe how you would select participants for this experiment. What is this method called?   (3)
   b) Identify **one** variable that should be controlled.   (2)

3 In writing the report of this study how would you present and summarise the data? Give **two** examples.   (4)

4 Why were twins used as participants in this study? Give **two** advantages and **two** disadvantages associated with the use of twins in experimental research.   (8)

TERMS TO DEFINE

control group   replication   statistics

A laboratory experiment is often seen as the most rigorous test of a hypothesis. In a controlled laboratory experiment the experimenter can isolate factors seen to be important from extraneous variables. However, the artificiality of the situation and the possibility of bias from experimental artifacts often results in a lack of confidence about the ecological validity of the research (i.e. whether the results would be the same in situations outside the laboratory).

Displaying the results of the experiment is also important. Activity 9.2 will give you the opportunity to do this.

By taking the research outside the laboratory into a natural setting we can be more confident about the generalisability of the results. Often the participants in a **field experiment** are unaware that they are participants in an experiment, so many experimental artifacts are eliminated. But this is not without its problems as can be seen in Reading 9.9.

One problem associated not only with research in the field but with all psychological research is that related to **ethics**. In the research discussed above, individuals were often involved without their knowledge or permission. Most social psychologists would find such experiments reasonable if the independent variables were normal occurrences in their daily lives and the setting was a public place. Much discussion has centred on this and other **ethical considerations** in psychology, some of which are discussed in Reading 9.10.

Activity 9.2

The results of an experiment demonstrating the effects of interference on memory are given below. If you were writing a report on this experiment, give **two** examples of how these could be displayed in the results section.

The Effects of Interference in Learning Pair-Associated Words		
	no. of trials to reach criterion performance	
S	Similar word pairs	unrelated word pairs
1	4	2
2	5	1
3	3	3
4	4	2
5	6	3
6	3	2

Reading 9.9   The Field Experiment

Although the field experiment may seem to be an ideal combination of the strict rules of experimentation with the realism of natural behaviour settings, it too has some disadvantages. These potential problems concern the nature of the independent variable, the nature of the dependent variable, the ethics of the experiment, and the practical difficulties involved.

Because the experimenter is working in a complex natural setting where many events may be occurring simultaneously, the independent variable in the study must be fairly obvious. For example, suppose you wanted to see whether people would help a person who dropped some packages. If the packages were dropped in the middle of a crowded rock concert, the behaviour would probably go unnoticed by the majority of people in the audience. Thus, the investigator conducting a field experiment must be sure that the independent variable is sufficiently strong to make an impact on potential subjects. Otherwise, a failure to respond will be difficult to interpret.

The dependent variable in a field experiment must also be selected carefully. The experimenters must be able to readily observe and reliably judge the dependent-variable behaviour. In the supermarket experiment, for example, it was very easy for the experimenters to record whether a person tried the sample produce and whether the product was purchased. In contrast, if the experimenters had been interested in more subtle facial reactions that might indicate approval of the product, their task would have been much more difficult. Because of these difficulties, the dependent variables in field experiments tend to be rather large-scale behaviours, frequently scored in a present-or-absent fashion.

K. Deaux and L.S. Wrightsman (1984) *Social Psychology in the 80s* (4th edn)
Brooks Cole

1 In a field experiment what problems are associated with:
   a) the IV
   b) the DV?   (2)
   Give **one** example of each.   (2)

2 a) A field experiment offers the most rigorous control of variables.   TRUE/FALSE
   b) The artificiality of the laboratory experiment affects external validity.   TRUE/FALSE
   c) The experimenter in the field has control over the independent variables.   TRUE/FALSE   (3)

3 Describe **one** research example of a field experiment.   (6)

4 Discuss, with examples, the advantages and disadvantages of field experiments.   (8)

TERMS TO DEFINE

field experiment

Reading 9.10   Ethical Considerations

Ethics in psychological research have become a controversial issue in the past decade or so. In large part this is because we are now more aware of the negative consequences that sometimes result from the procedures we use in studying human beings. Consider, for example, the following hypothetical studies:

A researcher is interested in studying the effects of punishment on children's problem-solving behaviour. Punishment is operationalised as a five-volt electric shock delivered to the child's palm whenever the child makes a mistake on a test item.

In a second experiment, a researcher decides to explore developmental trends in children's cheating behaviour. The young subjects are not told that the experimental setting has been designed to facilitate their cheating on a test; nor do they know that the researcher is watching them through a one-way mirror.

A third study is designed to evaluate the effect of environmental control on the mortality rate of nursing-home residents. Two groups of elderly adults are recruited. One group – the experimental condition – is given responsibility and control over scheduling their daily activities; the other group – the control condition – is exposed to the usual nursing-home procedure, which entails little personal responsibility and environmental control.

Each of the above examples raises a question about research ethics. In the first example, the question is very obvious: Is it necessary to use electric shock to study the effect of punishment on children's learning? Clearly the answer is no. Even if one argues that a five-volt shock is mild and unlikely to cause any physical damage, one cannot ignore the potential for psychological trauma to the child in such a situation. The problems in the second example are perhaps less obvious. Observing subjects without their knowledge and without their fully understanding the nature of the experiment not only undermines interpersonal trust, but may well place these individuals at risk from psychological harm (for instance, acute embarrassment and negative self-evaluation) should they later find out that others have observed them cheating. Finally, even the intervention study described in the third experiment raises an important question about ethical research practices. If the new intervention technique proves to be successful in reducing the mortality rate of nursing-home residents (or at least postpones death for a short time), is it ethical to withhold it from the control group? If it is not, how are we to gauge the effects of the new technique without employing a control group?

Evaluating the ethics of a particular research study can be a very complicated task, as the above examples suggest. While some studies (for instance, the first-described experiment) clearly violate standard ethical guidelines for research with humans, others are in an ethical 'grey area.' For example, standard ethical procedures require that subjects be informed about the nature of the experiment, including the procedures to be used. This requirement, however, jeopardises the validity of certain types of research – particularly studies that use deception. In such cases, the risk of withholding full information from subjects must be weighed against the potential benefits to be derived from the experiment. The final decision on whether or not to employ deception, or any other procedure, is usually made by a research ethics peer review board. This board, which is found in virtually every research institution, reviews all research proposals involving human subjects for possible violations of standard ethical practices.

It is generally recognised that research with children and other groups who are relatively powerless (e.g. the retarded, prisoners, inmates in mental institutions, nursing-home residents, etc.) poses even greater potential ethical problems for the investigator. For children, parental consent is always required before participation in research is allowed. Yet parental consent is no guarantee that the child will participate voluntarily. Sometimes subtle pressures (from parents, peers, teachers, or researchers) are enough to coerce the child into participating when he or she really does not want to. Such coercion, whether used with children or others, is in clear violation of research ethics.

D. Brodzinsky et al (1986) *Lifespan Human Development* (3rd edn)
Holt, Rinehart and Winston

1 Explain why each of the three studies reported above was not ethical.   (6)

2 Name **two** groups of participants most likely to create potential ethical problems for the experimenter.   (2)

3 What 'subtle pressures' are sometimes used to persuade people to participate in research when they do not wish to do so?   (2)

4 Discuss ethical problems involved in psychology and give examples taken from reported studies.   (8)

TERMS TO DEFINE

debriefing

Guidelines on a 'code of conduct for psychologists' are available from the British Psychological Society and full details are given in Suggestions For Further Reading at the end of the current chapter. All researchers (including students such as yourself) should try to ensure that every experiment undertaken is useful at some level.

Perhaps you have undertaken some psychological research and it is now time to write up your report. You might find Activity 9.3 helpful.

Activity 9.3

A repeated measures design was used in an experiment investigating how categorisation of anagrams improves performance. You will find below an extract from a student's report of the Methods and Results sections of this experiment. Read through the report and see if you can find at least **two** places where the description needs expanding to give more information, and at least **two** sources of possible bias.

METHOD

Design
A repeated measures design was used with participants solving anagrams in two conditions.

Subjects
Five students on an introductory course in psychology took part in the experiment.

Apparatus
1 Two lists of 36 anagrams were compiled. Each list was organised into six groups. One list was presented in categories and the other in random lists (see Appendix A).
2 Stopwatch (or watch with second hand).

Procedure
The group were presented with Set A (categorised anagrams) and advised not to turn over the sheet until requested. The following instructions were then given:

207

'On the sheet in front of you are a number of anagrams (jumbled up words). When requested I would like you to solve as many as you can until requested to stop. You will then be presented with a second set to solve. Do you understand? (Pause). You may begin.' After five minutes the group was asked to stop and the sheets collected. Set B was then administered and the process repeated for a further five minutes.

RESULTS

set A (categorised)	set B (non-categorised)
18	9
36	34
14	7
20	10
30	25

By now you should have a reasonable understanding of the discipline of psychology, and its associated problems and controversies. The time may well be approaching when this knowledge may be put to the test in the form of **exams**. It is at this time that, as a psychology student, you may like to put into practice many of the techniques you have come across during your studies. In Chapter Ten we shall try to apply some psychological knowledge and consider the question: **Can psychology help you study more effectively?**

SUGGESTIONS FOR FURTHER READING

Main texts

British Psychological Society (1985) *A Code of Conduct for Psychologists* in *Bulletin of the British Psychological Society* (1985) 38, 41–43.

F. Clegg (1982) *Simple Statistics* Cambridge University Press

N. Hayes and S. Orrell (1987) *Psychology: An Introduction* Longman

Other useful texts

S.J. Gould (1981) *The Mismeasure of Man* Penguin (a critical discussion of the use of psychometrics)

P. Harris (1986) *Designing and Reporting Experiments* Open University Press

S. Miller (1984) *Experimental Design and Statistics* (2nd edn) Methuen

Z. Rubin and E.B. McNeill (1985) *Psychology: Being Human* (4th edn) Harper Row (readable chapters on methods)

D. Shelley and D. Cohen (1986) *Testing Psychological Tests* Croom Helm

S. Walker (1985) *Experimental Design and Statistics* Methuen

Stimulus Questions

A psychologist wanted to study how experimenter effects could influence sense of humour. For her study, she used two male postgraduate students as experimenters. Both of the students were in their early twenties, but one of them (Experimenter A) always presented himself very formally and wore a suit and tie; whereas the other one (Experimenter B) usually dressed very casually and had a relaxed, informal manner. The experimenters were asked to act in their normal manner during the experiment, but the words which they had to say to the subjects were written down beforehand, so that both experimenters would use exactly the same words.

The subjects, who were college students taking courses in psychology, were asked to look through a set of 10 cartoons, and also to read through 10 written jokes. Then they rated how funny each one was on a 0–10 scale. Each experimenter tested 15 subjects. The table below summarises their results.

	Experimenter A	Experimenter B
mean rating for cartoons	6·3	7·8
mean rating for jokes	4·7	6·4

9.1 How many subjects were there altogether? (1)

9.2 Why were the words that the experimenters had to say written down beforehand? (2)

9.3 What is this precaution called? (2)

9.4 Suggest **one** disadvantage of using psychology students as the subjects in this experiment. (2)

9.5 Describe a practical method of obtaining a more representative sample for a study like this. (3)

9.6 What is a representative sample? (2)

9.7 If the psychologist wanted to introduce two more experimenters into the study, what should they be like? Give a reason for your answer. (3)

9.8 Why do you think that the cartoons were rated more highly than the written jokes overall? (3)

9.9 Suggest **two** reasons why the ratings were different for the two groups. (4)

9.10 If you were conducting this study yourself, describe **one** other control that you would introduce, stating why you think it would be important. (3)

Methodology Questions

You have been asked to do a study investigating how reliable observational studies are. You and your friend plan to make a set of written observations of the behaviour of a pet animal, taken at the same time, and then to compare them to see whether your observations are similar. Make your suggestions as practical as possible, such that you and your friend could actually carry out the study if you were asked to.

9.1 Describe how you will find the animal that you are going to observe. What type of animal will it be? (Remember that you want the animal to produce a range of behaviour that you can describe easily.) (2)

9.2 What would you consider to be a practical length of time to observe the animal for? Give a reason for your answer. (2)

9.3 What is reliability? (2)

9.4 Name and describe the three main ways of testing for reliability in psychological tests (e.g. intelligence tests). (6)

9.5 What is inter-observer reliability? (2)

One way of classifying observational reports is to count the types of descriptive statements which each observer has made in their report. Observational statements can be divided into three categories: i) descriptions of behaviour, ii) descriptions of motives or intentions, and iii) anthropomorphic descriptions.
9.6 What does anthropomorphic mean? (2)

9.7 Using those three categories, draw up a simple table which would allow you to compare your report with that of your friend. (You do not need to fill in any numbers.) (2)

9.8 What is a significance test? (3)

9.9 What significance test could you use to analyse your results? (2)

9.10 Describe one other way that you could present the results of this study. (2)

10

Can Psychology Help You Study More Effectively?

'. . . questioning, summarising, task setting and time allocating, coupled with the approaches for coping with anxiety, are a means of enjoying and succeeding in learning in almost every aspect of your life.'

D. Acres (1987)

Plate 10

Readings on 'Can Psychology Help You Study Effectively?'

Most of you reading this book have been approaching psychology for the first time, and may have found some of the concepts difficult to grasp, or to express clearly. What we hope to do in this chapter is to give you some practical help, based on psychological research, on how you can develop your study skills and be successful in your coursework and examinations.

Most introductory courses in psychology involve several aspects such as listening to talks or lectures and making notes, reading texts for information, answering questions and writing essays. Your understanding of psychology will often be tested by examinations. A few ideas on what might be helpful in these areas follows:

Taking notes

When taking notes it is extremely important that the central ideas or concepts are noted. The term **keyword** has been used to identify words or phrases which are most memorable and carry the essential information of the sentence or paragraph. In Reading 10.1 the use of keywords in remembering information is discussed.

Reading 10.1 Keywords

Howe and Godfrey (1977) designed an experiment to find out what the effect would be of asking students to write down the three words that they considered were important from each sentence of a prose passage, compared with writing down the whole of each sentence. In two separate experiments with 14 and 16-year-old pupils, no significant differences were found between the pupils who wrote down three important words and pupils who wrote down everything. This result confirms the findings of Howe, Ormond and Singer. It was found, however, that pupils who scored the highest on the test recorded a significantly greater number of words considered pertinent to the test questions, than had the low test scorers. This finding suggests that it is the actual words selected which is the important factor in aiding recall, and not that the number of words to be noted should be limited.

Since the above investigation did not include a review period, Howe and Godfrey carried out a further experiment with undergraduates acting as subjects and incorporating a review period. This led to the finding that those students who noted three important words from each paragraph (as opposed to each sentence), had significantly higher test scores after review than the students who were instructed to read, copy or write down the first three words of each paragraph.

There does seem to be a limited amount of evidence then, that using key words may have a beneficial effect on recall, especially if the words chosen for recording are genuinely key words.

L.S. Norton (1981) *Visible Language Journal* 15 (p. 75)

1 How old were the participants in the Howe and Godfrey (1977) experiment?   (1)

2 Note the findings in your own words.   (4)

3 In the later study with undergraduates which group had the significantly higher test scores?   (2)

4 Select a topic from your notes and pick out the keywords.   (6)

TERMS TO DEFINE

keyword

Hartley and Davies (1978), after reviewing over 60 studies made during a 50-year period, found that note-taking did appear to help people remember more about what they had heard or seen. Later research has suggested that the students who do best in tests not only take notes but also use the notes after they have taken them (Norton 1981).

Reading 10.2   Taking Notes

While you are taking notes remember the following points about layout:

1 Leave plenty of space to allow room for further notes to expand upon the original notes or to make them clearer. Other ways of leaving space are writing on only one side of the paper or allowing a large gap between each line of the notes.

2 Number each point and use headings. It is much easier to use notes later if they are arranged in a pattern.

3 Use different coloured inks for the same reason. You could use one colour for headings and another for notes or write important points in different colours.

4 Use diagrams, charts, graphs, drawings and other visual means as often as possible. Pictures are more easily remembered than words.

5 Use abbreviations to save time but keep to standard abbreviations; do not use several different abbreviations for the same purpose.

Another way of taking notes is described by Tony Buzan in his book *Use Your Head* (BBC Publications, 1974). With this method, the main idea of a lecture or chapter in the book is placed in the centre of the page. The related ideas and facts are written around this and linked to the main idea by lines which show their relationship to it and to each other. The more important the idea, the nearer it is placed to the centre of the page. In these notes only single words and, occasionally, phrases are used. The result is a diagram or pattern. The advantages claimed for this method are as follows:

1 Because only key words and phrases are used, the notes are much quicker to write.

2 For the same reason, they are much quicker to read.

3 The notes are much briefer than conventional notes so there is a saving in space and paper. It should be possible to get all the ideas of a chapter on one page.

4 There is space available to add new ideas. Also the new ideas can be integrated into the existing notes and not just tacked on to the end or at the side somewhere.

5 The notes resemble a picture or diagram and are much easier to remember than words on a series of lines.

6 Most important, the notes reflect in their arrangement the relationship between the ideas in the book or lecture. Provided the key words and phrases have been chosen carefully, it it should be easy by a process of association to 'hook' all the ideas out of the brain.

C. Parsons (1976) *How to Study Effectively* Arrow

1 Complete the following sentence from the text: 'It is much easier to use notes if they are . . . .' (1)

2 Give **three** advantages of taking patterned notes. (3)

3 Choose a psychological topic on which you have notes. Make patterned notes on this, perhaps using colours and numbers to pick out the important ideas. (6)

TERMS TO DEFINE

patterned notes

Most students prefer to take notes in a linear form but Buzan (1974) recommends the use of patterned notes. This involves **taking notes** in the normal way, and then after the lecture making a map or 'pattern' of the key concepts, as discussed in Reading 10.2. This technique is useful because it encourages you to review the lecture which will help in future revision. A comparison between the two types of note-taking showing the percentage of keywords to total words can be seen in Figure 10.1.

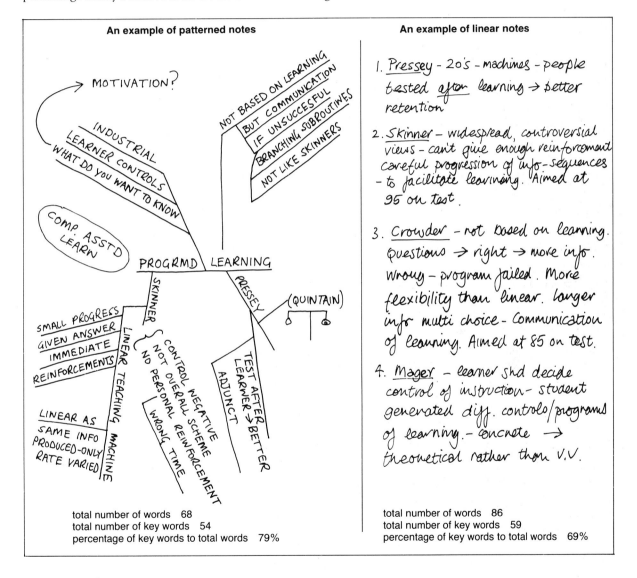

An example of patterned notes

total number of words   68
total number of key words   54
percentage of key words to total words   79%

An example of linear notes

1. Pressey - 20's - machines - people tested after learning → better retention

2. Skinner – widespread, controversial views - can't give enough reinforcement careful progression of info - sequences - to facilitate learning. Aimed at 95 on test.

3. Crowder - not based on learning. Questions → right → more info. Wrong – program failed. More flexibility than linear. longer info multi choice - Communication of learning. Aimed at 85 on test.

4. Mager – learner shd decide control of instruction - student generated diff. controls/programs of learning. - concrete → theoretical rather than V.V.

total number of words   86
total number of key words   59
percentage of key words to total words   69%

When identifying keywords in your notes it might be helpful to underline them or highlight them with a fluorescent marker. Although research into the value of highlighting and underlining is rather mixed, with some studies demonstrating the value and others not, many students feel that it helps them in revision. If you feel that it could help you then Activity 10.1 might prove advantageous to you.

Activity 10.1

Choose some notes which you have made on a psychological topic. Go through them and highlight the main points or keywords either with a fluorescent marker or by underlining in a coloured ink.

Go through the notes again and this time look at any headings. See if you can change each heading into a question. Then go through the following section trying to answer these questions.

Do you think this will help you to remember the topic better? Test yourself on the topic now and at regular intervals. Do you notice any improvement?

Reading texts efficiently

Many students complain that there is too much information for them to remember! This is a problem for all students and not only those studying psychology. Psychological research into memory has proved helpful in providing guidelines on how organisation in memory can aid recall of information. One technique for improving memory of written material, such as that in a textbook, is known as the **PQRST method** and was introduced by Thomas and Robinson (1982). This method is discussed briefly in Reading 10.3.

Reading 10.3 PQRST Method

The method takes its name from the first letters of its five stages: *Preview, Question, Read, Self-recitation,* and *Test*. We can illustrate the method by showing how it would apply to studying a chapter in this textbook. In the first stage, students preview the material in a chapter to get an idea of its major topics and sections. Previewing involves reading the table of contents at the beginning of the chapter, skimming the chapter while paying special attention to the headings of main sections and subsections, and carefully reading the summary at the end of the chapter. This kind of preview induces students to organise the chapter, perhaps even leading to the rudiments of a hierarchical organisation like that just shown. As we have repeatedly noted, organising material aids one's ability to retrieve it.

The second, third, and fourth stages (Question, Read, and Self-recitation) apply to each major section of the chapter as it is encountered. In this book, for example, a chapter typically has five to eight major sections, and students would apply the Question, Read, and Self-recitation stages to each section before going on to the next one. In the Question stage, students carefully read the section and subsection headings and turn these into questions. In the Read stage, students read the section with an eye toward answering these questions. And in the Self-recitation stage, the reader tries to recall the main ideas in the section and recites the information (either subvocally or, preferably, aloud if alone). For example, if you were applying these stages to the present section of this chapter, you might look at the headings and make up such questions as 'How much can the short-term memory span be increased?' or 'What exactly is the PQRST method?' Next you would read this section and try to determine answers to your questions (for example, 'One person was able to increase his short-term memory span to nearly 80 digits'). Then you would try to recall the main ideas (for example, 'You can increase the size of a chunk but not the number of chunks'). The Question and Read stages almost certainly induce students to elaborate the material while encoding it; the Self-recitation stage induces the student to practise retrieval.

The fifth, or Test, stage occurs after finishing an entire chapter. Students try to recall the main facts from what they have read and to understand how the various facts relate to one another. This stage prompts elaboration and offers further practice at retrieval. In summary, the PQRST method relies on three basic principles for improving memory: organising the material, elaborating the material, and practising retrieval.

R.L. Atkinson et al (1987) *Introduction to Psychology* (9th edn)
Harcourt Brace Jovanovich

1 '. . . . material aids one's ability to retrieve it.'   (1)

2 What does PQRST mean?   (1)

3 Note **two** principles on which the method is based.   (2)

4 Describe **one** study which demonstrates the importance of organisation in memory.   (4)

5 Discuss **two** ways of measuring memory. Give **one** experimental example of each.   (8)

TERMS TO DEFINE

cognitive maps   preview   retrieval

A central feature of this method is creating questions about each section and then setting about answering them. Anderson (1980) found that satisfactory questions can often be formed from section headings. Generating such questions and then trying to answer them helps you to organise the material in a way that is meaningful to you. Perhaps you can apply this technique as you read this book.

Writing essays

Essays can be of varying length, often determined by what is asked. Sometimes this is quite specific and can be answered briefly, and the question structures your answer. Other essays are more open to interpretation and demand that you structure your answer and decide what to include. Such essays may be coursework essays (where reference material has to be selected for use) or exam essays (where reference is to material available in memory).

It is often at the essay writing stage that the introductory psychology student begins to panic. Mature students who are returning to study after many years away from writing are especially vulnerable. Even students who are taking psychology as one of several subjects at examination level may find themselves confused because writing an essay in psychology is very different from essays written previously, such as on language and literature courses.

Figure 10.2 *Keywords in essay writing*

Questions in examinations vary in the approach they ask you to take. In every question there are certain key words (a number of these are verbs) which tell you the type of question it is and exactly which approach the examiner wishes you to take.

Two common groupings are *descriptive* and *analytical* questions. Below are listed fifteen descriptive and nineteen analytical words and phrases which occur commonly. Each is then defined.

Descriptive

Define – set down the precise meaning of a word or phrase. Show that the distinctions implied in the definition are necessary.
Describe – give a detailed or graphic account of.
Distinguish between – note the difference between.
Give an account of – describe in some detail.
How . . . – in what way, by what means or method, to what extent.
Illustrate – use a figure or diagram to explain or clarify, *or* make it clear by the use of concrete examples.
Outline – describe without detail, summarise.
Relate – narrate (the more usual meaning in examinations): to show how things are connected and to what extent (they are alike or affect each other.
State – present in brief, clear form.
Show how – make clear by what means.
Summarise – give a concise account of the chief points or substance of a matter, omitting details and examples.
Trace – follow the development or history of a topic from some point of origin.
What . . . – of which kind, which?
When . . . – at what time, on which day or year, etc.?
Where . . . – at/to what place, in what particular?

Analytical

Account for – explain.
Analyse – make a detailed description and criticism of.
Argue the case for – back your opinion by reasoning in favour of it.
Assess – determine the amount or value of.
Calculate – reckon or compute by mathematics.
Comment upon – offer an opinion (avoiding the use of 'I . . .').
Compare – look for similarities and differences between.
Consider – express your thoughts and observations about.
Contrast – set in opposition in order to bring out differences.
Criticise – give your judgement about the merit of theories or opinions or about the truth of facts, and back by a discussion of the evidence.
Discuss – investigate or examine by argument, giving reasons pro and con.

Evaluate – make an appraisal of the worth of something, in the light of its truth or utility.
Examine – inquire into, attempt to discover, investigate.
Explore – approach in a questioning manner.
Explain – make plain, interpret, account for, illustrate the meaning of.
Interpret – expound the meaning of; make clear and explicit; usually giving your own judgement also.
Justify – show adequate grounds for decisions or conclusions.
Review – to make a survey of, examining the subject critically.
Why . . . – for what reason(s).

Other types of questions

Some questions combine both types of questions as the examiner looks for a combination of facts and analysis, as in 'Describe and explain'.

Quotations usually indicate some kind of *analysis* is required.

'*Brief*' or '*List*' mean what they say. A paragraph for the first and a straightforward descriptive list, such as that above.

'*Compare and contrast*' type questions require you to point out the similarities and differences between two items, events or ideas. A good answer would focus on one *aspect* at a time and find the differences and similarities.

An example – Q. Compare and contrast cars and motor-bikes.

Aspects – Cost ———————— compare – similarities
contrast – differences
Safety ———————— compare – similarities
contrast – differences

The same applies to '*For and Against*' type questions, where, although you can argue all the points 'for' and then all the points, 'against' separately the answers which effectively argue for and against aspect-by-aspect can be the most successful.

In social science subjects such as History, Sociology and Economics, it is important to distinguish whether the examiner is asking you about the *causes* or *reasons for* or whether you are being asked about the *results of* events or actions.

• 'Factors', 'Account for', 'What problems faced?' – suggest you should write about reasons and causes.

• 'Achievements', 'Effects', 'Impact', 'How successful', 'The importance of' – suggest you should write about the results or consequences of an event, an idea or action.

Some useful advice on **essay writing** can be found in Table 10.1 and Reading 10.4.

Table 10.1 *Answering essay questions*

1 Before you start writing **read** the question carefully.

2 Look for keywords in the question. Several of such **keywords in essay writing** can be found in Figure 10.2.

3 Remember to refer to the question frequently as you write and answer what is asked, not what you would rather write about. This is especially important in an exam situation when you have revised topics. It is so easy to give everything you have revised, even if it does not relate to the question! This is a waste of time and effort as the examiner will only award marks for material relating to the question asked.

4 If you write as if writing to someone who knows nothing about psychology, you will find that you introduce the topic easily and simply. If you give your essay to a friend, or an older brother or sister, or parent, and they can understand what you have written then you are writing well.

5 You are supposed to write objectively (as if you are not personally involved and have no strong, biased views). This means avoiding the use of phrases such as 'I think . . .'. Instead you could say 'It is possible . . .' or 'Research shows . . .'.

6 Finally **presentation**. Now here your grandparents will be of help. Education 50 years ago stressed handwriting, spelling and the appearance of work. Although obviously the content of your work is the most important aspect, and some students will still gain high grades with bad spelling and writing, it is true to say that if the work **looks** good and is easy to read then the person marking is going to look more favourably at it, and this may be reflected in the grade given.

Reading 10.4 Essay Writing

Exam essays have a beginning, a middle and an end. The beginning or introduction will have several of these features:

● a summary of what you are about to argue or describe
● an indication of your attitude to the question asked
● the key words from the question incorporated into the above, to indicate that you have read and understood the question

- a back-up reason for any first statements made (this can be expanded upon or added to in the middle)
- definitions of any terms that clearly need to be defined in order for you to proceed with your answer
- it will be one or two paragraphs long
- it will indicate that more needs to be described, explained or argued to clarify what has been said so far.

It is my experience that introductions to essays are often of a very poor standard. Some candidates obviously get stuck in trying to express themselves. You can feel they are wondering what to write. Others simply restate the title and say something like 'I will now go on to answer the question': a poor start. Yet others start a long, long background account of a situation, event, period, etc. before beginning to make any relevant points in answer to the question. So I would suggest if you find introductions to essays difficult you try some of these alternatives:

- Practise them before the exam, using the principles outlined.
- Write a very short, one or two sentence, introduction before moving on to the essential core of the essay – the middle part.
- Don't waste time thinking of 'special' things to say in an introduction. Get on with answering the question in a straightforward manner, using your plan.

The middle
The middle will normally contain your key facts. They will be expressed precisely and specifically and in as much detail as the question appears to demand. Try to avoid generalisations or covering up phrases which attempt to conceal that you can't remember a piece of information.

Assemble your major facts in a clear manner and show how they are relevant to the answer. Where the essay involves you arguing a case, citing reasons, explaining causes, analysing consequences and other forms of analysis, let the facts support your arguments.

The end – your conclusion
Concluding paragraphs are often as inadequate as introductions! As with introductions it is best not to think of them as being special concluding paragraphs.

Ideally, you will reach a coherent logical conclusion at the end of your essay. It does not have to side with any particular issue that the question focusses on. You can argue that the evidence is conflicting, the fors and againsts evenly balanced or that evidence is insufficient. Practise this type of conclusion in your preparation for the examination.

If you find concluding paragraphs difficult, don't over-concern yourself with them. Simply answer the question to the best of your ability and when you have done so – stop.

Finally, in conclusion, try not to start your final paragraphs with 'Finally . . .' or 'In conclusion . . .' It is boring, repetitive and tends to cause examiners to yawn!

It is important to remember that the bulk of marks in the vast majority of essay type questions are awarded to the quality of the information and argument that forms the middle of most answers.

D. Acres (1987) *How to Pass Exams Without Anxiety* Northcote House

1 Describe **two** features of a good introduction to an essay. (2)

2 Note **two** faults you should avoid in writing an essay. (2)

3 Discuss **two** ways in which an essay written in an examination differs from one written as part of your coursework. (4)

4 What is an essay plan? Choose an essay from a past examination paper and draft an essay plan for this. (8)

TERMS TO DEFINE

analysis   essay plan   relevant

The essay writing that you practise during the course should prove useful in the exams. Obviously the technique has to be modified as you are writing in a fixed time period. Nearer to the exam you could practise **timed essays**. You may find this is done in class using past question papers. However, extra practice on your own could mean that you become even better at pacing yourself and making the best use of your time.

Topic-related Essays

1   How can the study of memory processes help people who are revising for exams?

2   Forgetting has been explained in many ways. Discuss, giving evidence, those explanations which you see to be most accurate.

3   Discuss the psychological concepts involved in managing stress in terms of their value for candidates taking important examinations.

Organisation

It is critical that you organise your study time and plan what has to be done. You will probably have deadlines to meet for essays and coursework, and in many cases there will be other subjects demanding your time also. Try to discipline yourself to work out a study timetable such as displayed in Figure 10.3, allowing at least one hour per day.

Some people find that they work better earlier in the day, whereas others find later in the day better. This is something that only you can decide. Perhaps you need to try various times of day to see which suits you best (this only applies if you have a choice of time available!).

Organisation is even more critical during **revision** prior to an examination. Some suggestions are made in Reading 10.5.

Acres (1987) recommends that you reward yourself by taking breaks between working periods. Learning theory principles, as discussed in Chapter Two, have demonstrated how such **positive reinforcement** strengthens learning. The social aspects of revision can also be helpful such as revising with a friend as suggested in Activity 10.2.

DAYS OF THE MONTH OF:	MON	TUES	WED	THURS	FRI	SAT	SUN
(Month)	7	8	9	10	11	12	13
a.m.	SUBJECT A	SUBJECT C	VOLUNTARY WORK	SUBJECT D	WHOLE DAY	SUBJECT E	SUBJECT E
p.m.	WALK SQUASH COFFEE – FRIEND	SHOPPING	SUBJECTS B&C	SUBJECTS B&C	VISIT TO	REVIEW OF ABCD	TV FRIENDS HOME
Evening	SUBJECT B (2 TOPICS)	SUBJECT A (1 TOPIC)	SUBJECT C	SUBJECT B	TOWN	MEET FRIEND AT DISCO	REVIEW CARDS PLAN NEXT WEEK
	14	15	16	17	18	19	20
a.m.							
p.m.							
Evening							
	21	22	23	24	25	26	27
a.m.							
p.m.							
Evening							
	28	29	30	31	1	2	3
a.m.							
p.m.							
Evening							
	4	5	6	7	8	9	10
a.m.							
p.m.							
Evening							

☐ time already committed during the Examination and Revision period e.g. social events, classes, exams

☐ time that may be available for revision: you would fill in subjects or topics in these spaces

Figure 10.3 *An example of a revision timetable*

Reading 10.5 Revision

(1) *Make a revision timetable* day-by-day from now until the examinations begin and for the period between examinations. The problem with revision timetables is that they often go wrong after the first day. To counteract this:
– Have a two week or one week trial period to enable you to determine what tasks you can realistically complete in a day.
– Be flexible e.g. different subject headings for each day will enable you to vary the topics you revise.

(2) *Pin up your timetable* or time plan on a wall in a prominent place e.g. above your table or desk. Coloured pens can make it clear and attractive.

(3) *Revise as you go:* start weeks before the exams. If you haven't started before reading this, start now. It's never too early to start and you can still revise until very close to your examinations. Starting 6 to 8 weeks before the exam is a typical revision period for most students.

(4) *Include in your revision timetable any unfinished work* you still have to do as part of your year's studies. You do not have to complete this work before starting revision. You can revise this subject work as soon as it is completed, so it can become part of your revision.

(5) *Know how you use the 168 hours in the week.* You can use the time chart to

The first week of this timetable is complete in some detail: other weeks can be completed in the same way, if you are continuing to attend full time education during the day, evenings or weekends will become more important and can be sub-divided into smaller units, if necessary.

If you have difficulty in making time to revise or in finding a balance between revision and other activities, completing this time chart may help you identify the hours when it will be most effective to revise. Fill in the spaces in this daily record at the end of each day indicating exactly what you did each hour period. It is important that you record what you did, not what you intended to do.

calculate exactly how you have used the time in one week and record hours in these categories, below. Alternatively, you can do a rough calculation and complete the table below. You have been provided with a daily and weekly column; complete either or both according to which you find easier.

(6) *Set yourself a daily target of revision hours.* An alternative to a large scale or weekly revision timetable is to set yourself a daily target of revision hours e.g. 4 hours a day. This time unit can be shown on a chart marked off in quarter hour units with your favourite colours, to show you effective and concentrated use of time. You could use this idea by itself or alongside marking off topics you have revised on a chart.

Angela, a final year undergraduate, combined this with positive self statements ('It's really working'. 'I've 40 whole days left') to successfully complete her revision. She monitored the quarter hour units on a chart and felt a sense of achievement and optimism: there are a great many quarter hours in 4 hours revision a day for 40 days!

(7) *Working late at night.* There are wide differences in people's ability to work effectively late at night or the early hours of the morning. For a typical student 3 or 4 hours work in an evening is likely to be as much as they can effectively tackle. It would certainly not be advisable to work very late or long the night before an exam. On other nights, developing the effective self-monitoring this book is encouraging, will enable you to decide whether you are working efficiently.

(8) *For routine revision, you can work in short periods of time* i.e. as short as 20–30 mins. Some topics and subjects call for longer periods but numerous sub-topics can be revised in this way. Mathematical, scientific or problem based revision will often require longer periods e.g. 1 hour, to follow through a sequence of techniques and knowledge.

(9) It is important to *set a time limit on completing a task* i.e. 'I will do X by . . .'

Time Chart

	Total hours
	Daily / Weekly

	Daily	Weekly
sleeping, dressing, washing, etc.	_____	_____
travel	_____	_____
classes, laboratories, etc.	_____	_____
going out socially	_____	_____
recreation and exercise	_____	_____
watching television	_____	_____
eating	_____	_____
domestic responsibilities and tasks	_____	_____
totals	_____	_____
hours remaining in the day/week that may be used for private study	_____	_____
	(total subtracted from 24 hrs)	(total subtracted from 168 hrs)

D. Acres (1987) *How to Pass Exams Without Anxiety* Northcote House

1 '. . . . is a typical revision period for most students.'   (1)

2 How many hours can a typical student work late at night?   (1)

3 Complete either a daily or weekly time chart.   (4)

4 Suggest at least **three** factors that would improve your concentration during revision.   (6)

TERMS TO DEFINE

revision   self-monitoring   timetable

Activity 10.2

When revising, it is useful to look at the studies which you have learned about, and see which ones of these are true experiments, and which have involved the use of non-experimental methods.

Begin by taking one topic area – such as might be represented by one chapter of this book. Take a piece of paper, and label one side 'experiments', and the other 'non-experimental studies'. Look at each of the studies which you have learned about in that area, and allocate each one to the proper column.

(If you are working with a friend, you could compare your two lists when you have finished doing this to see if your two lists agree.)

Now look at each of the experiments in turn. For each one, write down:

a The independent variable (the thing that caused the results)
b The dependent variable (what the psychologists measured)
c Any controls that were included in the study
d Any confounding variables that could have affected the results.

Then look at each of the non-experimental studies. For each one, write down:

a What kind of a study it is (e.g. case study, naturalistic observation)
b What kind of subjects were included (e.g. children, students)
c What the findings implied
d What other explanations could be put forward for these findings.

Again, if you are working with a friend, you could compare your answers and see if you have come to the same conclusions.

By doing your revision in this way, you will find that you have revised both the particular topic and the psychological methodology together – two lots of work in one!

N. Hayes and S. Orrell (1987) *Psychology: An Introduction* Longman

As noted earlier, organisation of memory is also important for good recall. Several techniques for improving memory named **mnemonics** have been developed, some of which are described in Reading 10.6.

Reading 10.6 Mnemonics

Some of the most commonly used mnemonic devices

A Method of loci ('method of places' or the 'house' technique)
You have to imagine a short walk through a series of locations, perhaps a journey through a familiar street, past well-known buildings or through the rooms in your house or college.

Take each of the (unrelated) words to be remembered in turn (e.g. the items on a shopping list) and associate it with each of your locations. The more bizarre the association, the greater the probability of recalling the words when needed.

B Associations
You find a relationship between the unrelated words by weaving them into a sensible story.

C Rhyme and rhythm
e.g. 'Thirty days hath September' . . . etc.

D Numeric pegword system ('Pigeonhole technique')
Numbers are associated with a rhyming object and you picture the items to be remembered in relation to the relevant pegword.

e.g. one   – bun   egg   ('egg on a bun')
      two   – shoe   sausage   ('sausage in a shoe')
      three – tree   potatoes   ('potatoes growing on a tree')

The items to be remembered are hooked onto the pegword by constructing an image which includes the first item with the bun, the second with the shoes etc.

R.D. Gross (1987) *Psychology: The Science of Mind and Behaviour* Arnold

1 a) What are mnemonics?   (2)
    b) Give **one** example.   (2)

2 The method of loci is . . . . .   (2)

3 What is the difference between the pegword system and the method of loci?   (2)

4 Give **one** example of when mnemonics could prove useful. Critically discuss the value of mnemonics.   (10)

TERMS TO DEFINE

concrete words   dual coding   imagery   mnemonics

Whether such techniques are useful is often questioned. Baddeley (1976) commented on the use of the method of loci for remembering shopping items: '. . . *I must confess that if I need to remember a shopping list, I do not imagine strings of sausages festooned from my chandeliers and bunches of bananas sprouting from my wardrobe. I simply write it down.*' The choice is yours! Any verbal or visual links or associations you make in memory may aid recall.

Revision

Revision is usually associated with the period prior to an examination for most students. This is often seen as 'cramming' information into memory in a few weeks (or in some cases a few days!). Research finds this to be a most ineffective method. Baddeley and Longman (1978) have demonstrated the effectiveness of **distributed practice**, whereby practice spread over a period of two days led to more efficient learning than cramming the learning into one day. Such distributed practice can be used to advantage in revision, as discussed in Reading 10.7.

PEANUTS   by **Schulz**

Reading 10.7   Distributed Practice

Try to organise your revision so that you give at least four sessions to each topic, like this:

Session 1
The preparatory stage, in which you collect and organise the material you are working with. Try starting by writing out sets of exam questions, then reading through all the notes you've got to see what would be relevant to them. Use this session to provide yourself with a file of useful information for that topic, but put any 'just in case' notes on one side – it's probably too late for them anyway. It may not seem as though this is 'real' revision, but the very act of reading through your notes to decide what's relevant and what isn't is effective: you're reading actively this time, for a purpose, and so you'll remember more of it than if you just tried to read through it all.

Session 2
The memorising stage, where you sit down and work with the material to learn

it. This is where you really use those revision exercises that I was just talking about: tree diagrams, mental images etc. Just one of the main ones for each topic – if you have any extra time later you can always come back, but it's important to get through everything at least once.

Session 3
The testing stage, where you try out sample questions as if you were in the exam, and see how well you do. This bit is where you practise the high-powered stuff. You have to get used to working at high speed for longish periods of time. Even though you may know that you can only really do it at peak efficiency on the day, practice always makes it easier, so you do even better! . . .

Session 4
The final stage where you develop a set of last-minute summary notes for checking over on the morning of the exam. This is where you condense all that work down to a few last-minute reminders. Make them as brief as possible – remember that by then it will be far too late to learn anything new, and you'll just want to refresh your memory on the main themes. A small set of postcard-sized reminders should be all you'll need. It will certainly be about all you have time to read on that morning, anyhow!

   If you can fit in any extra sessions for any topic, devote them to work from sessions 2 and 3. Remember that nobody expects you to be superhuman: the important thing is for you to do the best that you can in the time that you have available. This is one way of making sure that you use the time you've got as effectively as possible, and that you don't waste it, either by useless reading or by being bored and not being able to make what you are learning 'sink in'.

N. Hayes (1990) The GCSE Survival Guide Longman

1 Complete the following and put them into the correct order:
   'The testing stage . . . .'
   'The preparatory stage . . . .'
   'The final stage . . . .'
   'The memorising stage . . . .'   (8)

2 Prepare a topic for revision as suggested above using:
   a) a tree diagram/patterned notes
   b) any other mnemonic system such as suggested in Reading 10.6.

3 Which system seems best for you? This may help you to decide which technique you will use most in revision – or perhaps you will use a mixture? This is something only **you** can decide, as some techniques seem to work for some individuals better than for others!   (10)

TERMS TO DEFINE

distribution of practice effect   forgetting curve

   The memory systems previously discussed support the **levels of processing** viewpoint suggested by Craik and Lockhart (1972) (see

Chapter Four) in finding that the more meaningful the coding the better the recall. Using this technique in revision is discussed in Reading 10.8.

Reading 10.8   Levels of processing

The levels of processing theory of memory tells us that if we process the information that we are receiving in some way – in other words, if we actually do something with it, and change its form – then we are likely to remember it better. It also tells us that things are processed most deeply if we have to deal with their meaning, or semantic content, rather than if we just concentrate on more superficial aspects, such as how it looks on the page.

Either on your own, or working in small groups of not more than four people, think about the revision that you will have to do for your next set of exams. (It's a good idea to start by naming a couple of actual topics that you know you will have to learn.) Then, between you, work out six different revision strategies that you could use, which would force you to process the material in a different way.

For example, even a simple thing like making a tape of the information, and playing it back to yourself at times when you are doing other things, means that you have processed the information in a different way than if you simply read through it. Drawing up flowcharts which summarise topics means that you have processed it semantically, as you can't draw up a flowchart of a topic unless you have thought about what the information actually means. Doing it forces you to process the information differently, so the drawing up of flowcharts becomes a strategy that you can use when you revise.

When you have developed your six strategies, think again about what you have to revise, and decide which of the strategies are most suitable for which material. Then compare your list with those of the other groups, if you are working in class.

Are any of them the same?

Which strategies involve processing the information most deeply?

Most important of all, try putting these into practice next time you have an exam coming up. You won't regret it.

N. Hayes and S. Orrell (1987) *Psychology: An Introduction* Longman

1 In your own words explain what is meant by the levels of processing approach.   (3)

2 Fill in the missing terms:
   Drawing up .... which .... topics means you have processed it ..... (1)

3 Describe **one** study which illustrates the levels of processing approach.   (4)

TERMS TO DEFINE

coding   levels of processing approach

An optimum level of arousal is needed to enable you to concentrate and remain attentive. If this level is exceeded then stress may interfere with learning (see Chapter Three especially Readings 3.7 Stress, 3.8 Type A Behaviour and Chapter Eight, especially Reading 8.5 Occupational Stress, for further discussion of the effects of stress on behaviour). Involving friends and other students can be extremely valuable at all times but particularly in times of stress.

Several ways of **coping with anxiety** are suggested in Reading 10.9.

Reading 10.9   Coping with Anxiety

Correct mental attitude
The first step in overcoming the problem of pre-exam nerves is to develop a positive mental attitude. There are a number of ways of doing this.
- Convince yourself first of all that you are **studying for your own benefit** (no one else will benefit or lose if you pass or fail!)
- Try to develop a genuine **eagerness and willingness to study**. As you come to enjoy your studies more, you will find yourself actually looking forward to the exams as the culmination of your course, and the means by which you can reap the rewards of all your hard work.
- Above all, be **confident**.

Awareness
Stress is largely caused by fear of the unknown, which all of us experience to some extent. So try to make yourself aware of the exam and its various aspects well in advance – the marking schemes, structure of the papers and so forth. This will break down the mystique which often surrounds exams, and which causes so much unnecessary pre-exam anxiety.

Preparation
Try to become **well prepared** both physically and mentally, well in advance of the exam. Make sure you really do understand your work as you go through the course; when you come to revise you will be able to do so easily and avoid needless panic. **Be organised**; work to your own timetables as suggested elsewhere; make sure you have everything needed for the day itself. On the night before each exam organise all the things you will need, and the right clothes to wear. All this helps you *feel* well prepared, and gives an important boost to your confidence.

Other remedies
If you have done all these things, and still feel exam nerves building up:
- try going out for a long walk
- get some good fresh air, take some deep breaths and give yourself a good talking to
- try taking some other form of vigorous exercise (swimming, cycling, playing a match, and so on) and put exams and exam nerves right out of your mind.
It may help to talk to someone about the problems – parents, friends, instructors. If you do, make sure the person you talk to is someone you can really trust to be sympathetic, not someone who will only make you feel worse! Sometimes stomach pains can be caused by nerves giving symptoms of

indigestion, or nausea. This can usually be cured quite easily by taking antacids such as Milk of Magnesia, Rennies and so on, from any chemist. Tension-headaches can be cured with aspirin or paracetemol. If you experience severe headaches, or migraine, stronger analgesics would be needed, and you should see your doctor if these persist.

C. Parsons (1987) *How to Study Effectively* Arrow

1 Note **two** ways which can help in developing a positive attitude.   (2)

2 Describe **two** methods which can help to relieve exam nerves.   (4)

3 Relaxation techniques are used in association with clinical therapies. Discuss, with examples, **one** behavioural technique which uses such techniques.   (8)

TERMS TO DEFINE

anxiety   coping strategies   relaxation techniques

We are becoming increasingly aware of the value of **relaxation techniques** in reducing stress levels. Activities such as talking over problems with relatives and friends who are sympathetic, breathing exercises which encourage you to breathe slowly and deeply, and imagining or visualising stressful events, have all been found helpful. Activity 10.3 includes some of these suggestions.

Activity 10.3

Draw up a list of situations which cause you anxiety. Make it detailed and specific, e.g. writing a timed essay, sitting in the exam room, giving a talk in class. Put these into hierarchical order, the most stressful at the top and the least stressful at the bottom.

Start working through these from the least stressful upwards. For each situation, try to pretend that you are actually in that situation (try to visualise or simulate it), trying to maintain a state of relaxation. If you cannot relax then try to subdivide this stage into smaller units, again putting them into hierarchical order, and start again with the least stressful aspect. Gradually move upwards through your list. If you feel anxious at any point, stop and relax and see if you need to split it up once again into smaller steps. This may help you to relax in the real situation.

On which behavioural techniques is this activity based?

Any students who are parents may well be familiar with breathing exercises used in the pre-natal period to help relaxation during the birth.

Preparation for examinations

You can help reduce your anxiety by making sure that you have given yourself adequate time for revision as suggested above. However, some people find the period prior to the examination very stressful and this may interfere with eating and sleeping. The previous reading on coping with anxiety should prove useful here. Whatever happens do not add to your stress level by worrying about not sleeping! Remember that you can lose sleep for short periods without it having any long-term effects. Taking enough exercise and eating a balanced diet helps. Remember how important diet is to the functioning of the brain (refer to Reading 3.6 Malnutrition and the Brain). It is also important that you have sufficient breaks during which you have a complete change of activity from studying. Mature students, many of whom have family commitments, often feel frustrated when they have to break from studying to deal with domestic matters. Try to look on this as a bonus – at least it is giving your brain a chance to **consolidate** the learning!

Reading 10.10   In the Exam

In the examination itself, follow this procedure:

1 Find out if a particular part of the room (or a particular seat) has been assigned to you. If not, and you can choose where you sit, place yourself where there is plenty of natural light and where you can see the clock clearly.

2 Make sure that your watch and the clock in the exam room tell the same time. Take your watch off and put it in front of you.

3 When you are given the exam paper, check that it is the correct one. (There may be two or more exams taking place in the same room.)

4 Read the instructions. How many questions have to be answered? Are any compulsory? Are there answer booklets to be completed? Are there any objective test questions? If so, where are the answers to be recorded? How much time have you got for each question?

5 Read through all the questions and tick those you think you can do.

6 Re-read the questions you have ticked. Check the phrasing, noting particularly the key words. These will indicate what the examiner is looking for.

7 Make notes for each question. Switch from one question to another, jotting down all the ideas that come to mind. Visualise the essay plans. Use the memory devices you learnt during the year.

8 Put your name, candidate number, course and any other information required on the exam answer sheet.

9 Break up the number of questions to be answered into time limits, e.g. first question by 9.55, second question by 10.40, etc. Start with what you think is the easiest question and, using the notes, write your first essay. Remember the advice on essay writing. . . . . . . Glance at your watch frequently to make

sure you are keeping within the time limit. Write clearly and neatly. When you have finished the easiest question, go on to the next easiest and so on.

10 When you have finished all the questions check your script. Is your name on each piece of paper? Are all the answers numbered? Read over your answers for misspellings, omissions, miscalculations, etc. Join the answer sheets together. If there is an answer booklet, attach any additional sheets to it.

It is very important for you to finish the required number of questions; otherwise your paper will not be marked out of the maximum number of marks. If you miscalculate the time, so that you are left with, for example, two questions to do in 40 minutes, write two plans rather than one complete answer – one good essay may collect 14 or 15 marks out of 20 but each plan could get 8 or 9, that is 16 to 18 marks.

When you leave the examination room, it is not usually a good idea to discuss the paper with students as, for no good reason, you may get the impression you have not done well. Mix instead with people on other courses.

Take the rest of the day off. If you have other examinations over the next few days, try to keep your work down to light revision.

C. Parsons (1976) *How to Study Effectively* Arrow

1 Note **three** steps you should take before starting to write an answer to an exam question.   (3)

2 Complete the following:
'It is important for you to finish the .... questions.'   (1)

3 Describe **two** techniques you have used while making notes that might help you remember information in the exam.   (4)

TERMS TO DEFINE

compulsory questions   examination   pacing/timing

Once the examination starts there are techniques which may help you to maximise your performance. Remember to keep as relaxed as possible – deep breathing helps. Once you are **in the exam** the procedures noted in Reading 10.10 may help you to get the best out of your performance.

Usually students get together after the examination for a postmortem. Try not to get depressed by hearing of points that you missed. From your study of memory research you know that the memory of what you have written is imperfect, as is that of the people you are listening to! Some people find this 'group therapy' helpful – in discovering that they are not alone in finding certain questions difficult! For others, however, it can prove stressful. If you are one of the latter then make a quick escape after the exam and go away and **relax**. Even if there are still exams to follow, have a break and give your mind and body time to recover before starting any further revision. Have some time off. You've earned it!

Now the course is complete. We hope you have enjoyed your introduction to psychology and will find the knowledge useful in the future.

SUGGESTIONS FOR FURTHER READING

Main texts
D. Acres (1987) *How to Pass Exams without Anxiety* Northcote House
N. Hayes and S. Orrell (1987) *Psychology: An Introduction* Longman

Other useful texts
R.L. Akinson et al (1987) *Introduction to Psychology* (9th edn) Harcourt
    Brace Jovanovich (further details on the PQRST method)
A.D. Baddeley (1983) *Your Memory: A User's Guide* Penguin
D. Cocker (1987) *Successful Exam Technique* Northcote House
J. Hartley (1984) 'How Can Tutors Help Students Write Essays?' in K.E.
    Shaw (ed) *Aspects of Educational Technology XVII* pp 74–79 Kogan
    Page
N. Hayes (1990) *The GCSE Survival Guide* Longman
Z. Rubin and E.B. McNeill (1985) *Psychology: Being Human* (4th edn)
    Harper Row (good section on improving memory)

Objective Test Questions

Chapter 1 – What is Psychology?

1.1 'Psychology is the study of behaviour'. To which school of thought does this definition belong?

1.2 Underline the area of study in the following list which does **not** form part of cognitive psychology:

      memory   language   perception   conditioning   attention

1.3 Which of the Gestalt Laws does this diagram best illustrate?

```
XXXXOO      OOXOXX      OXOXXX      OOOOxO
COXXXO      XXOCOX      OXXXOO      XXXXOX
XXOOXX      XXXXOO      XOOOXX      OOxxOO
```

1.4 Name **one** psychologist associated with the humanistic school of thought in psychology.

1.5 Are the following statements true or false? Mark each one with a T if it is true, and an F if it is false:

Social psychology is the study of society and its institutions. ....

For the behaviourists, thinking was more important than action. ....

Freud believed that a large part of the mind was unconscious. ....

Phenomenology is the study of unexpected events. ....

Most applied psychologists work in laboratories. ....

1.6 What does the S–R in 'S–R psychology' stand for?

1.7 Match **two** items in List A with **two** items from List B by drawing appropriate lines between them.

List A	List B
social interaction	management decision-making
visual information processing	instinctive behaviour
industrial psychologist	dream analysis
phi phenomenon	conditioned reflexes
functionalism	principle of closure

1.8 Tick the statement which does **not** apply to the phenomenological approach within psychology.

  a) Personal Construct Theory is a good example of it. ....

  b) It is important to be objective when studying human beings. ....

  c) It is not possible to understand a situation unless you see it from the point of view of the people involved in it. ....

  d) Carl Rogers adopted this approach in his therapy. ....

234

1.9 What psychologist is famous for developing psychoanalysis?

1.10 Rearrange the following terms in their correct order.

the cognitive revolution   behaviourism
Gestalt psychology   introspectionism

Chapter 2 – Nature and Nurture

2.1 An empiricist psychologist believes that:

   a) development occurs mainly through genetic influences

   b) development always occurs in stages

   c) development comes from cross-cultural influences

   d) development occurs mainly from environmental influences.

2.2 Fill in the missing word in the sentence.

A period in which learning must take place, if it is to happen at all, is
known as a . . . . period.

2.3 Explain briefly what a twin study is.

2.4 Match **two** items in List A with **two** items from List B by drawing
appropriate lines between them.

List A	List B
imprinting	Skinner box
shape constancy	frustration-aggression hypothesis
superstitious learning	adoption studies
perceptual discrimination	sensitive period
babbling	physical punishment

2.5 Name a researcher famous for studying imprinting.

2.6 Indicate whether each statement is true or false by writing T or F in
the box provided.

   a) Chimpanzees can be taught to use language as
       grammatically correct as a typical six-year-old child.

   b) Adopted children tend to have higher IQs than children
       who remain with their natural parents.

   c) Violence on TV does not affect people's behaviour.

   d) Children's perceptual discrimination is fixed at birth.

   e) Even pigeons adopt superstitious rituals at times.

2.7 What is the term used to describe the idea that aggressive behaviour
happens because of difficult or frustrating circumstances?

2.8 Which of the following statements apply to perceptual development?

a) People need active movement to develop it properly.

b) Maternal deprivation seems to produce problems with it.

c) Infants prefer simple stimuli to complex ones.

d) It can be speeded up by an enriched environment.

e) Size constancy seems to be an innate ability.

2.9 What is wrong with this sentence and how should it be corrected?

Newson and Newson found that middle-class parents tended to encourage their children to 'stand up for themselves' against other children.

2.10 Which of the following is the odd-one-out?

Lana   Nim Chimpsky   Washoe   Genie

Chapter 3 – Brain and Behaviour

3.1 Match the following two lists by drawing a line from the appropriate word in List A to the appropriate word or phrase in List B.

List A	**List B**
caffeine	receptor site
fight or flight response	autonomic nervous system
neurotransmitter	Wernicke's area
understanding speech	electrical stimulation of the brain
	CNS stimulant
	dreaming

3.2 What are the **two** divisions of the autonomic nervous system?

3.3 Fill in the missing word(s) in the sentence.
'GSR meters are used to study . . . .'

3.4 Tick the appropriate box(es) to show which of the following statements are true:

a) The angular gyrus is active when we are reading.

b) Neurotransmitters do not affect moods or emotions.

c) Animals can adapt completely to high stress without experiencing any ill-effects.

d) Rats have been known to press a lever five thousand times an hour for electrical brain stimulation.

e) We spend most of our nights in REM sleep.

3.5 Explain the difference between Type A and Type B behaviour.

236

3.6 Iatrogenic disorders are:

   a) problems which only affect special individuals ☐

   b) problems in comprehending or producing speech ☐

   c) disorders of electrical activity in the brain ☐

   d) disorders which have been caused by medical treatments. ☐

3.7 On this diagram, draw one line pointing to the visual cortex, and another to the auditory cortex.

3.8 Which **two** of the following are used to measure brain activity?

galvanic skin resistance   electro-cardiograms
electro-encephalograms   tomography

3.9 Which of the following is the odd-one-out? Put a tick in the box opposite the correct answer.

   a) cerebellum ☐

   b) serotonin ☐

   c) hypothalamus ☐

   d) medulla ☐

3.10 Name a researcher famous for investigating long-term stress reactions.

Chapter 4 – Cognition

4.1 Match the following two lists by drawing a line from the appropriate word in List A to the appropriate word or phrase in List B.

List A	**List B**
attention	receptors
divergent thinking	language acquisition
sensation	eye-witness testimony
event memory	non-verbal interaction
	cocktail party phenomenon
	creativity

4.2 What is this figure called?

4.3 Fill in the missing word(s) to complete the sentence.

'Dichotic listening tasks are used to study . . . .'

4.4 Which of the following statements apply to Vygotsky's theory of language acquistion?

  a) Language is completely dependent on thinking.

  b) Egocentric speech vanishes as the child 'decentres'.

  c) Egocentric speech becomes internalised as 'inner speech'.

  d) Vocabulary and grammar determine our thought processes.

  e) Language and thinking have independent origins.

4.5 Name a psychologist famous for investigating hypothesis-testing in perception.

4.6 Noticing mainly what you are expecting to see is called:

  a) pattern recognition

  b) instrumental conditioning

  c) mnemonics

  d) perceptual set.

4.7 What is meant by the term symbolic thought?

4.8 Which of the following is the odd-one-out?

  a) perception

  b) mnemonics

  c) free recall

  d) short-term memory.

4.9 'Divergent thinkers are people who tend to look for just one correct solution to a puzzle'.

What is wrong with the above definition and how should it be corrected?

4.10 Which of the following statements are true?

  a) Perception is unaffected by the state of your emotions.

  b) Some drugs can produce altered states of consciousness.

  c) Dichotic listening tasks are used to test verbal memory.

  d) Eye-witness testimony is usually quite reliable.

  e) Functional fixedness can limit success in problem-solving.

Chapter 5 – Social Influences

5.1 Fill in the missing word(s) in the sentence.

'Sherif used the autokinetic effect to study . . . .'

5.2 Match the following two lists by drawing a line from the appropriate word in List A to the appropriate word in List B.

List A	**List B**
intergroup conflict	non-verbal communication
paralanguage	social norms
scapegoat theory	halo effect
diffusion of responsibility	social comparison
	prejudice
	bystander apathy

5.3 Name **two** factors shown by Milgram which may make someone more likely to obey authority.

5.4 What psychologist is famous for investigating cognitive dissonance?

5.5 What is meant by the term audience effect?

5.6 Which of the following is the odd-one-out?

   a) authoritarian personality

   b) scapegoat theory

   c) social facilitation

   d) stereotyping.

5.7 'Social norms are the written rules of a group or community, governing the behaviour, attitudes and beliefs of its members.'

What is wrong with the above definition and how should it be corrected?

5.8 The phenomenon of people working less hard when they are in large groups than when they are in small ones is described by which term?

   a) cognitive dissonance

   b) social loafing

   c) the fundamental attribution error

   d) obedience

   e) depersonalisation.

5.9 What is the name given to discrimination which is based on someone's gender?

5.10 Which of the following statements are true?

   a) Primacy effects are relatively unimportant in person perception.

   b) Bystander intervention is more common if there are few people about.

c) People usually make situational attributions about themselves but dispositional ones about others.

d) People only obey authority if they think the instruction is reasonable.

e) The 'foot-in-the door' technique is relatively useless for salesmen.

Chapter 6 – Individual Differences

6.1 What psychologist is famous for studying the self?

6.2 Fill in the missing labels on the personality diagram.

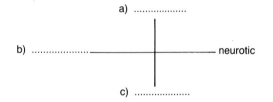

6.3 What is the term that Spearman used to describe inherited intelligence involving quickness and alertness?

6.4 Which **two** of the following are established personality traits?

a) intelligence

b) stability

c) mechanical aptitude

d) Downs syndrome

e) psychopathy.

6.5 Fill in the missing word in the sentence.

'When administering an IQ test, it is very important that the tester follows the . . . . procedure.'

6.6 What does the term compensatory education mean?

6.7 Which of the following statements apply to Personal Construct Theory?

a) People always classify their ideas into formal groups called concepts.

b) The human being acts like a scientist in everyday living.

c) People use bipolar constructs, with opposite personality characteristics at each of the extremes.

d) Some constructs that people use are more important than others.

e) Personal constructs can be used to measure objective reality.

6.8 What is wrong with this sentence, and how should it be corrected?

'Systematic desensitisation involves suddenly teaching the subject to relax in the presence of the feared object.'

6.9 Are the following statements true or false?

		True	False
a)	Psychotherapy has been proved to be more successful than any other treatment.	....	....
b)	Carl Rogers developed client-centred therapy.	....	....
c)	Rosenhan showed that medical staff could distinguish clearly between schizophrenics and normal people.	....	....
d)	Existentialist psychology concerns the choices that people make in their lives.	....	....
e)	Family therapists view the family as a dynamic system in which each member affects everyone else.	....	....

6.10 Which of the following is the odd-one-out?

a) behaviourism

b) humanistic psychology

c) introspectionism

d) existentialist psychology

e) psychoanalysis.

Chapter 7 – Human Development

7.1 What psychologist is famous for studying attachment in young monkeys?

7.2 Which is the odd-one-out?

a) the concrete operational stage

b) assimilation

c) the Oedipal conflict

d) mastery play.

7.3 What is meant by the term accommodation?

7.4 During which of Freud's psychosexual stages does gender identification take place?

a) the latency period

b) the genital stage

c) the oral stage

d) the anal stage.

7.5 Fill in the missing word in the sentence.

'During Freud's first psycho-sexual stage, the . . . . is focussed on the mouth.'

7.6 Match two items in List A with two items from List B by drawing appropriate lines between them.

List A	List B
imitation	accommodation
body-image	Piaget
the Oedipal conflict	autonomous morality
play therapy	adolescence
	identification
	imprinting

7.7 What is the single word used to describe the young child's inability to understand the world from an objective or external point of view?

7.8 Are the following statements true or false?

a) Sex-role learning is completed by the age of five or six.

b) A schema is a kind of mental plan.

c) Kohlberg said that autonomous morality was the highest stage.

d) Older workers can learn just as quickly as younger ones.

7.9 In what order should the following terms be put?

object constancy   abstract reasoning   conservation   body-schema

7.10 Which **two** of the following are skills involved in observational learning?

a) the observation of special features of the behaviour

b) the ability to make accurate social judgements

c) the maintenance of positive reinforcement

d) the adequate replication of actions.

Chapter 8 – Life-Events

8.1 A social role is:

a) the paid work which people do

b) any recognised part that we play in society

c) an actor in a psychological experiment

d) a way of looking at social interaction.

8.2 All but one of the following are important factors in coping with retirement. Which one is not?

self-esteem   locus of control   previous career change   social roles

8.3 Which of the following diagrams illustrates most clearly the relationship between how much stress we experience, and our average level of health? Health is measured on a scale from 0 = very unhealthy to 10 = very healthy.

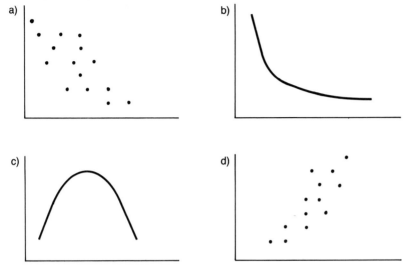

8.4 What is meant by the term disengagement?

8.5 Fill in the missing word in the sentence.

'People who have been unemployed for a period of time show lower . . . . than those who are in employment.'

8.6 Match **two** items in List A with **two** items from List B by drawing appropriate lines between them.

List A	List B
empty nest	disengagement
lifestyle	career transition
social readjustment	family life-cycle
locus of control	bereavement
retirement	stress

8.7 Are the following statements true or false?

	True	False
a) Dentists have a high suicide rate.	. . . .	. . . .
b) Unemployed people find it easier to start a new job than employed people.	. . . .	. . . .
c) Girls benefit from having working mothers.	. . . .	. . . .
d) Married men die earlier than widowed men.	. . . .	. . . .

8.8 What is the term used to describe the process of refusing to believe that someone is going to die?

8.9 Pining, searching and numbness are the three stages of bereavement described by Parkes. In the boxes below write down the three stages in the order in which they occur.

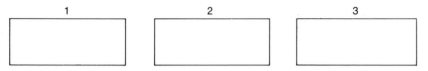

8.10 The family life-cycle is:

a) a system of assessing how old members of a family are

b) a description of stages which families go through

c) a way of measuring stressful life-events

d) an alternative to compulsory retirement.

Chapter 9 – Planning Psychological Research

9.1 In psychological investigations, a psychologist should take care not to:

a) invade the privacy of the subjects . . . .

b) carry out interviews . . . .

c) cause subjects pain or distress . . . .

d) control environmental variables. . . . .

Tick the **two** answers which correctly complete the sentence.

9.2 What is this type of diagram called?

9.3 Which is the odd-one-out of the following?

standardisation sampling validity reliability

9.4 Match the following two lists by drawing a line from the appropriate word or phrase in List A to the appropriate word or phrase in List B.

List A
experimenter effect
scattergram
pilot study
generalisability

List B
field experiments
questionnaire design
quota sampling
correlation
confounding variable
double-bind control
external validity

9.5 What is meant by the term demand characteristics?

9.6 Fill in the missing word(s) in the sentence.

'A good experimental sample should be representative of the . . . . from which it comes.'

9.7 What is wrong with the following sentence. How can it be corrected?

'A case study is the in-depth study of a group of individuals.'

9.8 Link together the report section titles with the definitions of what they should contain by drawing lines to connect them:

discussion   a brief summary of the whole study
introduction   the data and calculations
results   the theoretical background to the study
method   a summary of the main findings of the study
appendices   the problems and interesting outcomes of the study
abstract   an exact account of how the study was done

9.9 What is counterbalancing and when would you use it?

9.10 An experimental hypothesis is:

i)   a tentative idea which is to be tested to see if it comes true

ii)   a system for preventing experimenter effects

iii) a way of dealing with uncooperative subjects in an experiment

iv) a statement that no differences will be found in the study.

Chapter 10 – Study Skills

10.1 Which is the odd-one-out?

a) cognitive psychology

b) educational psychology

c) occupational psychology

d) clinical psychology.

10.2 What is a schema?

10.3 What is Adorno famous for studying?

10.4 Are the following statements true or false?

a) Parents with high expectations often have high-achieving children.

b) People often remember what they expected to happen rather than what really did happen.

c) Authoritarian personalities come from warm, loving homes.

d) We usually attribute the same kinds of motives to other people as we do to ourselves.

e) A variable-ratio schedule is the strongest form of partial reinforcement.

10.5 What is the term used for an experimental control which involves balancing the order of experimental conditions for the subjects?

10.6 Which **two** of the following do **not** form part of comparative psychology?

conditioning   attribution   ethology   imprinting   conformity

10.7 Locus of control refers to:

a) the motives that you ascribe to other people for their actions

b) the hypothesis-testing model of perception

c) learning to control blood pressure and heart rate through biofeedback

d) whether you believe that your own efforts are largely responsible for what happens to you.

10.8 What are negative after-effects?

10.9 Which of the following is **not** assessed using psychometric tests?

a) job suitability

b) creativity

c) fashion sense

d) personality traits

e) mechanical aptitude.

10.10 The following terms refer to the Gestalt principles of perception. Number them in the correct order, finishing with the most dominant one.

good Gestalt   similarity   proximity   closure

References

ACRES D. (1987)
How to Pass Exams without Anxiety   Northcote House: Plymouth
ANASTASI A. (1982)
Psychological Testing (5th edn)   Macmillan: New York
ARGYLE M. (1979)
The Psychology of Interpersonal Behaviour   Penguin
ARGYLE M. AND HENDERSON M. (1985)
The Anatomy of Relationships   Heinemann
ATKINSON R.L., ATKINSON R.C., and HILGARD E.R. (1983)
Introduction to Psychology (8th edn)   Harcourt Brace Jovanovich
ATKINSON R.L., ATKINSON R.C., SMITH E.E. and HILGARD E.R.
(1987)
Introduction to Psychology (9th edn)   Harcourt Brace Jovanovich
BADDELEY A.D. (1976)
The Psychology of Memory   Harper Row: London
BADDELEY A.D. (1983)
Your Memory: A User's Guide   Penguin
BARON R.A., BYRNE D, and KANTOWITZ B.H. (1980)
Psychology: Understanding Behaviour (2nd edn)   Holt, Rinehart and Winston
BEE H.L. (1985)
The Developing Child   Harper Row: London
BERGER K.S. (1980)
The Developing Person   Worth: New York
BERKOWITZ L. (1986)
A Survey of Social Psychology (3rd edn)   Holt, Rinehart and Winston
BERRYMAN J., HARGREAVES D., HOWELLS K. and HOLLIN C.
(1987)
Psychology and You   BPS: Methuen
BIRCH A. and MALIM T. (1988)
Developmental Psychology   Intertext: Bristol
BLAKEMORE C. (1983)
Mechanics of the Mind   Cambridge University Press
BRODZINSKY D., GORMLY A.V., AMBRON S.R. (1986)
Lifespan Human Development (3rd edn)   Holt, Rinehart and Winston
BROOKFIELD A.P. (1980)
Animal Behaviour   Nelson
BURNS R.B. and DOBSON C.B. (1984)
Introducing Psychology   MTP Press
CLEGG F. (1982)
Simple Statistics   Cambridge University Press
COCKER D. (1987)
Successful Exam Technique   Northcote House
DAVEY G. (1981)
Applications of Conditioning Theory   Methuen
DEAUX K. and WRIGHTSMAN L.S. (1984)
Social Psychology in the 80's (4th edn)   Brooks Cole: California

DUCK S. (1986)
Human Relationships   Sage: London
EYSENCK M.W. (1984)
A Handbook of Cognitive Psychology   Erlbaum
FONAGY P. and HIGGITT A. (1984)
Personality Theory and Clinical Psychology   Methuen
GESELL A. et al (1940)
The First Five Years of Life   Harper Row: London
GLEITMAN H. (1986)
Psychology (2nd edn)   W.W. Norton and Co: New York
GOLDSTEIN E.B. (1984)
Sensation and Perception   Wadsworth: Belmont
GREENE J. and HICKS C. (1984)
Basic Cognitive Processes   Open University Press: Milton Keynes
GROSS R.D. (1987)
Psychology: The Science of Mind and Behaviour   Edward Arnold
HALL C.S. and LINDZEY G. (1985)
Introduction to Theories of Personality   Wiley: New York
HARRIS P. (1986)
Designing and Reporting Experiments   Open University Press: Milton
Keynes
HASSETT J. (1984)
Psychology in Perspective   Harper Row: London
HAYES J. and NUTMAN P. (1981)
*Understanding the Unemployed: The Effects of
Unemployment*   Tavistock
HAYES N. (1984)
A First Course in Psychology   Nelson
HAYES N. (1988)
A First Course in Psychology (2nd edn)   Nelson
HAYES N. (1990)
Exams: The GCSE Survival Guide   Longman
HAYES N. and ORRELL S. (1987)
Psychology: An Introduction   Longman
HEIN P. (1968)
More Grooks   Hodder: London
HOTHERSALL D. (1985)
Psychology   Merrill: Ohio
KAGAN J., HAVEMANN E. and SEGAL J. (1984)
Psychology: An Introduction (5th edn)   Harcourt Brace Jovanovich:
San Diego
McCONNELL J.V. (1983)
Understanding Human Behaviour (4th edn)   Holt, Rinehart and Winston
McKENNA E.F. (1987)
Psychology in Business   Erlbaum
MANNING A. (1979)
An Introduction to Animal Behaviour (3rd edn)   Arnold: London
MATLIN M. (1983)
Cognition   Holt Saunders: New York

NORTON L.S. (1981)
'Patterned Note-taking: An Evaluation', *Visible Language* 15: 67–85
PARSONS C. (1976)
How to Study Effectively   Arrow
PECK D. and WHITLOW D. (1975)
Approaches to Personality Theory   Methuen: London
RAAHEIM R. and RADFORD J. (1984)
Your Introduction to Psychology   Sigma: London
RADFORD J. and GOVIER E. (1982)
A Textbook of Psychology   Sheldon: London
ROEDIGER H.L., RUSHTON J.P., CAPALDI E.D. and PARIS S.G.
(1984)
Psychology   Little, Brown and Co: Boston
RUBIN Z. and McNEILL E.B (1981)
Psychology: Being Human (3rd edn)   Harper Row: New York
SHELLEY D. and COHEN D. (1986)
Testing Psychological Tests   Croom Helm: London
SHOBIN E.J. (1954)
'Theoretical Frames of Reference in Clinical Psychology' in L.A.
Pennington and I.A. Berg (eds) *An Introduction to Clinical Psychology*
(2nd edn)   Ronald Press: New York
SYLVA K. and LUNT I.
Child Development: A First Course   Basil Blackwell: Oxford
TAYLOR A., SLUCKIN W., DAVIES D.R., REASON J.T., THOMSON
R. and COLMAN A.M. (1982)
Introducing Psychology (2nd edn)   Penguin
WILLIAMS K. C. (1981)
Behavioural Aspects of Marketing   Heinemann

Index